TH_
SOLAR
ANGEL

A
COMPILATION
FROM
PUBLISHED AND UNPUBLISHED WORKS
BY TORKOM SARAYDARIAN

COMPILED
BY MARY SENTER

T.S.G. Publishing Foundation, Inc.
Complete Line of Torkom Saraydarian's Works
P.O. Box 7068, Cave Creek, AZ 85327 USA
Tel: 480-502-1909 * Fax: 480-502-0713
www.tsgfoundation.org

Library of Congress Number: 89-83490
ISBN: 0-911794-62-X

Cover Design by Fine Point Graphics, Sedona, Arizona

Printing by Delta Lithograph Co., Valencia, California

NOTE: The exercises and meditations given in this book should be used only after receiving professional advice. Use them with greatest discretion thereafter, and at your own risk.

Dedicated to all those
who seek contact with their Souls

This book has been compiled and edited from the following works of Torkom Saraydarian with his permission:

Bhagavad Gita
Challenge for Discipleship
Christ, The Avatar of Sacrificial Love
Cosmos in Man
Five Great Mantrams of the New Age
Hiawatha and the Great Peace
Symphony of the Zodiac
Talks on Agni
The Fiery Carriage and Drugs
The Flame of Beauty, Culture, Love, Joy
The Hidden Glory of the Inner Man
The Legend of Shamballa
The Psyche and Psychism
The Science of Becoming Oneself
The Science of Meditation
Triangles of Fire
Unpublished writings

Contents

Preface

*O*ne afternoon in spring
under a great oak tree,
hundreds were gathered
around Hiawatha.
Rising from His carpet,
He addressed the people,
saying,

> "Our Soul
> has Its language.
> It speaks with us
> through dreams.
> Our Soul has Its visions,
> and sometimes
> It shares with us
> Its visions,
> to evoke striving for a new dimension
> of consciousness.
> Our Soul watches
> over us
> and warns us
> about things which
> prevent
> our advancement

toward the future.

"Your guidance
depends upon your sensitivity
to listen to the language of the Soul,
and upon
increasing
the sensitivity
of your consciousness.

"The Great Spirit
gave you mountains,
lakes and rivers.
Commune with them
as if they were alive,
as if they were living
entities,
and you will build
higher sensitivity
to the events of life.
Do not destroy Nature.
It is your body.

"Do not destroy your body.
It is the Nature.

"Our Souls,
the flowers of Nature,
the messengers of Nature,
speak to us
about the harmony
between Nature, the Great Spirit,

and our existence.
Follow the suggestion
of your Soul,
and you will experience
beauty.
Live in beauty.
Sing in beauty.
Be in beauty.
The Soul is beauty.

> *"Once beauty begins*
> *to sing within you,*
> *you find the path*
> *leading you to the contact*
> *with the Great Spirit.*

"Beauty becomes
the language
between you and the Great Spirit.
Our Soul
knows that language
and tries to teach it to us.
In the mountains,
in the rivers,
near the lakes,
in the forests,
you may learn that language,
and especially during the night
watching the stars.

"The Soul is our guide
in the stormy sea of life.

If we do not follow
the guide,
we invite upon ourselves
the destructive currents
from Space
and develop pain
and suffering,
and we die.
If we follow
all the desires of our Soul,
we bloom
and grow in strength,
in beauty,
and find the way
leading to contact
with the Great Spirit."[1]

---

[1]*Hiawatha and the Great Peace,* pp. 29-31.

Introduction

The Legend of the Human Spark

*T*here is a great deal of confusion in the minds of spiritual searchers about the Monad, the Spark, the Solar Angel, the human developing soul, personality, Soul infusion, Ego, ego and Self. The meanings of these terms have occupied the attention of individuals for many thousands of years.

We need to have clear definitions in our minds in order to understand the Teaching given in the Ageless Wisdom:

Monad — The Monad is a contact point with the matter of a ray which is projected from the Central Spiritual Sun. Thus the Monad is an appearance of a nucleus of the fiery seed that has *fallen* into the ground of the Monadic Plane.

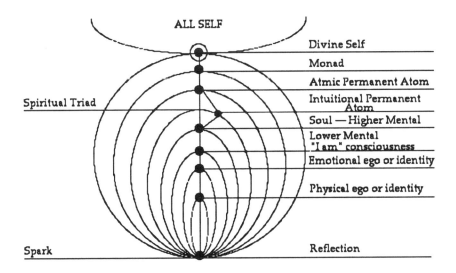

Spark — The Spark is a fiery root projected by the Monad toward matter, buried in the physical plane as a fiery essence. This Spark, through millions of years, builds bodies to come in contact with the physical, emotional and mental planes and uses them to develop *consciousness*. Gradually It reaches a point in evolution when a human body is built with the help of angelic beings, who in past globe cycles were Sparks Themselves. In our globe, some of these angelic beings are called Solar Angels, Who inspire the Spark on Its journey back Home.

Human soul — The Spark advances toward the emotional plane, building an appropriate emotional body. When the Spark enters into the mental plane, It develops "I am" consciousness. Often he thinks his body is he, his emotional body is he, his mental body is he. This stage of development is called the stage of the human soul. The Spark becomes a human soul because he tries to develop his *humanness*.

Personality — At this stage the relation between him and his Solar Angel deepens and because of this help he tries to integrate his personality into a mechanism which functions as a unit. This stage is called the stage of personality. The human soul totally identifies himself with this unit. He is a personality, which means the human soul identifies with his three bodies as if he was his three bodies. This stage lasts many, many incarnations, during which the potentials and talents of the human soul are used for the interests of his physical, emotional and mental bodies.

Soul Infusion — The next stage starts when the human soul begins to realize that he is not a body, emotions, thoughts, but a fiery essence, buried in them and has capability to use his bodies, rather than to be used by them.

This is the stage of emancipation of the human soul. He achieves this emancipation with the help of the Solar Angel, and because of this emancipation process he develops a powerful attraction toward the Solar Angel. This attraction slowly makes him fuse with the Solar Angel Who is in some literature called "The Beloved," or "Bridegroom," and other names, and identifies with the Solar Angel. This phase is called Soul infusion.

Ego — In some esoteric literature, Ego written with a capital "E" refers to the Solar Angel.

ego — Ego with a small "e" refers to the developing human soul. This ego is the Spark plus the matter with which he is identified. This ego is the self-centered state of the Spark. In this stage the ego is an egotistic, self-seeking entity, who tries to use all that he can for his own self-interest.

A time comes in the evolution of the human soul when he slowly realizes that the Solar Angel is not him, but he was nourished by It, as a baby, and now he can slowly have his new identity.

In that phase the human soul relates with the Solar Angel as his Teacher and Real Guide, Who slowly prepares the human soul to learn the steps how to be independent, and eventually be graduated and born anew. Such a birth takes place between the phase when the Solar Angel trains him for independence, and the phase in which the human soul strives to make a breakthrough and enter into the Intuitional Plane. As the human soul penetrates deeper into the Intuitional Plane, the Solar Angel slowly withdraws, and eventually departs.

The human soul progresses toward Intuitional and Atmic Planes, expanding his activities in the higher mental planes.

As he tries to be aware in these three planes, he realizes that some very advanced entities were watching his progress from darkness to light. Eventually he cultivates a high relation with them, and becomes the focus or the central point between these three entities. In this stage he is called a *Spiritual Triad*.

After this stage he travels to the Monadic Plane and identifies with his source, the Monad. Here he is called an *individuality*.

Self — After many thousands of years, because of his striving, service and sacrifice rendered on various planes, he penetrates into the Divine Planes, and understands that he is a Ray, rooted in the Central Spiritual Sun. This stage is called the stage of the *Self* — not self hood.

A Self is one of the All Self which is the Central Spiritual Sun with all the Rays. The Self lives not as an individuality anymore but as a One.

The Great Sage, M.M. says that, "A great Oneness reigns in Cosmos as a powerful Law. Only those who adhere to this law can verily take part in cosmic cooperation...."[1]

---

[1]Agni Yoga Society, *Infinity*, Vol II, para. 48.

1

The Solar Angel

*T*he Solar Angel is a subject that is so close to us. This subject is the axis of light around which all our lives turn and evolve, but most of humanity is not aware of this subject.

Man has a habit to accumulate. Why? Because he wants to meet his own needs. This was the first path made by man. It was a very simple process at the beginning of human history because man wanted to satisfy his physical needs, then his emotional needs, then his mental needs. He collected all kinds of objects for his physical needs. He tried to collect objects to satisfy his emotional nature. Then he collected objects to meet his mental needs.

Throughout centuries he lost some of these objects and he developed a theory or an idea that he may again be in need of these objects. Because of this fear he started to accumulate more and the result became greed. So man became an accumulator, a person really oriented toward having more and more. He thought his joy came from his havingness. Throughout ages, experience showed him that havingness did not satisfy his needs, because the things he was accumulating were sometimes lost. For example, he gathered lots of objects, cars, houses, money, furniture, clothes and many material things for the physical body. When he lost the physical body, none of these objects were able to satisfy him. So experience gathered throughout incarnations taught him that his joy, beauty and happiness do not depend upon the physical nature.

When this experience was gained he started to have the emotional experience. He discovered that the emotional body and nature could be lost and those things that satisfied the emotional body were no longer attractive and important to him.

Then he entered into the next stage of development which was the realization that mental objects were not really dependable. What were the mental objects? Lots of knowledge. People base their happiness and future on their knowledge, but suddenly they see by the smallest test that their knowledge does not answer their needs.

I was talking to a heart surgeon. He said, "You know, I think I have a heart problem." "You are a heart surgeon, you shouldn't have heart trouble. You know all about these things." "You know," he said, "sometimes I think I don't." What is happening? Man is putting his faith in things that are outside and giving all his energy and life to accumulate things to secure his physical, emotional and mental happiness. But when critical times come he realizes that all he has gathered does not help his inner search. Man is searching for something and he does not know what it is.

In one of the temples I saw a very interesting drama. There was a girl on stage looking for somebody. She knew his name and everything about him, but she did not know what or who that man was. A man came on the stage and she asked, "Are you, John?" "Yes, I am John." "Oh," she said, "I love you," and started to embrace him. Then she asked, "Is your family name Johnson?" "No." Downcast, she remarked, "Oh." She was searching for something and when she found it, she tried to get all her happiness through that object. But that object vanished.

Then a second man came and she asked, "Is your name John Johnson?" "Yes." "Oh," she said, "you are the one I am looking for." She embraced him a little and they started to talk. Then she inquired, "What is your father's name?" "My father's name is Peter." "Oh," she said, "you are not what I am looking for."

Another man came and she asked again, "Is your name John?" "Yes, and my family's name is Johnson and my father's name is Peter." "Oh," she said, "it is you." She jumped and hugged him and then asked, "What is your mother's name?" "My mother's name is Rebecca." "You are not the one I am looking for." "What should be my mother's name?" "Marie," she answered. So both of them were disappointed.

This continued in a very dramatic and musical way. Every time she was disappointed she danced in a way as if she was crying and searching for something. It was not there. Every time somebody came, that person did not satisfy or fill her innermost needs, giving her joy and bliss. Eventually she said, "Maybe what I am looking for is within me, let me start within myself." She started to search and travel on a path to find the jewel within herself.

There is a presence hidden within man and throughout centuries, man has lost that presence and he is now going back to find it. This path is not controlled by having, accumulating or gathering objects but it is a path on which you always search, always sacrifice, so that eventually the one which you were looking for appears and establishes conscious contact with you

What is the Solar Angel? Throughout centuries people felt that there was a source of inspiration within themselves, a retreat, a place of rest and joy, in which men enter and when they come back they shine, are creative, happy, healthy and radioactive.

This Inner Sanctuary, this inner source of beauty and creativity, is called by different names. In psychology It is called the Higher Self but simple psychology does not know what is meant by Higher Self. They also call It the Psyche. Other people call It the Inner Guide, Inner Leader, Inner Master. In Christian terminology, It is called the Inner Christ or Inner Glory. Buddhists call It "the Land of Happiness," the "Fountain of Love and Compassion." In Sufi literature and in a classic love poem written by Solomon, It is called "The Beloved." It is not a girl or woman he is looking for, but he is looking for something that is not tangible, something that can totally satisfy all his urges, drives, inspirations, searches and consciousness. It is called also the "Inner Sun." In occult literature It is called "Lord of Flame."

Why is It called "Flame?" We are told that the Inner Presence within us is a fiery creative nucleus. In Tibetan literature It is called the Dhyani, which means the Meditative One. The Tibetan Master says there is a Presence within us Who throughout ages meditates and tries to harmonize with the physical, emotional and mental bodies of the human being and slowly reveals the *jewel* that is hidden within these three bodies.

In a modern definition, It could be called the nurse or gardener who tries to make the seed bloom that is hidden under the layers of physical, emotional and mental bodies, and to evoke and call that beauty out into expression. This is the hidden joy of the Solar Angel.

The Solar Angel is within our aura as a friend, great mother, guide, leader, protector, and a source of treasure. When one of our teachers gave this information, he said man has a treasure box, but he does not want to open it because it takes labor, and he searches everywhere else for the treasure. If he would only start to labor, struggle and strive, that treasure box will open and in it he will find all satisfactions. The treasure box is within ourselves. We are trying to open it, to walk up the mountain to see if we can touch that box.

The Solar Angel is not the human soul. Those esoteric books which show that Solar Angels and human souls are the same, are in error.

The Solar Angel is a Guardian, and we will read about It in this book. The human soul is a developing Spark of God, the real human essence, you, the True Self.

The Solar Angel's duty is to guide the soul to higher realms and help him to reveal the Inner Glory in man.[1]

---

[1]Taken from the lecture, "Solar Angel," September 8, 1973.

2

The Human Soul

What is the human soul? The soul is you, the immortal being, who occupies physical, emotional and mental bodies, then leaves them one by one and reincarnates again to go through the school of life.

The soul has three major characteristics:

light — seeing things as they are,

love — seeing others as they are, and

energy — service to all.

The human soul is like a bud which opens its flower, and as it opens, it radiates more light, more love and more energy.

The soul is the one who makes the bodies to:

1. act,
2. feel,
3. think,
4. change,

and thus the soul controls the bodies, masters them and recreates or improves them.

The soul can travel in astral, mental and Intuitional planes. The soul can come in contact with subjective Ashrams and teachers.

People are very concerned about their financial situation, and want to know if they made money. If they are building a house, they want to see it progressing. If they have a fruit tree, they want to be sure it bears fruit. If they have a child, they want to be sure the child is well, and always has good things for his growth and perfection. People want the bad things to decrease and disappear such as crime, war, hatred, revenge, pain, suffering, sickness. But people are very seldom interested in the growth of their soul.

To inspire interest in soul growth, we can ask ourselves the following questions:

Am I more conscious about my future?

Am I maturing?

Am I repeating my mistakes less?

Did I gain more control over my habits, negative emotions, words and thoughts?

Do I see a meaning in life?

Am I interested in my future?

Am I more giving?

Do I have any experience that I am not the body?

Do I see that life does not end with this earthly incarnation?

Do I have a planned study?

Do I have a planned meditation?

Do I feel that whatever I am is my own creation?

Am I grateful for all the help I receive?

People think that the progress of the soul can be purchased or achieved by:

reading,

listening to a lecture,

hypnotism,

magic, etc.

The soul is the hardest seed and needs labor and work if you want it to grow. It took millions of years to pass from one kingdom to another, going from human to the kingdom of God.

The progress of the soul can be achieved through:

study,

meditation,

service,

actualization, and

transmutation.

Study — Study of yourself, of your hatred, blind urges and drives. Study of your emotions, thoughts, mechanical thinking.

Meditation — Think of the wisdom of the Great Ones. Be systematic in writing down the result of your meditation and experiences.

Service — Find a way to serve: service for yourself, family, nation and humanity.

Actualization — Try to manifest the following virtues:

gratitude,

solemnity,

perseverance,

reticence,

nobility,

enthusiasm,

joy, and
serenity.

Transmutation — Change the substance of your physical body, emotional body and mental body.

Your bodies are composed of corresponding substances: physical, emotional, mental. But the substance of each body is graded. The highest level is called atomic substance, which is the purest one in each body. As this substance increases in your body, you pass into higher and higher initiations. For example:

Atomic Substance Percentage in Initiation

30%	first
60%	second
75%	Third
90%	Fourth
100%	Fifth

The percentage is recorded in your permanent atoms and in the next life your bodies start from the same standard.

The progress of the soul is:

1. mastery over one's vehicles,
2. Soul-fusion,
3. dedication to a great goal,
4. intuitive flashes,
5. psychic powers,
6. expanding influence, and
7. higher creativity.

Most of the time the human soul is subject to the physical machine, which has its own interests. Often it is subject to emotional interests and mental interests. But the soul cannot grow until these interests become his own.

The physical elemental does not care for the emotional elemental. The emotional elemental does not care for the mental elemental, and the mental elemental does not care for the physical and emotional elementals.[1] It is only the human soul who is concerned with the well-being of these three bodies, and for his own sake he liberates himself from these three bodies by transforming them.

Man has been enslaved in these bodies for billions of years and is making very little progress. We can estimate that ninety-nine percent of the people are under control of their physical, emotional and mental elementals, and one percent of the people are almost breaking the control and liberating themselves from their physical, emotional and mental bodies.

In every century only a few people are able to do this. It is not because it is impossible, but because the lure of the physical, emotional and mental bodies is greater.

The first step toward liberation is to know sincerely and really that you are a slave. Unless you know it, you will not take action to gain freedom.

How will you know it? Try to observe how much control your body has upon you through sex, food, clothes, shelter, sickness.

Try to see how much control your emotional body has upon you through fear, depression, happiness, misery, greed, jealousy, anger, touchiness.

---

[1] Read *The Psyche and Psychism,* Chapter 17, "Elementals."

Then see how much power your mental body has upon you. Can you differentiate between you and your thoughts, between knowledge and opinion? How much can you disidentify yourself from your thoughts, worries and opinions of others about you?

How many thoughts do you fabricate? With how many thoughts do you deceive yourself? How much do you lie? How much do you take advantage of others?

Through such observation you slowly move from physical, emotional to mental plane. But it is impossible to liberate yourself from the mental plane, unless you first liberate yourself from the physical and emotional planes.

Liberation is possible only when you transform your bodies and increase the atomic substance in them.[2]

---

[2]Unpublished writing, January 27, 1985.

3

Mystery of the Soul

One day my father said, "Prepare your horse, we are going somewhere." I had a white horse and his was black. I prepared my horse and jumped on his back. Under the light of a full moon we headed toward the desert. After two hours, three people stopped us. They blindfolded me and turned my horse around a few times so that I would not know the direction in which we were heading.

After one hour of riding they removed the blindfold from my eyes. We were in front of a great cave. We went into the cave. It was huge. At first I could not see anything, then I started to see human beings all over the cave. There were around five hundred people. Inside the huge cave there was another cave opening which was used as a stage. There were three candles on the stage.

We all sat in meditation in great silence. Then a man went to the corner of the stage and started to play the flute. It was some kind of music that takes you out of the body. If people only knew the power of sound, of how to quiet the body and emotions and expand the consciousness through sound! When the sound of the flute started, my consciousness started to expand. I felt that I was not the body. I felt that the universe was my home. I felt that there was only Space and that man has unlimited power.

Then I saw seven shadows pass across the stage. After the seven shadows passed we saw a huge rosebud of golden color. The big petals were closed. As the music became more rhythmic and beautiful, the petals started to open one by one into a huge golden rose, radiating its color. When the music hit its highest note and stopped, a bird flew from the center of the rose.

We sat again in silence. Then three musicians came and started to play extraordinary music, so rhythmic and beautiful that it affected all the cells of my body and brain.

Next a man dressed in grey came and danced, but it was a very erratic dance. He was not in rhythm with the music. A second man dressed in silver came and danced. A third man dressed in yellow joined the other two. But they were not in harmony with the music. Suddenly the bird that had flown from the rose returned in the shape of a girl with wings. She began to dance around the three men, but they wanted her to dance to their inharmonious rhythm. But the girl resisted. She took the hands of the man dressed in grey and started to dance with him in rhythm. Then she danced with the man in silver. Then she danced with the man in yellow. Her dance was so exciting and beautiful, it created a tremendous joy in us.

When the dance was over, we saw the rebirth of the rose. The rosebud opened its petals and the bird again flew from the rose. A huge man came on the stage and said, "Let us think about this." Everybody meditated. What was it? The thought energies were breaking my crystallizations. I was making a breakthrough into a world of meaning.

Afterwards, we got on our horses to leave. They blindfolded me again and after an hour they removed the blindfold so I could see.

"Daddy," I asked, "what was the rose?" "Did you count the petals?" "Yes, there were twelve petals." "And did you see the bird that flew away?" "Yes." "Well," said daddy, "those twelve petals are twelve virtues in which your soul lives. As your virtues manifest and like fragrance radiate throughout your life, the bird which is you makes a breakthrough. You release yourself from the limitation of Space and time and become your real Self." "What are these virtues?" I asked. He told me they were:

1. striving	7. service
2. courage	8. compassion
3. daring	9. patience
4. discrimination	10. fearlessness
5. solemnity	11. gratitude
6. harmlessness	12. responsibility

"Daddy," I asked, "when these twelve petals open, how does the Spark fly out?" He said, "That is God. The bird you saw was the symbol of your innermost you. You are within the twelve petals and not until you open these twelve petals — which means not until these twelve virtues are actualized in your life through your thoughts, emotions, words and actions — does your soul bloom and expand itself. So the first thing to do in your life is to be a virtuous human being."

"Who were the three men?" "The man in grey was a symbol of your physical body who could not dance to the rhythm of the soul. He could not dance to the music."

"What is the music?" "The music is Divine Will. The dance is the Plan. When a man can dance to the Divine Plan under the Divine Will, he becomes synchronized with the music. All his movements express Divine Will. Everything he does is in harmony with Divine Will. He is integrated and fused with Divine Wisdom. He becomes a manifestation of the Divine Presence in everything."

"You are lucky," I said to my horse, "to be listening to these things."

"What is the man dressed in silver?" "He represents your emotional nature, which takes time to adjust to the music and dance. Your emotional nature is not in harmony with the Divine Presence, with Divine Will."

With the consciousness that we have, we get depressed, we become fearful, we gossip. Because of our many negative attitudes, our emotional body creates funny movements instead of rhythmic movements in response to the music. It has taken many lives in tension, suffering, pain and joy for the emotional body of man to learn how to adjust its movements to the music.

Then my father continued, "The man dressed in yellow is your mental nature. The mind does not obey the dignity within you. You know what is right, but the mind says, "Do it another way." The mind is so cunning. The whole dance symbolizes harmony of the physical, emotional and mental natures with the highest that we know, with the best we believe in or with the divine intent, the divine vision. It takes time for all three bodies to come together and become synchronized. It takes an Angel to come and teach man how to dance."

How can one be in harmony with the laws and principles of health, happiness and joy? It is not easy. The Angel first helps man to make his physical body rhythmic and harmonious, then helps organize the emotional nature in such a way that it becomes purified, rhythmic and harmonious to reflect the divine beauty.

The next conquest is the mental nature. There was a great Sage called Krishna who was teaching Arjuna, His disciple. Krishna said that the ultimate victory to be achieved was to conquer the mind. But Arjuna told Him that the mind was like a wind. This is true. Your thoughts play a great circus in your mind. You try to meditate, and your business, girlfriend, boyfriend problems, taxes come to your mind. How to control the mind?

Krishna agreed that it was difficult to control the mind, but He told Arjuna that there is nothing in the universe which cannot be conquered by the Divinity living within him.

The cave represents the human nature. The three candles in the cave symbolize the three lights in your cave called beauty, goodness and truth. Goodness must dominate your life. Everything must be done in truth. Your life must be beautiful. Always light three candles in your home and say, "This is beauty, this is goodness and this is truth." Say, "I know I am going to be beautiful, good and truthful, and I am going to do my best." Then you will see a transformation coming into your nature.

The three candles in your head are your head centers, which are the three glands called pineal gland, pituitary body and alta major center. Light them and you will see your life becoming a mystery school. You become an expression of mysterious beauty.

The seven shadows symbolize your seven vehicles. Your physical body is a shadow, which means it is not reality. Your emotional nature and mental nature are shadows. Your four higher natures are shadows. After you reach perfection, you are going to leave these seven shadows behind.

What is the difference between one musician and three musicians? One musician is concentration. The flute is the symbol of the tuning fork. One is the tuning key, and your three bodies must be tuned to the three musicians.

The three musicians are the perfection of your physical, emotional and mental bodies, which are learning, synchronizing and harmonizing themselves with the Divine Angel within you.

The bird symbolizes the human soul. In Egypt a bird is seen flying out of the coffin. Four thousand years before Christ, a bird was the symbol of the human soul. In the play, the bird that came back was like the human soul, but it was different. It was the Guardian Angel, the Solar Angel.

There are five words that people think are synonymous. They are Spark, ego, soul, Self and Solar Angel.

1. Spark. To explain the beauty of the Spark, Christ did something that was unusual. He took a piece of bread and said, "This is My body; take it and eat it." Eating the body, the disciples became one with the Christ, and one with each other. The Spark within you came from the One. You are part of that great Spiritual Sun from which everything originated. The Spiritual Sun is the bread and parts of it that went to the Universe are from the same Spiritual Sun.

You, as a Spark, were projected into Nature at the beginning of time. The Spark went throughout the Universe and built a physical, emotional and mental manifestation, until the human being came into existence. It is the same Spark coming from the same Source. In every creation, in every atom, exists the One that is the basis or the foundation of the brotherhood of all existence.

We say "brotherhood of humanity," but this is wrong. It should be "brotherhood of everything." Animals are our little brothers. Birds are our little cousins. Flowers are our grandchildren. Each Spark throughout the Universe first of all condensed and built the atom. From the atom the Spark graduated into the vegetable kingdom and built millions of forms, and then entered into the animal kingdom. Eventually the Spark graduated from that kingdom and became human.

In the human kingdom you, the Spark, built a human emotional body, the correspondence to the vegetable kingdom. You built a mental body as the correspondence to the animal kingdom and eventually you will learn to build another body which will be the angelic body.

2. ego. When the Spark is identified with the mental, astral and physical bodies, you have an ego. Ego serves the bodies, instead of the bodies serving you.

When you are an ego, you are an egotist, which means you always search for the benefit of your body at the expense of others. That is ego. When you identify with your emotional nature, you have an emotional ego. If somebody hurts you, you want to bite and beat the one who hurts you.

The mental ego has vanity, pride, hypocrisy. It means the Spark in the mental nature is serving, obeying, working for the mind, instead of making the mind work for you. If you are working for the body you are an ego. If the body works for you, you are a soul.

So ego is the Spark identified with the physical, emotional and mental vehicles.

3. soul. If you know that you are not the physical body, you are a soul. Are you? Do you really know by experience, by realization, that you are not your physical body? If you know that, you started to be a soul.

When I was looking at the stage in the cave, there were three steps that a person could climb to enter the cave and touch the three candles. The first step was that the soul knows he is not the physical body.

How does a soul know that he is not the physical body? He will not obey physical demands. He will make the physical body obey him. If you want to be a perfected spiritual being, then you are going to pay for it. What does it mean to pay? It means to labor, work, strive.

People think if they go to lectures and read books, they become perfect. That is not so. Perfection is the improvement of life, the evolution of life. It is a steady, heavy labor to dominate and to conquer your nature. The first aim is to control your body. When you resist the temptations and demands of the body and say, "No, I do not want it," you are becoming a soul and entering the first step.

The second step is when you start conquering your emotional nature, especially the five devils: hatred, fear, anger, jealousy, greed. When you really conquer these five things and control your emotional body, you are becoming a soul, a shining candle on the second step.

Then eventually you realize that you are also not the mind, that you can use the mind, and like a jacket hang it up and say, "Do not bother me now; I am going to sleep," or, "I am going to concentrate." When the mind is controlled, you have conquered three steps. You are on the stage of light as a soul.

You are withdrawing, growing, becoming a soul. People think they are souls. They are not. Most of them are their body, stomach, sex, marijuana, whiskey. Where is the soul? The soul is a victorious human Spark.

The Spark travels and eventually on the mental plane, the Spark looks at himself and sees his face in the physical, emotional and mental mirror. A great Apostle said, "We see our faces in the mirror now, but one day we will see ourselves face to face." We are not there yet. We are going to see our face one day and know we are a soul.

4. Self. The Self is something deeper. The soul thinks in terms of family, nation and one humanity. On the first step, there is physical victory. You live in your family as a group-conscious human being. Then on the second step of emotional victory, you become nation-oriented. You sacrifice yourself for the nation. On the third step you conquer the mental body and realize the mental body is not you, and you become oriented toward one humanity. But when you conquer your separate self, you become cosmic, universal; you become a Self.

The Self has no limitation. It is totally cosmic. Your Self and the All Self that is energizing and giving life to everything in the Universe is one with you. That was the stage of the Christ consciousness when He said, "I and My Father are one."

You reach the Self in everything, the Self in the Universe. Self stands for the Cosmos, and everything that you do, think, speak and feel is done for the whole. Holism includes everything, synchronizes everything. It becomes a symphony in everything. That is the Self.

There is an ancient, beautiful prayer called THE SELF:

> *More radiant than the sun,*
> *purer than the snow,*
> *subtler than the ether*
> *is the Self,*
> *the Spirit within my heart.*
> *I am that SELF,*
> *that SELF am I.*

You are not the body; you are the sun. What is the sun? The sun is a little candle in comparison to the One Who created it. If you go out on a starry night, you see billions of constellations and suns like little stars, but the One that contains them is the Self. That Sun is within you, and you are that Sun. Can you reach that realization? If you reach that realization, you become a free bird. You are beyond your body, emotions, thoughts, worries and anxieties. You are free from them.

Can we reach that freedom? Of course we can. If any man has done it, we can do it. If Great Ones, great Masters, great Initiates, great Angelic Beings did it, we can do it, because we are the same Spark traveling on the same path, going to the same destiny.

What a destiny awaits us. But if anything small happens, we lose our balance, our head, our heart. Conquer them. The Spark, the Self, can conquer everything! Do not give up. When the body controls, you give up. When you control the body, you gain a little. Emotions control you; you give up. When you control the emotions, you are a victor. When the mind controls, you are in depression. When you control the mind, you enter into everlasting joy. Here you find the secret of joy. The secret of joy is mastery. Everything you master and expand increases your joy.

Each of you can do this. You must hear and read these things over and over so that you start practicing. A man can become illuminated in one second. Who knows who you are or where you are? Maybe for a million years you accumulated and have now reached the point where you must burst.

Christ held the hand of a dead girl and told her to get up and walk. She got up. If the Divine Presence can work through your Master, that same Divine Presence can work through you. Hold the hand of your body and say, "Get up!"

There are four steps through which we can achieve Self-awareness:

A. Hard work and labor. Whatever you are doing at your home or in your business, do it with all your might and soul and concentration. Even if you are writing a letter, be in the letter. Give your heart, mind, emotions and concentration. If you are in the kitchen cleaning utensils, really concentrate. Do not do anything in hatred, in a hurry, in the dark. Whatever you are doing, do it as if you are doing it for the Lord. If you are polishing shoes, say, "These are the shoes of God. I am going to make them so beautiful." When you clean the house, clean it as if a Divine Angel or Christ is going to visit.

If you are selling or buying something, be extremely concentrated and honest. You will see that you will slowly awaken on the physical plane to your Self-awareness. Whatever you do, do it with great love, dedication and concentration.

There was a great saint, named Saint Teresa. When she went to the convent she thought she would spend her time singing, praying, be dressed in beautiful vestments and be glorified, but what happened to her? They told her to wash the dirty sheets of the patients, which smelled and were covered with blood, sweat and stains. The first few days she was depressed and then she asked herself, "How can I conquer this?" She thought awhile; then the idea came to her to imagine that the sheets were Christ's sheets. Her sadness turned into joy. She was asked why she was so happy, and she said, "I am washing Christ's sheets." All her chores were done in the same spirit. She became clairvoyant, clairaudient, and continually in contact with angelic forces. She eventually became a saint. She labored.

What is labor? People think to labor is to sit and meditate. You cannot sit and meditate if the work is not done in your kitchen, not done in your bathroom.

B. Pain and suffering. Pain and suffering teach you that you are not the body. Sometimes you curse pain and suffering because you do not know that pain and suffering have divine intention. When you suffer emotionally, mentally or physically, there is a lesson to be learned. That lesson is not for the body. You are realizing little by little that you are not the body, that you must stand beyond the body.

C. Observation. You are going to observe your hands, your motions. When you are feeling, you must observe it. When you are thinking, you must observe it, so that eventually you come to the realization that you are not the body. When you walk, observe yourself. When I was thirteen I went to a monastery in the mountains. When a man asked me what I wanted, I said, "I want to see what the soul is." "What else son?" "I want to know how I can achieve immortality." He said he would teach me.

The next day he took me to a yard and I was told to walk to the wall, hit it, and then walk across the yard to the other wall and hit it. "Then what?" I asked. "In a few minutes you will be enlightened. But," he added, "there is one piece of advice I want to give you. When you walk, all your attention must be on your walking. Be alert, observe your muscles, how you are walking, how your feet feel. Be really conscious."

The first day I walked, cursing all day. I said, "I do not want to do this. I am going to get my horse and...," but there was no escape; the horse was gone. I was in the mountains and could not leave.

I thought maybe they had something secret. So I started to concentrate. I discovered that when I walked with negative emotions and mind, I was exhausted at night. But when I started to walk with concentration, I could go until morning without getting tired. Then I came to the conclusion that concentration generates energy to your body. That is why the Bible says anything you do, do with all your might and heart. There is a great secret in it.

I walked for six months. I was feeling better and better. One day before the six months were over, I saw my body walking. I was watching my body walk. My teacher cried out, "You did it!"

Observation detaches the soul from the body. This was learned from practical knowledge, six months of practical knowledge. My body became so beautiful, strong. My mind was so concentrated. The energy was flowing.

You can start doing this. When you paint, concentrate. When you play, concentrate. Anything you do, be completely there. That is observation.

D. Mastery. When you give an order to your body and make it obey, that is mastery.

One day my teacher told me to teach my body something daily so that it learned to obey. I created many different things. One thing I did was to tell it to stand on one foot without moving for two minutes. Then I daily extended the time until I was able to do it for fifteen minutes. Then I told it to stand and not think. The body must be controlled.

I would go to eat dinner and with everything smelling so good, I would tell my body, "You are not going to eat." Or I would be thirsty and go to get a glass of water. I would say,

"You are not going to drink." Can you come to the realization that the body is not you? Who are you? The Self has no name. The Nameless One is you. The Nameless One is the Divinity within you. It is the Nameless One who says, "Stop that smoking!"

Do not be a slave. Be the master. Those who are slaves of their bodies serve the lowest interests of humanity. Those who are masters of their bodies serve God. If you see a criminal committing a crime, he is a slave. When you see a person creating beauty, he is the master.

The next step is to control and master your emotions. Five of the emotions are: fear, anger, hatred, jealousy and revenge. Try daily to be above these negative emotions. It is not an easy labor. When you conquer these negative emotions and pass various tests, you are almost a saint, because when these emotions are conquered, your intuition begins to develop, and you become an intuitive person.

Intuition is one of the tools of all success. Through intuition you develop Self-awareness on the astral plane. Self-awareness on the mental level is reached when you start conquering your mental body, your thoughts. The first step is to be aware that you are not your thoughts. You create thoughts. Thoughts come to you, but you are not thoughts. You are not your plans. You are not your opinions. You are not even your knowledge. All these things are furniture in your mental body.

Can you reach the awareness that nobody is going to put you into an elevator and send you to the mental plane? You are going to do it by yourself with hard work. If you start thinking of something negative, stop it immediately and say, "I do not want to think about this; I want to think of something else." If you think of something that is fearful, change it to something that is joyful. If you think of something ugly, change it to something that is beautiful. If you think of something that is destructive, change it, make it constructive. In that way you learn how to control your mind. Say, "I do not want these depressing thoughts. Let me put elevating thoughts in my mind."

You will discover that you can create your own thoughts, and instead of bringing trash into your house, you bring beautiful flowers. Ugly thoughts create suffering and complications in your life. Change your thoughts and bring bouquets of flowers, fruit and jewels instead. Once you learn that trick, your health will improve; your magnetism will increase.

A few years back a lady came to me and said, "I always attract the wrong man. Can you help me so that I attract the right man?" I answered, "The law says that you attract people according to the level of your consciousness. Change your consciousness and you will attract the right man." "How can I change my consciousness?" I gave her a meditation and advised her to live in a state of beauty, goodness and truth. Six months later she married a very beautiful man. "It was so interesting," she later told me, "it really worked!"

If you control your thoughts, create thoughts of beauty, goodness and truth, you will see that you are achieving Self-awareness on the mental plane.

The Teachings of great Masters say that the soul comes first to build his body. The theory that the soul comes three months or six months after pregnancy is false. You need a nucleus to build the fruit. The nucleus comes first. The nucleus is the human soul, the human Spark. When the Spark comes, the etheric body is formed.

5. Solar Angel. Solar Angels are our Guardian Angels. Every human being has a Guardian Angel. According to *The Secret Doctrine* and esoteric teachings, Solar Angels came to human beings eighteen million years ago.

At that time human beings were having a hard time entering into human consciousness. They were still attached to animal behavior, animal consciousness. Because of this the progress of human souls was retarded. We are told that a Great Being on this planet Who in the Ageless Wisdom is called Melchizedek, Sanat Kumara, asked Almighty God to send hosts of Angels to come and guide humanity.

About eighteen million years ago, these hosts came in three great waves. The first wave came and looked at humanity. They said that humanity was not ready. The second wave came and planted into the mental body the bud, which in Ageless Wisdom is called the twelve-petaled Lotus.

The third wave came and dwelled in the Lotus, also called the Chalice, and used it as an anchorage. The intention was to expand the consciousness of humanity in such a way that it mastered its physical body, emotional body and mental body step by step.

This great Teacher within you, the Christ within you, the Light within you, shines from the beginning of your life. The intention was to make you the master of yourself.

Until you reach that state of mastery and to the consciousness of the Self previously explained, the Solar Angel or Inner Guardian is with you. When you reach that destination — the mastery of all your bodies — the Solar Angel leaves you and proceeds on Its own evolution. The bird flies away.

One day when I was with my teacher on the seashore, I said, "Master, how many times was this Universe created?"

"I have something to do in the Temple," he said, "and while I am gone count how many waves are hitting the rocks."

He went and I started counting. I kept counting. He finally came and asked, "How many waves did you count?" "I stopped at three hundred." "Do you realize," he said, "that after you stopped counting, still the waves continue, and before you started, millions and millions of waves had already hit the shore?" "Yes," I answered. "That is what creation is, my son; there is no end, no beginning. The snake bites its tail. Do you understand that symbol?"

Billions of years ago, Solar Angels were human beings in another solar system. They conquered; They achieved mastery. They passed through all the initiations and eventually became Angels. Then the call came. They came back to the human realm to help Their little brothers. The relationship between the Solar Angel and you, the human soul, is like mother and son, or teacher and student.

Our first intention is to have a contact with the Solar Angel within us. Once you have a contact, It will guide all your steps. It is the Inner Light. It is the Inner Source of wisdom, goodness, beauty, strength, courage and striving. Every human being must come in contact. Immediately after one comes in contact with his Solar Angel, he gradually grows into It and a day comes when a Divine Marriage takes place. Esoterically we call it Soul infusion in which you as a human soul, become equal to the light of the Solar Angel and you become the inheritor of Its wisdom, beauty and energy.

There are hindrances that prevent us from making contact with our Solar Angel:

A. Physical hindrances:
  1. alcohol,
  2. hallucinogenic drugs,
  3. marijuana,
  4. meat,
  5. excessive sex,
  6. crime.

Alcohol prevents you from contacting your Solar Angel. Hallucinogenic drugs create a wall. They destroy the bridge between you and your Solar Angel. The greatest danger to our youth is drugs. Drugs make them criminals instead of angels.

Marijuana prevents Soul contact. The greatest danger of marijuana is that it puts the user in contact with dark forces. The odor of marijuana attracts dark forces. Eventually the user loses his health and sanity.

Meat creates hindrances because it pulls you into animal consciousness. As much as possible, avoid meat unless it is necessary for health reasons.

Excessive sex depletes your energy and prevents contact with the Solar Angel. When sex energy is sublimated it creates some kind of substance through which you can come in contact telepathically with your Solar Angel. That is why in old monasteries, great advanced sages used sex very economically or became celibate. If you want to reach higher realization, minimize your sex life slowly, slowly, until you reach your destination.

Excessive sex is determined when it leaves you weak. You cannot concentrate. You become irritable. Your voice loses its beauty. You have more tendency toward negative things than harmless things. These are signs that your sex is excessive. You must watch yourself. It is like spending money. When you spend money that brings something beautiful, spend it. But if it is taking away beautiful things, do not spend it.

B. Emotional hindrances:

1. hatred,
2. jealousy,
3. fear,
4. anger,
5. greed,
6. depression,
7. irritation,
8. revenge.

As much as you can, stand on your own feet. Find strength from your Soul. Instead of looking for help from others, help yourself. That is very important. There is a saying, "God helps those who help themselves." If you do not help yourself, God does not help you. You are first going to learn to help yourself. Stand on your own feet.

Irritation is a hindrance that creates tremendous walls between you and your Solar Angel. It creates poison. It is responsible for diseases and cancer. Doctors and scientists are proving that the first enemy of the heart is irritation, and that cancer is directly the result of irritation.

The best method to avoid irritation is to try to see beauty in everything, and expand your compassion. If lightning and thunder start and you think for a moment that is the end of the world, you become irritated. But if you think that lightning and thunder are blessings, cleaning the air, burning bad thoughtforms and creating beauty and peace, you do not have irritation. We must do the same thing for each other. Try to see the beauty in each other.

C. Mental hindrances:

1. laziness;
2. hypocrisy, bribery, flattery;
3. prejudices;
4. superstitions; and
5. preconceived ideas.

If you want to stand in front of God, you must be a humble man. If you think you know everything and can do everything, you are in vanity. You must be humble. Go outside and look at the stars, then you will learn humility. We had two great presidents, Roosevelt and Truman. After the war when the Allies had conquered, they became very proud and said, "We did it!" But then they looked at each other and one of them said, "Let us go to the balcony of the White House and look to the stars." And they did it to keep their humility alive. Humility is the beginning of wisdom. Those who want to be great human beings must first of all be humble. To be humble is to have exact awareness of where you are and who your are. Unless you have that inner awareness, you cannot increase yourself.

The real Solar Angel looks like a five-pointed star. But because of our imagination, our aspirations and visualizations, we change the form to what we want to see. If you visualize your Solar Angel as a beautiful girl, you see your Solar Angel as a beautiful girl. If you visualize your Solar Angel as a beautiful boy, that is what you see.[1]

---

[1]Taken from the seminar, "Mystery of the Soul," August 27, 1982.

4

The Beginning

*T*o better understand our own existence and why Solar Angels came into our life, I am going to start from the beginning of how our solar system came into being, and the building of our chain.

Our planet is a globe. Each globe always has six companions. These seven globes together make a chain. This is called the earth chain. In this chain there are three planes of existence: physical, emotional or astral, and mental.

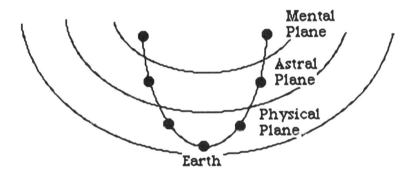

You will note that the highest globe, which is actually our globe, is in the lower mental plane. For example, if you think of something you are going to build, you have that form in your mind. If you are going to build a chair, the form of a chair is in your mind. The same is true in the Divine Mind. The first globe is our planet, but it is in the mental plane. The next globe, which is still our planet, is in the astral or emotional plane, which is condensed a little. Then we have our planet condensed in the physical plane.

There are seven chains and our chain is the fourth one. In the seven chains are found all planes of existence: Divine, Monadic, Atmic, Buddhic, mental (higher and lower), astral, etheric and/or dense physical.

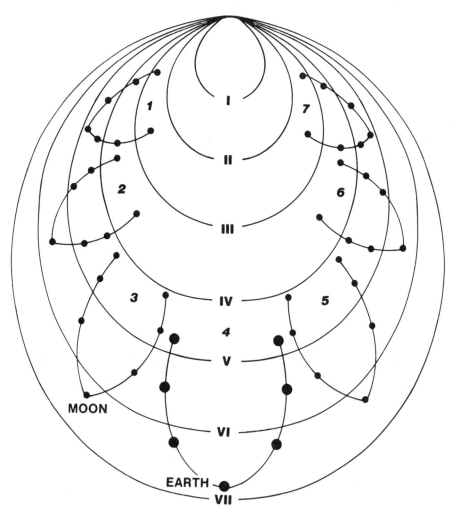

THE SEVEN CHAINS OF OUR SCHEME AND THE COSMIC PHYSICAL PLANE

Our solar system started from the Atmic Plane of the first chain. From there it proceeded to the Buddhic Plane, to the higher mental, lower mental and then astral. We traveled until we reached the earth chain where we are now. The next chain we will enter is the fifth chain, and from there to the sixth and then to the seventh.

These seven chains are called one scheme of evolution. You start from the beginning and graduate at the end. Seven or ten of these schemes make one solar system. These ten schemes are created three times. There was the first solar system, the second solar system which is our present solar system, and there will be a third solar system.

The planets that you see are all on this scheme. We have for example, Venus chain, Uranus chain, Jupiter chain, etc.

There are seven globes in a chain. Seven chains make one scheme. A solar system of ten schemes has four hundred ninety globes, but they are on different levels. The first ones are all physical. Then there are globes that are all etheric, globes that are all astral, globes that are all mental. This seems to be something beyond our comprehension. It shows to what depth God is. Imagine people on globes in the atmic level with atmic bodies built of very refined elements, as in the Bible where it says that lightning is God's messengers — lightning bodies.

Seven globes exist at the same time. When the last one disintegrates, the first one on the next chain starts to build — disintegrate and build, disintegrate and build. The material of one is magnetically kept in Space to be the substance for the next one, then substance for the next one, and so on.

This is all happening on ten schemes simultaneously. This means that there are ten physical earths like ours, each one in its own scheme, but we cannot see them because they are in higher planes; they have not materialized. There are planets in our solar system which have not materialized as they are still in the etheric stage.

If you want to build a temple, the temple is in your mind. Then it is emotional. Then it is etheric. Then it is physical. It exists on all levels, but in different dimensions; it is a continuous process. The ten schemes, including this one, are going on simultaneously. It is simultaneous but here it is sequential. It is a different rhythm. If forty-nine people dance seven different dances, it is like what is happening to the planets and solar system — one fading, one coming, one turning, one slowing down, and so on.

If we have seven people, each representing a scheme, they exist simultaneously. Although simultaneously present, each one in his own scheme is progressing.

All planets exist as seven brothers or sisters, but one planet exists in the physical plane, two in the etheric, two in the higher astral and two in the lower mental plane. They are all in existence and you can travel to them if you know how. You can go to the etheric, astral and mental planes. This is referred to as the inner rounds.

When we reached the lowest condensation of energy which is matter, our Earth, we reached halfway toward our destination. There are people who are striving to break away from matter, possessions, luxuries, ego, and going toward their spiritual evolution, for they are realizing there is no other way.

The first solar system was Holy Spirit, the Third Ray or Intelligence. The second solar system, the one we are in now, is Second Ray or Love-Wisdom. The third solar system will be First Ray or Will. So our scheme is under the Second Ray of Love-Wisdom. Our scheme is part of this whole solar system, and the entire solar system is related to our Earth, to our earth chain and our earth scheme. We are in the fourth chain of the earth scheme, and in the fourth globe, halfway through our journey in this scheme.

The chain before this one is called the moon chain. Only the emotional body of the moon remains. The mental body is going and eventually will evaporate. The moon will slowly disappear in Space. There is no life there. The astral plane is keeping the form together, but it is dissipating.

It is the measure of the condensation of the etheric body that makes a planet visible or invisible. The moon was in our scheme. It was our Earth. We came from the moon. That is our trouble.

Our sun is in the center in relation to the schemes, the solar systems.

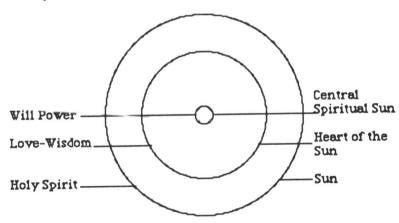

Will Power —— Central Spiritual Sun

Love-Wisdom —— Heart of the Sun

Holy Spirit —— Sun

The first ten schemes of the first solar system were created and have finished. Another ten schemes, which are related to our solar system, were created by Love-Wisdom. The next ten schemes, the third solar system, will be created by Willpower.

When the Ray of Intelligence or the Third Ray of the Holy Spirit aspect created the first ten schemes and then became annihilated, or dissipated, the whole substance was charged with the aspect of Holy Spirit. That is the consciousness in the atom.[1] We use this substance now as material to build our solar system, the second solar system. When the third solar system comes into being, the substance will be a combination of Third Ray, Second Ray and First Ray, or Holy Spirit, Love-Wisdom and Willpower aspects, all in the substance itself.

The first solar system, which was Third Ray, was the Law of Economy. The second solar system is Law of Attraction and Repulsion and Law of Economy together. The third solar system is going to be Law of Economy, Law of Attraction and Repulsion and Law of Synthesis, or the First, Second and Third Rays. These three Rays will be synthesized in the third solar system.

The Law of Economy is the matter aspect. The Law of Attraction and Repulsion is the love aspect. The Law of Synthesis is the will aspect.

When the three solar systems are finished, it will be only three days for the sun. A day of the sun is billions of years — 8,640,000,000 years, to be more precise.

As we have day and night on Earth, so do we have day and night in the solar system, which in Sanskrit is called manvantara and pralaya. Manvantara is when there is activity or action. When the period of manvantara finishes, a great night, a great period of rest elapses until the next solar system comes into being. That period of time is called pralaya. "Laya" means center. "Pra" means stop of center.

---

[1]See *The Consciousness of the Atom*, by A. A. Bailey.

There is no activity. It is just like night time. You work during the day for twelve hours and at night you go to sleep. There is an activity period and a rest period. The same happens between the solar systems. Until the next solar system forms, you go into a long sleep or into pralaya. You are suspended and unconscious. When a new solar system is created you start something, but you do not know your past because you do not have continuity of consciousness.

The day of Brahma, the day of God, of our Sun, is measured in time. If you do not make it in that period, you are out. We hear people say, "If I do not make it in this incarnation I will make it in the next." They play like rabbits on the path. The tortoise reaches the goal, and the rabbit is late. When such people are late, they are suspended. They remain asleep in space for millions of years. They are thrown out from the system for a long time. When they come back, their former pets or animals are their teachers. So it is up to each of us.

Real discipleship on the path is not standing wherever you are. It is a tremendous striving and expanding process. If something easy is given to you, do not accept it. You want something to fight, to battle, to wrestle so that you grow. Sooner or later you are going to grow, so start now and endeavor and strive to expand your consciousness. Once you make a breakthrough, it is so easy. Do not be afraid when a book or a lecture is difficult to understand. Just attack it.

When we finish the seventh round of our earth chain, we will go into pralaya. Then we start the next chain. Those who do not build their continuity of consciousness go into pralaya. Those who build their continuity of consciousness will proceed to the next chain.

If you do not make it during the seven schemes, then you have to enter a chain in another scheme, some place else on a lower level. When a university expels a student, he wanders until a university is built that will take students on his level so that he can return to school and start learning again. There are many people on this planet who have previously flunked in other systems. That is why our planet is really in danger.

A round is a life-wave that comes seven times through our scheme. We have finished the first, second and third rounds, and are now in the fourth round.[2] Every time a life-wave comes, seven root races develop in each globe, and from each root race, there are seven subraces or forty-nine subraces for our seven globes. A life-wave comes and brings the Monads, the Sparks. They are mineral monads; they are atoms. The atoms graduate and become vegetables in the second round. Each time the life-wave comes, the atoms graduate to a higher level, to become etheric, then astral, then mental — mineral, vegetable, animal, human and Divine kingdoms.

You are going to become etheric, astral and then mental beings. Mental being means that you do not have an astral body. There are lots of angels and devas who are mental. They do not have astral bodies. There are some devas who have only astral bodies. There are violet devas, higher etheric and lower etheric devas. Then we have earth devas.

As we descended the chain we added to our bodies; we descended from lower mental, to emotional, to etheric and then to the physical level. As we ascend we start subtracting these bodies until we again reach the lower mental plane, but this time consciously.

---

[2]See pages 29-31, *Cosmos in Man.*

We are presently in the fourth globe. Seven races developed on this globe, which was a recapitulation of the process going from the first, second and third globes to the fourth. We had a first root race, second root race, then the third, which was called the Lemurian race. The fourth root race was called the Atlantean race. The fifth root race is called the Aryan race, which is us. The sixth race may be called the Aquarian race, and then there will be the seventh root race. Seven races develop in one day of this life-wave called the fourth round.

The chain before this one was called the moon chain. Something wrong happened there. Some people advanced to higher levels in their astral and mental bodies. Then there were those who were concrete or physical like us who caused a cataclysm, which could have been an atomic war. As a result, Shamballa or the Hierarchy had the planet removed from the chain. But before the destruction of the moon, those who were advanced enough were brought to our globe. That is why H. P. Blavatsky in *The Secret Doctrine* says that humanity came to our globe first, then the animals came.

Those who did come did not graduate. They were late in the solar system time table. For example, in two million years these students should have reached the degree of a Fourth Degree Initiate, but they did not make it.

What could be done for this humanity? They were suffering; they were not progressing. They were like animals, some half animal, half human. The whole scheme was dependent on their progress. It was in trouble.

The Planetary Logos had a consultation with the Solar Logos. They decided to bring one hundred and five great Beings, called Kumaras, from the Venusian scheme, and sixty thousand million Solar Angels. Solar Angels were those beings Who in many previous solar systems, schemes and chains had graduated from being human to become Fifth Degree Masters. They were waiting for another scheme in order to continue Their evolution, but They were called to duty. They sacrificed Themselves to save humanity. These are the Solar Angels that are within you, great Masters watching over you all these years. What patience They have to watch over us.

They are also called Nirvanis. "Nirvani" means They penetrated into the Buddhic Plane, the Intuitional Plane, and are living in Their Buddhic or Intuitional vehicles.

The one hundred and five Kumaras went to the Gobi Desert. That is where Shamballa started. They made a nine-year study on how to help humanity. They called the Solar Angels to watch humanity to see if They could do something.

The first wave of Solar Angels came and watched humanity. They said They could not do anything. Millions of years passed. They called the second wave of Angels. They came and hovered and said, "The mental body is a little ready; let us put a Spark in it." From Their Causal Body, a Spark, a seed, was planted in the mental plane of the human being so that the human being could eventually be "leavened." That was the second wave of Solar Angels.

The third wave of Solar Angels came and said, "The human being is ready," so They occupied them. And when They did, millions of humans cracked, and died. Such an aggressive entrance was needed in order to save humanity and to make humanity progress in its evolution.

The Solar Angels occupied the third mental plane and started building "the temple not made by hands." It is also called the "Temple of Solomon," "the Lotus — the twelve-petaled Lotus," or the zodiac in man. It has many names.

The Lotus has twelve petals. The first petals are called knowledge petals. The second ones are called love petals. The third ones are called sacrifice petals. When the Solar Angels came, these petals were a bud. It was the third wave of Solar Angels, also called Agnishvattas, which means fiery lightning, Who came and dwelt in man, in his little bud. They entered into deep meditation so that They slowly radiated, to help integrate the physical, emotional and mental bodies, and to produce a personality.

The Solar Angel in deep meditation tries to contact the human soul with Its magnetic love, to pull the soul up and awaken it. The "sleeping giant" is within you, and you are the Spark of God awakening. One inch of awakening opens one of the petals one inch. It is reaction to the Solar Angel's energy or influence that makes the petals unfold. As the petals unfold, they give more knowledge, more love, more willpower.

Each knowledge petal goes in three directions. The first knowledge petal is linked to the physical body. The second knowledge petal is linked to the emotional body. The third knowledge petal is linked to the mental body. There is physical knowledge, emotional knowledge and mental knowledge. If the Spark is progressing in knowledge, knowledge petals are opening. If he is awakening into love, love petals are opening. If he is sacrificial, the sacrifice petals are opening.

When man awakens to the mental plane, this is when meditation must start. Meditation is the first technique to contact the Solar Angel. Meditation is a must. A person may start meditating for one minute or two minutes. It is important to discipline oneself and do right meditation.

As meditation starts the human soul takes initiation. In the first initiation, the first three petals open. In the second initiation, four, five and six petals open. In the Third Initiation, nine petals open. When nine petals open, a light from the innermost petals shines so brightly that it is said, "He took the Third Initiation." When Moses was going to the mountain to receive the Ten Commandments, his face was radiating. When Christ went to the mountain and was transfigured, nine petals opened. When Buddha was under the tree and became enlightened, nine petals opened. As your petals open, your Solar Angel makes a secret marriage. That is what is called "marriage in heaven."

The marriage in heaven is explained in mystic and Sufi literature. Jalaluddin Rumi, who was a Sufi and Persian writer in the fourteenth century, wrote a beautiful anecdote to explain this mystical marriage. He wrote about a man who fell in love with a girl. One day he knocked on her door and said, "My love, open the door." "Who is it?" she asked. "Don't you know me, I am...." She said, "I am sorry I don't have a place for you." He left, but days later he returned, knocked on the door, and said, "My love, open the door, I have come to marry you." Again she asked, "Who are you?" He gave his name, but she said, "Go, I am not opening the door because there is no place here for you."

Years passed, lives passed, during which time the man searched and inquired of religious people, philosophers, and learned people in all professions to find out why his love was not allowing him to enter and be one with her.

Then one day a man gave the Teaching to him. He got the secret. He knocked on the door. The girl, who was his Solar Angel, asked, "Who are you?" He answered, "You." She said, "If it is me, come in."

This is the Soul marriage which happens at the Third Initiation. It continues until the Fourth Initiation which may take seven, seventy-seven or seven hundred and seventy-seven incarnations to make. If you really work hard, you will make it. You will marry and become one with your Solar Angel. In esoteric literature, we call this stage Soul infusion. It is during this period between the Third and Fourth Initiations, that the Solar Angel watches to see if you are ready to make it on your own before leaving you. When that time does come, three inner petals start to be radioactive. Suddenly there is a conflagration. The temple is destroyed, the Angel leaves and the man becomes a Soul. He becomes a King in the Universe. His physical, emotional and mental bodies are under his control. There is nothing that can bother him and he is ready to give his life, whatever he is, whatever he knows, to the service of one humanity.

This is called the great sacrifice or renunciation through which Buddha and Christ passed, and through which others are passing. At the time of Its departure, the Angel becomes free and in a position to aid the animal kingdom, to initiate animals. Our success in freeing our Angel is a means of helping our little brothers. To be a Solar Angel to an animal is a very heavy duty. The Solar Angels are so wise and cosmically expanded, time is nothing to them. Personal progress is nothing. They want to sacrifice for the Divine Will. This is the greatest joy for Them. Because of Divine Will They came to animal humanity; still They watch us and the many secret, stupid things we do. But slowly Their inspiration and courage take root in our system and we expand and progress.[3]

---

[3]Taken from the seminar, "Solar Angel," 1975.

5

Path
of the Soul

editation means the process of penetrating into the secrets of Nature, and the power to use these secrets for the betterment of life and for the progress of evolution.

Meditation is a process of using the mind and intuition through which man penetrates into the secrets of Nature. The secrets of Nature are laws hidden from the simple human mind, but those who know how to approach the world of laws and principles find them. Once these laws and secrets are found, they are used for the betterment of life on the planet and to create various methods to further the plan of evolution for all humanity.

Meditation is also a process of transmutation in which the nature of man changes and enters into a process of transfiguration. This can be symbolically described as a process in which the charcoal of man changes and becomes fire. Literally, the substance of the physical, emotional and mental bodies changes. The atoms of the physical, emotional and mental bodies vibrate in a low frequency. Through meditation, their frequency increases to a very high frequency and they become more responsive to the corresponding waves of impressions coming from different sources.

For example, our first television set was able to receive only one station. That was our physical body at that stage. Fifteen years later because of our increasing knowledge and skill in action, we are now producing more advanced television sets with a choice of multiple stations.

This can be likened to our physical body. It is entering into a process of change, a process of development, and because of this change, the human body is able to respond to more stations and register new impressions from the Universe. This is also true for our emotional and mental bodies.

Meditation is also a transformation and transfiguration process. Meditation not only brings things from the outside, accumulates knowledge, opinions, energies, laws or principles, but brings change in man himself. It is a mental effort of changing, unfolding and making a man bloom.

You are a Spark and you are unfolding. Unfoldment means more enlightenment, joy, happiness and readiness to respond to Nature, but you do not have the instruments to come in contact with Nature. Then you make a telephone line between you and her and call that your vehicle of communication. You touch and say, "This is my nose, my eyes or ears, my vehicles of communication." You inhale Nature to smell her flowers, to see their patterns and feel their texture.

All your mechanisms were built to come in contact with Nature. The little Spark throughout ages is building mechanisms. First It built a very little instrument, a worm, an insect, a little animal, a more developed animal, a man, then a very advanced man. The Spark is not only developing a physical body, but is also developing a tremendously complicated mechanism in Its emotional nature. Still, there are millions of gaps between the Spark, the mechanism and Nature. Some men are not sensitive to the beauties of Nature, to the needs of other people, while others are so sensitive.

Then we have the development of the mental mechanism. One man cannot learn the ABC's, but another man is a very advanced scientist or artist. The difference between these people is in the development of their mental mechanism.

The real Self in you is the Spark, the drop of light. That is you and that Spark is developing.

We are told that the development of the Spark depends on communication with the whole. Let us say he was a whole before, but was not conscious of it, and now he has become a drop and individualized. He is now going back to wholeness, to unity again, consciously and with experience.

Animals are mechanically and naturally very much in tune with each other and have some kind of group consciousness. But then listen to a symphony. You can hear how the violinists and other instruments are adjusted, harmonized and in tune with each other and with the creative source of that music to radiate a tremendous beauty. This is also an example of group consciousness but far more advanced than herd consciousness.

I was watching a small group of birds and was amazed how they moved together as if they were connected. They did not look at each other. But that is not conscious movement; it is mechanical, natural and instinctual, unless it is based on conscious geometry, physics or with an understanding of the purpose and goal of the motion.

In the Ageless Wisdom, an initiation is the moment when a little life unit with a special pattern becomes a cell or a leaf, then becomes a flower, a tree. What a tremendous Cosmic urge is needed to make an unmoving life unit become a moving life unit! Imagine how the life of the vegetable kingdom moves ahead and becomes an insect or an animal or a bird. Now he can fly. Such advances are called initiations. Trees, dogs, cats, horses and elephants will take human initiation one day.

Let us come again to the globes.

What will happen on the fifth globe? When humanity passes to the fifth globe, it will lose its physical body and will live mostly in an etheric-physical existence, as advanced Masters or Initiates now live.

The Masters have both a physical and an etheric body. But when They want to go somewhere etherically, They send Their etheric body. They can appear the same time at seven to ten places by sending thoughtforms of Their physical bodies. These bodies are called Mayavirupas.[1]

Masters have mastered the substance or the matter of the mental plane. Just as you build forms with clay, They build forms with the substance of the mental plane. They animate the form and project it in order to give the messages They want. But if you touch the form, it is not there, it is an illusion.

You can touch the thoughtform; you can touch the physical body; but if you touch the etheric body, you will receive a shock. The etheric body is energy.

The Masters have Cosmic business and have arranged Their lives in a way that They can reach people by such reflections at different times, in different manners, to communicate and give light. It would be wasteful for Them to

---

[1]"The Mayavirupa is literally the illusory form; it is the body of temporary manifestation which the Adept creates on occasion through the power of the will and in which He functions in order to make certain contacts on the physical plane and to engage in certain work for the race." *A Treatise on Cosmic Fire*, by Alice A. Bailey, p. 761.

go physically to see me or you. They can send Their reflection, give the message and disappear.

Every chain is named by its fourth globe. We are the fourth globe, and this chain is called the earth chain. "Chain" means seven globes. We must have seven chains so that life reaches graduation. Those who were not able to graduate will be left out from evolution for many, many ages. They will wait in darkness. Life will continue until some appropriate planet or chain is built to carry the evolution of such suspended souls.

The globes are the bodies of the Planetary Logos in which He incarnated. The first globe was His first incarnation; then He had His second incarnation, the third, and now the Planetary Logos is incarnated with this planet. Then He will focus His consciousness on the fifth, sixth and seventh planets in given cycles.

The first three planets are involutionary. The fourth planet is the globe of opportunity. It is on this globe that you can go upward or backward.

What did we do to this planet? We trapped ourselves. We are in confusion. Our seas, oceans, earth and air are all polluted. Day after day, pollution is increasing. All our knowledge trapped us. We emphasized accumulation, the gathering process, havingness, but in having we neglected *to become*.

M.M. said if humanity had waited and not created the telephone and television, it would have been able to develop those psychic powers through which man could communicate great distances. But we searched for things outside, not inside. We did not need television. We did not need telegrams, for telepathically in one second a contact could be made to see what is going on at any given moment.

But we did not work for inner realization, becomingness. Instead we started to depend on outer means instead of inner means. We satisfied our outer thirst instead of searching for the inner treasure.

In the New Testament there is a story about a man who was looking for a jewel. He went and found his land. "Land" means another plane of existence, a level of consciousness in which there is a jewel. He said, "I am going to sell everything. I have to buy that land and have that jewel." So what was the process? To sell it, give it away, sacrifice, serve, and lose oneself is the key process in the science of becoming.

The first three globes are involutionary. The last three, (five, six and seven), are evolutionary. The first three are the seeds. The last three are the flowering. The first is the seed and the seventh is the total flowering of that seed.

The mental plane is divided into two levels: higher mental and lower mental. Our evolution started from the lower mental plane. The mental plane is divided into seven subplanes: seventh, sixth, fifth and fourth are called the lower mental plane and third, second and first are called higher mental plane. The first four are involutionary; the last three are evolutionary.

When you miss the turning point from involution to evolution, you delay your progress and create lots of pressure, tension, suffering and destruction, because you did not feel and sense the timing, the turning point.

The turning point is when you really sense and say, "I must go back to my Father's house." That is the story of the prodigal son in the Bible, who reached the lowest identification and was lost in matter, and then sensed there was something that he lost. He began to look for *the jewel* within him-

a wonderful boy and needed my support. He became a lawyer. Ten years later when he was making good money, he called and offered to give back the money. But I told him he had a great debt. He asked what it was. I told him to give the money to those who needed it for their education. He was very beautiful; he understood. He sent ten boys to school from Jordan to London to educate them to become engineers, lawyers and doctors. That is how we clean our debts. Do good. Spread the instructions of the Hierarchy, of the Ageless Wisdom, and serve. Your karma will become less and less.

My father was a pharmacist and because of the war and shortage of doctors, his services were needed as a surgeon in a big hospital. There was a window in the pharmacy where people came to pay. My father would look at the man or woman and would sense that they did not have money. He would mark their bills paid. My mother would ask who was going to pay for all these bills. But many times I would hear my father say, "What I pay to poor people, God will pay to your children."

One day while riding in a car with four other people going from Jerusalem to Jericho, the car accidentally jumped the rail of a bridge and fell thirty-four feet below in the mud. We sat there. I was stunned at first, then I felt that there was no pain, nothing broken. "Get up," I told them. But nobody answered; they were all dead. Five days later I went to my teacher and asked him, "Do you know what happened?" "Oh," he said, "your father paid for you!"

Another time, during the war, I was walking with three friends. A machine gun was opened on us. I thought I was finished. I walked through the bullets. Nothing happened to me. I laid down. I touched myself. Was it a dream? One boy took thirty-six bullets, and another twenty-nine bullets. Not a bullet touched me. Either my daddy paid for me or I paid in past lives.

The Soul, the Solar Angel, is one of the greatest mysteries that the temples protected, and even writers of esoteric books never wanted to clearly define It until the time was right. The Soul is one of the greatest mysteries in the human being. Curiously enough, some psychological schools are discovering that another being exists in man who is greater, has greater wisdom and depth than the surface man. They call that being the Transpersonal Self.

The Solar Angel does not belong to our nature. When we are ready to go to the Father, It will say, "Good-bye, I did my work." We are going back to the Father or to our Monadic Consciousness, step by step. These great steps going toward the central Core of our inner Self are called initiations.

In the first initiation the Spark is controlling the physical body. In the second initiation, he is controlling the emotional body. In the Third Initiation the mental body is controlled, and these three are enlightened and transfigured.

Not only have you been watched by the Solar Angel, but also whatever you say, do and think are being recorded, especially those acts which are against the Law of Love.

The Law of Love is the source of all laws. All transgressions or sins are nothing else but acts against the Law of Love. All vices are nothing else but lack of true love. Killing, stealing, jealousy, hatred are all expressions of those actions that are against the Law of Love.

There are six ways your Inner Guide or Solar Angel communicates with you:

1. Through revealing dreams which confirm the steps you are taking or showing the dangers confronting you. Prophetic dreams warn you if you are about to do something wrong. They can be symbolically given so that they develop your mind and understanding if you are ready.

If you are not remembering your dreams it means that you are in agitation, emotionally, physically and mentally. You have some worries or irritation. These are the two main things that prevent you from being impressed by dreams through your mind. You may see lots of dreams when you have worries or are irritated, but they do not come from the Solar Angel. They are static recorded in the radio or television machine of your mind. They come from your stomach, solar plexus, sex center, and sometimes from your throat center. They build a drama on the stage of your mind and are called dreams, but they are not dreams, they are just static that takes shape in your imaginative faculty. A dream is of higher quality, such as the dreams and visions of a prophet.

If you dream without sleeping we call it vision, but you can dream daydreams. Close your eyes and say, "I wish I had a nice girlfriend or boyfriend." That is called daydreaming. If you are daydreaming, it is wishful thinking.

2. Through direct telepathy, thoughts, images. Urges come and impress themselves on your mind and you follow them, confident that they are coming from your Inner Guide.

I remember once while in Middle East I was looking for a friend. Where could I find him? While reading a book in a library I suddenly got a message to go out and walk on the street. I went out, started walking, and there he was, the man I had been looking for. We had not seen each other for ten years. This was telepathic communication.

3. Through warning sounds in your ears or at the center of the head. You hear a sound when you do something wrong or when you speak things not necessary or fitting to a situation. Anytime you do something wrong it buzzes and you stop whatever you are doing.

It is a very high pitch. It comes in your mind, in both ears. Suddenly you feel your head enter into total silence and then the voice comes. If you hear a voice before that silence, it is not coming from your Solar Angel, it is coming from the solar plexus or entities.

4. By making you meet the right person to find the right book through right timing and right conditions. Once I met a lady in a library. I was looking for a certain book. She checked to see what books I was looking for and then said, "Take this book, it is a book on spiritualistic mediums." I looked at it and said, "Oh, good." I did not want to offend her. Then I gave her one of the Alice Bailey books and said, "You read this one." I took another book and left. She followed me and asked for my address. Later that night, she called, "May I come and see you." I said, "Come."

She was the lady who inspired the forming of the Aquarian Educational Group. She gave the spark. She said, "I want to learn these things from you." I told her I did not have time to teach just one person. The next day she brought eight or nine people, her father, mother, sister and others. That was when I started teaching.

We had a St. Bernard dog. He was getting so big and because of the care he needed, we decided to put an ad in the paper to find a home for him. A girl with her girlfriends came and bought him. But an hour later they returned saying they could not keep the St. Bernard as he picked on their little doggy and they were afraid he would kill him. I gave back their money. The girl had brought her mother with her, and the mother asked, "What is this place?" I told her about the classes and showed her the books. She bought four books. Now she comes to all the classes. She says that doggy fished for her. He was the excuse to get her to come. Things happen in very mysterious and complicated ways.

5. **Through inspiration and creative urges toward sacrificial service.** You decide to do a service, to make a great sacrifice, to be of use for a great cause. You no longer like your life to be empty and full of nonsense. You want to make your life worthwhile for something great. That is a very high communication.

6. **Through direct appearance and direct instruction of the Plan of the Hierarchy, and for the service of humanity.** Your Soul never talks about anything else except the Plan of the Hierarchy and service for humanity. If anything else is said, be careful and alert. The Soul is not concerned with your personal life, your sicknesses, problems, husband, wife, divorces, unless such problems cause your consciousness to dim.

Direct appearance means that the Soul stands in front of you and speaks. This does not happen until the Third Initiation. If it happened before the Third Initiation it would create glamors and illusions, pride and vanity. You should be totally purified before you come in such a contact with your Solar Angel. Before that, a contact could create a tremendous "I," an ego problem, that a person would think he is a Master, the incarnated Jesus Christ. Such people exist claiming that they are Jesus Christ. They create tremendous glamors and illusions in your mind, and distort the incoming great Teaching.

After the Third Initiation it is possible for you to contact the Solar Angel. How can you know that you are a Third Degree Initiate? When you really have mastered and purified your physical, emotional and mental bodies, and there is not a single lie in you, you are a Third Degree Initiate. You should not have any depression, hang-ups, fear and habits controlling you.

When you are a Third Degree Initiate, your Soul can speak to you, sit by you, take you to the Ashram of your Master.

7. Your Soul contacts you and introduces you to your Master, with Whom you will consciously carry on the Divine Plan even after the Solar Angel leaves. He sends you to another great Teacher and leaves you alone.

Those who think they have met their Master before the achievement of Third and Fourth Initiations are in illusion. They are meeting wolves dressed in sheepskins. Many people of good will, who have possibilities to be beautiful, are trapped by such wolves. Sometimes they give certain teachings for one, two, three, five months until you have faith in them. Once you put all your faith in them, they mislead you in various ways.

Solar Angels do not protect you from such wolves. They have no right, for you must reach your destiny by your own merit. It is the same as telling your daughter that it is not good to smoke, but no matter what you say, she does as she pleases. You cannot beat her. The Solar Angel respects your freedom and karma.

The following meditation is on how to contact our Solar Angel. This is not a face-to-face contact. To contact means to become sensitive to impressions and to reorient yourself in such a degree that the Soul's message is not like water lost in the desert but reaches to a fountain and fills a bucket.

1. Sit as comfortably as you can. Your spine must not touch anything.

2. Purify your mental, emotional and physical atmosphere from any irritation, negative emotions, negative, limiting or destructive thoughts.

3. You are going to promise three things: harmlessness, givingness, forgiveness. These are very great concepts and they create a true atmosphere in the human being. Then consciously and willingly promise these things to the Almighty One Who is everywhere. You will be harmless, as much as possible. You will be giving as much as you can. You will be forgiving. Forgiving means also detachment from the "I" identification.

4. After that you are going to love all beings. You are going to express a tremendous love starting with your beloved ones and then expanding it to the whole surface of the earth to all beings, to all life. A great love will start to flow; you must feel that love.

5. In your imagination sit on a mountaintop. The mountain is foggy and there are lots of clouds, but you feel that the sun is shining beyond the clouds. Make a tremendous effort to disperse these clouds, create cloud rents, to contact the sun. Eventually the sun will shine on you.

6. Say, "Oh Self revealing One, reveal Thyself in me." That is the prayer of the Solar Angel. It is the Solar Angel who really reveals yourself to you.

7. Say three OMs. With the first OM, see a blue star, and then from that blue star a blue light will come to your head center, which is one foot above your head. When it hits the head center you will see a blue light coming out. Then again, see the star. A golden light will come to your heart center which is one foot away from the body. You are concerned with the centers in the etheric body, not the physical body. Group formation eliminates any danger when doing this meditation.

You will see the third light which is orange coming to the ajna center. You have three lights coming, blue, gold and orange. Blue is going to the head center, gold is going to the heart center, orange is going to the ajna center. These three form a triangle.

The first OM is for the head center. The second OM is for the heart center, and the third OM is for the ajna center. Link them together.

8. After you make the triangle, imagine again your head center as a big lotus one foot above the head and see the blue light, and in the blue light a little Angel sitting there. Sit by Her or Him and feel tremendous joy.[2]

---

[2]Taken from the seminar, "Solar Angel," September 8, 1973.

6

The Search

SEARCH FOR THE **J**EWEL

...Christ told the story of the rich man who was searching for a jewel. Although he was rich, he was searching for a *special* jewel. One day he heard that in a certain field there was buried a rare jewel. To find the exact location in such a large area was difficult, so he sold *everything* he had and bought the land. The word *sold* is very significant. He renounced all that he had to obtain that one precious jewel because that which he sought was his own essence. Nothing was more valuable than that jewel, his *real Self*.

When man finds his real Self, he becomes aware of the fact that in every man there is a jewel, a real Self, and this knowledge makes him love and respect everyone. He is ready to sacrifice himself to help others find their own jewel and live according to the level of that awareness.

The "land" to which the parable refers is the higher mind where the jewel in the Lotus is kept. It is our supreme duty to "sell" everything, to sacrifice, to labor, to renounce our lower activities, to buy the land, to make it our own, to experience it, and find the jewel. Once you "buy" that land you will have a deeper sense of justice, deeper love for your fellowman, deeper aspiration toward cosmic values and an all-embracing compassion.

As I was traveling from country to country, from temple to temple in quest of the jewel, I met a man one hundred fourteen years old. His home was a one-room hut in the middle of a forest. He devoted his time to reading and meditating. When I told him that I was searching for something real that lasted after death, something that would make me live this life more joyously in helping others to love and be joyous, he looked at me steadily with great, green eyes, and made a sign to me to rest on my knees in front of him. Placing his hands upon my head, he went into deep meditation. Then he read from an old book a few pages which made my body feel electrified.[1] After he had finished, he told me these beautiful truths:

> *There is a mystery in man. There is a Presence beside him which is the path leading to the jewel. The shortest way to find that Presence is to watch, to observe your behavior, your emotional and mental actions, reactions and activities. You must always remind yourself that these activities do not originate in your real Self, but have two different origins. One originates in your lower vehicles mechanically. The other comes from a higher source, which is your Guardian. If you practice observation enough, you will discriminate between these two. One is mostly selfish, negative, separative, materialistic, narrow and limiting. The other is selfless, joy-giving, courageous, fearless, sacrificial, all-embracing, group-conscious, spiritual, progressive, enlightening; leading to service, dedication and gratitude.*

---

[1]This book, called *Nareg,* was written by a monk in the 10th century in Armenia.

Once you are able to discriminate between these two, the next step will be to tune yourself to the higher one, and express the impressions that you receive from that Inner Presence, which eventually will lead you to your Self, to the Jewel.

I followed his advice, and the first thing I saw in myself was a duality. Besides this duality there was a deep, misty point of awareness, which I was not able to identify, but which I knew to be there.

I found a level of consciousness in myself which was receiving special impressions from a source within, encouraging me to change the way I was living, reacting emotionally and mentally. There was also a resistance in me which was laughing at these suggestions, and making me feel at ease with my way of daily living. Sometimes I was following the deeper guidance. Sometimes I was rejecting it and listening to the voice of my mechanical self, of my body, emotions and superficial thinking.

FOLLOWING THE INNER GUIDANCE

When I was obeying the deeper guidance, my joy, my energy, my creativity were increasing, and I was feeling closer to the beauties of Nature. When I was obeying the mechanical calls of my nature, my worries were increasing. I was feeling less secure, less joyous, even depressed, and my creative energy was nil.

Then the most crucial questions came to my mind. Who is the Guiding One? What is It? Is It "me"? The more I thought about this Guiding One, the clearer became my understanding of It, and I knew It to be different from the "me" I had always known. The choice was mine to reject Its suggestions and act mechanically, or to accept these suggestions and adapt them to my own level of consciousness and the point in time.

Many, many times it happened that when I was very thirsty and about to drink a cup of cold water, the command not to drink came from within. This was surprising to me. Sometimes during dinner I was advised to leave the table and write a letter to a friend, and to keep on fasting. Sometimes It suggested that I depart from a joyful party, go home and carry on with my studies, or go and visit a sick friend. Very often It impressed upon me the command to stop talking, or to change the subject. It also suggested that I confess my lies and other thoughtless acts to an old man, or to those whom I had wronged.

For example, once in a monastery I took the protective cover away from an electric switch in the bathroom where our principal used to lead the students. He, himself, always turned on the light. That night, he was joking with us and, without looking, extended his hand to the wall to turn the switch. Of course he received a terrible shock, which resulted in his being pale and nervous for several hours. I was delighted because he was often very harsh with the students.

It was midnight when an inner suggestion came to go to his room, awaken him, and tell him what I had done. Not expecting such advice, it made me hot and uncomfortable as I lay in my bed. For some time I tried to rationalize, to politely reject the suggestion and go to sleep. Then I noticed that the pressure of the advice from within lessened and I felt free to follow it or not. Just at that moment, I remembered the suggestion of my old teacher: "Obey the inner real voice if you are sure that it speaks of courage, truth, beauty, selflessness." Yes ... yes ... now, what to do? Should I disobey and lose the line of communication, or obey and suffer the humiliation brought on by my act?

At last I decided to go to my superior, my principal, and tell him how and why I had uncovered the switch. I knocked at the door three times. A faint voice told me to come in.

I entered and said, "I came to see if you need any help." This was completely rejected by the Inner Guidance and I felt like a coward, a hypocrite, and I knew that I was lying.

Immediately I collected myself and said, "I really came here to confess to you that it was I who took the cover from the switch."

He looked at me in great surprise, became sad, and in a very serious voice said, "Come closer."

I ran to him and embraced him, resting my head on his heart. For a few minutes we did not speak.

Then he said, "Go and sleep."

This was a great moment for me. A great source of love and respect was released in me, and I was truly sorry that he had suffered because of me. I returned to my bed with tears in my eyes and a great joy in my heart. From that day on, he loved me and I loved him deeply. I was the one on whom he depended when he was in difficult situations and under trying conditions.

The Inner Guidance, day by day, increased. It was so real that I felt a presence around me every day, every moment. I found myself talking with It during the day and at night.

Often it was suggested that I take dangerous trips. On one trip I saw that a huge pine tree had fallen across a deep river. I was on my way to a friend's home to borrow a book for one of my teachers. As I walked along, I was gathering flowers and looking for the shallowest place to cross the river, when the command, or the subtle suggestion, came, "Cross the river on the fallen tree."

"No," I said, "you are joking. It would be the end of my life if I should fall." No answer came.

I sat down at the foot of a tree and began to think, "Will I be insane to try to cross the river on this great tree? Was this the suggestion of the Inner Presence, or...?"

For perhaps half an hour I sat there, unable to decide. Then I said, "It takes courage, fearlessness, daring. Yes, it would be dangerous, but selfishness is being afraid of danger. At least I can try!"

When I came closer to the river, I saw that it was very swift and very deep. Again I hesitated, warning myself, "Don't be foolish. You will die!" I waited for opposition from inside, but there was not the slightest indication of opposition to this warning. This fact gave me inner courage, a feeling of self-dependence, and I said, "I can do it!"

With great caution I sat down on the tree. Just at that moment a monkey-thought came to me, "Never mind, you can go back any moment you wish." I immediately rejected the thought as the voice of my physical, emotional and mental existence. I began to move along the tree in a sitting position with the help of my two hands. I focused my eyes upon the tree and moved on, but when half-way across, I looked down at the churning waters below. It was terrifying, but it was too late to turn back. I closed my eyes long enough to establish my balance. My hands felt weak and the tree seemed to be moving under me.

I wanted to touch, to come in contact with that mysterious Presence, to ask Its protection and guidance ... but It was not there! I was completely on my own! For the first time in my life I knew the meaning of courage and fearlessness — *I seemed to be one with the tree, with the river, with the whole existence!* Some hidden source of energy and joy burst within me, washing away all fear and anxiety. I began to move along the tree with an electrified feeling. Upon reaching the other side I looked back at the tree and the swirling waters of the river. I said, "Do you know what great danger you passed?" I rejected this thought at once and told myself that it had been a great joy and that there had been no danger at all.

I proceeded on to the home of my friend where three boys lived. It was very quiet. No one was in the garden, so I went up the path and knocked at the door. There was no answer. Climbing up to a window and looking into the hall, I was horrified! They were all dead!

I hurried back, crossing the river on the same tree, and gave the news to my teacher. Later, we learned that someone had killed the boys and robbed the home at the very same time that I was trying to make up my mind to cross the river by way of the fallen tree.

Another time a suggestion from within told me to enter a burning house in our neighborhood, to run upstairs, look into a certain room and return. This was a dangerous thing to do, but without hesitating, I did it. This incident was a source of joy in my heart for weeks.[2]

---

[2] *Cosmos in Man*, pp. 19-23.

*"All creation is contained in the call of the heart.
The entire Cosmic expanse is permeated with a call
and the Heart of Cosmos and the heart of an Arhat
are permeated with the call."*[3]

The call is the magnetic pull of the Heart of Cosmos, the call for perfection. It is heard sometimes as your duty, responsibility and high calling. It is heard sometimes as an urge to improvement, service and sacrifice. It is heard sometimes as an affirmation of your labor. It is a call to striving and daring, a call to bloom your Innermost Divinity, a call to lay down your life for the sake of your fellow human beings.

This call may come from your Soul; it may come from your Master, directly or through your teacher, your friend or even through your enemy. It may come from the Lord Christ, or from the Youth of Eternal Beauty, but the source of all these various calls is the heart of manifestation which calls every Spark back Home. Evolution in all its various aspects is the answer to that call.[4]

---

[3] Agni Yoga Society, *Hierarchy*, para. 6.
[4] *The Psyche and Psychism*, p. 175

7

Temple Dramas

ach Initiation into the Mysteries contained the question—"Is thy ear open?" Such opening signified first of all the ability to maintain keen vigilance.[1]

—M.M.—

I was very young when my father took me to a secret meeting. We rode together on horseback under the bright light of a full moon. It was a very still and beautiful night. I could see the branches of the trees bending low as we brushed past them in the moonlight. The stones were shining in the path under the horse's feet.

After riding for an hour we arrived at the meeting place, a deep, natural cave with capacity for no less than five hundred people. Many people were sitting cross-legged in silence on oriental rugs. The atmosphere was heavy with the scent of sandalwood and pine. The soft, soothing music of a flute was penetrating into my heart as some kind of energy.

When the members were all assembled the doors were closed. A huge man with a heavy beard appeared upon the stage and spoke in a clear, strong voice, "Today we are going to search for the Treasure, the Treasure within all of us. We shall find the way to the Treasure." After a few moments of silence, beautiful, rhythmic music floated through the air.

---

[1]Agni Yoga Society, *Fiery World*, Vol. I, para. 226

We could hear the soft, steady beat of drums and the plaintive tones of the flute.

Suddenly a man leaped on to the stage and began a beautiful dance, moving in perfect harmony with the music. Then, to my amazement, the dance began to degenerate. The dancer changed his movements until he was completely out of harmony. He reached a point where the rhythm of his dance was in direct contrast to the rhythm of the music. A few moments later three men rushed on to the stage and attacked the dancer. The first man struck him with a sword and the dancer fell to the floor as though dead. All lights were extinguished and for several moments there was complete darkness. Then a candle began to glow on the stage, and by its light we could see the half-naked figure of the dancer lying upon a long, low table. A man of radiant, angelic beauty entered. In rhythmic step he moved to the table. With his dagger he opened the chest of the man lying there and ran away into the darkness. Then one of the three men who had attacked the dancer came forward, put his hand into the chest and brought forth the heart, a glowing fluorescent heart. Raising it above his head he chanted a few words. Fiery music burst forth and he began to sing an ancient mantram. His deep, powerful voice flowed through the hall like a great, surging river rushing down to the sea.

The music stopped abruptly and he chanted a few more words. The heart began to open like a lily. I saw that the first tier of petals was slowly opening. The second tier opened and as I watched intently the unfolding of the third tier of petals, a blue light flashed forth from the very center of the flower. Myriads of flying sparks filled the darkness, illuminating the hall and revealing the presence of the angel who had wielded the dagger. I was beholding a sight of rare

beauty, inexplicable beauty. As we sat spellbound by his
radiant splendor, the angel disappeared into darkness. The
man still holding the flower, now in full bloom, placed it
back into the breast of the man on the table. Again, there
was a period of total darkness and absolute silence. I was
aware that these intervals of silence were periods of deep
meditation.

As the meditation came to a close we could hear again
the soft strains of music. A single beam of light shone upon
the man lying on the table. Slowly he arose. Clad in a beautiful robe of radiant white and brilliant blue, he stood in the
center of the stage under the bright beam of light. He looked
about in wonder and ecstasy as he said,

> *I was dead in body, in heart, in mind,*
> *but I killed my dead body.*
> *The Angel opened the gates.*
> *I took my heart from within and*
> *by the hands of my mind,*
> *dedicated it to Cosmos, to the Future.*
>
> *And it opened,*
> *radiating the glory of love.*
> *I am alive! I am awake!*
> *Salutations to the Inner Glory of man!*
> *The seed of the Sun is free!*

Heavy darkness fell upon the room during a long period
of meditation. I remember closing my eyes and trying to
recall the drama again and again; each time in greater
amazement and each time thrilled to the center of my being.
At the close of the meditation a member of the audience led
the crowd in a short, simple chant, which expressed in
words and melody gratitude to all creation and to the Light
beyond understanding.

We were again on horseback returning home under the clear, bright light of the full moon. I noticed that my father was still in meditation as we rode over the stony, white path. For a long time I dared not speak, but when we had traveled for some distance I said, "Father, I know what they were doing. I know the message." "What?" he asked. I did not answer, but fell into deep silence and meditation. We arrived home in silence. Never again did we speak of the drama.

Years passed ... difficult and painful years which brought about great changes within myself. I began to realize more fully the depth of meaning behind that beautiful temple drama, still vivid in my memory. It portrayed the release of the Inner Glory of man and presented in dramatic manner the technique to be used in achieving that glory. The dancer who first appeared upon the stage was the divine Monad in tune with Its Source, but as It symbolically descended into matter, Its rhythm and beauty were lost, killed, or put to sleep in the body. The three men who entered next represented the physical, emotional and mental bodies. These bodies "attacked" and killed the Monad. This meant that through the glamors, illusions and inertia of these bodies, the Real Man had fallen asleep spiritually.

The Angel was the Lord of Flame. The Angel opened the gates or established communication between Itself and the awakening Spark. This was accomplished through centuries and centuries of meditation by the Solar Angel. The heart was touched. The real heart is the Causal Body, the Chalice or the Lotus, upon the third plane of mental substance. The flower of the Chalice had opened tier by tier in full glory, and the divine light, love and power radiated from Its petals. As Its radiance increased and reached its greatest heights, the Solar Angel, the Lord of Flame, left, and the Chalice was destroyed. The Solar Angel had completed Its task and was no longer needed; for man, the Monad, was fully awakened. He had arisen and gone to his "Father," his true Self. Man had become Himself.

This drama was a technique used in mystery temples to explain the relationship between the Real Man and his Solar Angel and between the Solar Angel and the vehicles of expression.[2]

Temple Drama II

The relation of the Monad to the Soul and the state of the Monad in the arc of creation and evolution was very beautifully expressed in a temple dance which I saw in Asia.

There was a huge cave and in it was a great stage where a king was sitting on his throne. He had long hair, and a beautiful, ornamented coat. Light was focused on him, but the other corners of the big stage were dark.

As he was sitting, he decided to go into the darkness. So after removing his crown and stepping down from his throne, he started to walk. The beam of light still shone on the empty chair where the crown lay.

As he descended, he met a woman who gave him a cup of drink. He drank it, and his steps became confused. Then he met another woman and bowed to her, and touched his head to the earth. He went to another one — and as he went he entered into more darkness, and finally disappeared. There were seven women who gradually took him into darkness, until he lost his light and kingship.

---

[2]*Cosmos in Man*, pp. 43-45.

As he was in darkness and lying on the earth, a piercing voice tore the silence, calling him:

> *Where are you,*
> *my Self,*
> *the source of beauty,*
> *truth and goodness?*

And he started to move and to show signs of living again, walking as a blind man or as a drunken man.

In the meantime, the seven women tried to prevent him from walking and finding his way to the throne. As he was struggling to walk and find himself, he cried out:

> *Where am I?*
> *Who am I?*
> *Where are you — Me?*

The women were confusing him, answering his call:

> *Here you are. Come and find yourself*
> *in the wheel of the Seven Rivers of pleasure.*
> *Here is the body.*
> *Here is glamor.*
> *Here is illusion.*
> *Here is pride, possession.*
> *Here is hate.*
> *Here is power, you!*

He yielded himself often, but sometimes he endeavored to reject one of them or even two.

As the conflict continued and while he was falling and getting up again, a radiant angel appeared in a golden robe, and approached him. The angel touched him with his sword, giving him a shock. He turned to the angel with an expression of fear and adoration, but the next moment he turned toward the seven women. The angel gave him another shock. This time the adoration and attention were longer, but again he turned back.

This drama continued for awhile until he jumped toward the angel and embraced him, saying:

> *My Self. Me!*

After this moment, the Solar Angel, holding the man's hand, started to do rhythmic movements and dancing, forcing the man to do the same. As he became able to follow more and more the rhythm of the angel, the light increased until suddenly the man saw his throne. He made a cry which was both extremely sad and extremely joyful.

He went five steps toward the throne, and as he came closer, the angel disappeared in the light.

Eventually he reached his throne, and sat there as a victor.

Seven virgins appeared and put a crown on his head, which had a five-pointed star on the front. They knelt in front of him, and with one voice they said:

> *King!*
> *Your glory is seven times more now.*
> *You have overcome matter, the sea and the red*
>   *fire.*
> *You have become a Soul ... and now you are*
>   *the SELF.*[4]

---

[4] *The Science of Becoming Oneself*, pp. 178-179.

8

Individualization

T *here is a sun.*
 Another sun arises over the horizon.
 Between these two suns a form arises.
 The second sun obliterates the first,
 And then these two suns blend and merge...
 A third is seen.

Here we have three Suns. First, "there was a sun." This *was* the Spark, the Monad, which, as the prodigal son, went into materialization and identified Itself completely with the mineral kingdom. Ages and ages passed until It was able to initiate Itself into the vegetable and the animal kingdoms. During the Fourth Globe these Monads were initiated as the first animal-humanity on earth.

Here Its progress was very, very slow, so much so that the Ancient of Days and the Solar Angels decided to hasten the progress of humanity through the process of individualization. Sanat Kumara reincarnated on the higher etheric planes, and the Solar Angels entered into those bodies which were ready to receive them.

Each Solar Angel was a "Sun." And each human being who was ready had a Solar Angel, a Sun, Who was empowered to give life and light and love to each animal form called a human being, in which the first Sun was lost or asleep.

Immediately when this second Sun appeared in the higher mental realms of the human being, a form became visible between these two Suns. This form was the bud of the Lotus or the Chalice.[1] This form is used by the Solar Angel to impart Its light, love and power to the first Sun, and to make It able to climb the ladder of evolution, to fulfill Its destiny.

Eventually this first Sun, who was identified with the physical, emotional and mental worlds, gradually was absorbed into the light and the reality of the Solar Angel, and became one with It. Thus as a separate Sun It was obliterated, though not lost.

Ages passed. This obliterated Sun slowly became born from the womb of the Solar Angel, climbed the spiritual ladder and became Itself. This is the third Sun that is "seen," the Monad in all Its glory.

The first and the third Suns are one. The first was lost in maya, glamor and illusion and became a mere reflection of Its True Self.

The second Sun, the Solar Angel, liberated the first Sun, the reflection of the Monad in the three worlds, and led it to Solar or Soul consciousness (to the consciousness of the Solar Angel Itself) where it was obliterated (lost itself to find Itself.) Then the Solar Angel led the third Sun to Its true Self. Once the first Sun became Its true Self "a third Sun was seen." The reflection, the third sun, was lost in Its true Reality.

The Spark fallen in the densest matter tries to actualize the archetypes impressed upon Its Core. The pressure of the outer world evokes It out, and the Spark magnetically

[1]See Chapter XII in *The Science of Becoming Oneself*, and Chapter XII in *The Hidden Glory of the Inner Man*.

[2]*The Science of Meditation*, pp. 54-55.

attracts those elements which contribute to the formation of the physical body, throughout millions of ages.

Through Its bodies the Spark gathers experiences, acts and reacts toward matter and the forces of environment, and tries to build a mechanism which secures contact with the physical world for Its survival.

Self-actualization at this stage for the Spark is to build a reflection of the archetype impressed upon Its Core, age after age, adding on It and carrying It into perfection. A similar thing is done for Its subtle bodies.

We can say that evolution for the Spark is the actualization of the archetype, of Its bodies, organs, senses, centers and so on. It slowly climbs on the ladder, through the bodies It builds, and thus gradually achieves a new stage of consciousness.

In the Spark are recorded all experiences It gathered throughout ages — during the period of building Its mechanism.

In this building process a time came that It had crises. It is in this period of time that angelic Beings incarnated in man and helped the Spark to continue to build more subtle bodies.

The angelic Beings acted as a reflector for the ideal, for the archetype, focusing it partially on the consciousness of the Spark.

These angelic Beings were called Solar Angels, or various names. They were the Inner Teachers, the Light shining in the human form. They reflected the archetypes on the consciousness of human beings and made the Spark able to actualize them throughout long ages. They were in a sense reminders to the Spark about the "Father's Home."

The actualization process will go on until the lower bodies are highly developed, and are in a state of transfiguration.

After the transfiguration, the Spark, which is the human soul, will have a very close relation with the Solar Angel. It is during this time that the human soul will begin to build higher contacts and higher mental mechanisms, eventually to pass into the Intuitional Plane, and let the Solar Angel depart and pursue Its own evolution.

Age after age the Spark unfolds and actualizes the "dreams" of the Higher Power. As It actualizes, It expands Its light, consciousness, love, power and becomes a better engineer to build those bodies which will put It in contact with the centers of higher evolution.[3]

Long, long ages ago, there came a time when the Universal Soul as a huge and unmeasurable Cloud *"precipitated."* This was the greatest victory of Creation, when the spiritualized substance or materialized Spirit divided into particles to carry on the Act of Creativity and growth. Throughout ages these particles or "drops," passing through numberless forms accumulating experience, reached the stages of self-consciousness ... and became "the Sons of God" Who saw the mystery of God in the mirror of matter and to some degree identified Themselves with that mystery, Their real essence. When some of these "Sons of God" reached a certain high degree of development, They were called "Souls," Sons of Mind, or Solar Angels. They put the mental spark in the evolving man, and then incarnated in him to lead him into the heights of Divine understanding and creativity because at that time the man-form was no more than an animal in consciousness.[4]

---

[3]Unpublished writing, January 21, 1989.

[4]*The Hidden Glory of the Inner Man*, p. 43.

STORY OF INDIVIDUALIZATION

During the middle period of the Third Root Race, a most remarkable event took place — the act of *individualization*. *The Secret Doctrine* says that:

> ...Having passed through all the kingdoms of nature in the previous *three* Rounds, his physical frame ... was ready to receive the *divine Pilgrim* at the first dawn of human life, i.e., 18,000,000 years ago. It is only at the mid-point of the 3rd Root Race that man was endowed with *Manas* [mind]. Once united, the *two* and then the *three* made one; for though the lower animals, from the amoeba to man, received *their* monads, in which all the higher qualities are potential, all have to remain dormant till each reaches its human form, before which stage manas (mind) has no development in them.[5]

This story is given in detail in the following quotation:

> The Sons of Wisdom, The Sons of Night, ready for rebirth, came down. They saw the vile forms of the First Third. "We can choose," said the Lords, "We have wisdom." Some entered the Chhaya. Some projected the Spark. Some deferred till the Fourth. From their own Rupa they filled the Kama. Those who entered became Arhats. Those who received but a Spark, remained destitute of knowledge; the Spark burned low. The Third remained mind-less. Their Jivas were not ready. These were set apart among the Seven. They became narrow-

---

[5]Blavatsky, H.P., *The Secret Doctrine*, Vol. II, p. 255, 1947 ed.

headed. The Third were ready. "In these shall we dwell," said the Lords of the Flame.[6]

This was most fascinating to me. I continued to read and read, feeling deeply that in these ancient writings was the key to the human mystery, and to the identity of my Inner Guide. I continued my studies in *The Secret Doctrine* wherever I went in Asia. Gradually the whole picture of the human psyche became clearer and clearer. I began to grasp the meaning of the passages which had so captured my interest when I first began reading *The Secret Doctrine*.

The Sons of Wisdom. The Sons of Wisdom were very advanced Beings, Angels Who were emerging from Their Night and coming into the Day of a new creation. It was on the fourth chain and at the fourth globe that these Celestial Hosts came to our planet. They came during the period of the Third Race, ready to start a new cycle of experience and expression.

[They] came down. This means that these Beings came from Their state of development to the lower spheres of creation, to the physical earth.

They saw the vile forms of the First Third. "Vile forms" were human beings, with huge, animal-like bodies, possessing no intellect. They were devoid of intelligence. The "First Third" refers to the first half of the Third Root Race which was a senseless, unintelligent race.

"We can choose," said the Lords. This means that these Beings were Lords of mind, discrimination, and choice.

Some entered the Chhaya. "Chhaya" means shadow, the copy, or the etheric body of human beings which is the pro-

---

[6]*Ibid.*, p. 18.

totype of the physical body. Some of the Lords of Flame entered into this electromagnetic atmosphere of man. Others, instead of entering into the atmosphere of man, projected a spark of intelligent substance into man's elementary mental cloud.

Some deferred till the Fourth. Some of the Lords neither entered nor projected a spark, but went away to wait until the Fourth Root Race came into being.

From their own Rupa they filled [intensified] *the Kama.* Those Lords of Flame Who entered into the atmosphere of man stimulated the astral or desire body of humanity. They filled it with Their essence, with will power, which changed in the vehicles of primitive man and became desire.

Those who received but a Spark remained destitute of knowledge. It took ages and ages to inflame the spark of mind, and to make it a real tool for the acquisition of knowledge. The knowledge referred to here is higher knowledge, abstract knowledge, which could be assimilated only as the spark of intelligence developed.

The Spark burned low. The spark of intellect was in a very slow process of development and unfoldment.

*The Third remained mind-less....*The "Third" refers to those human-animal forms that received neither the spark nor the Lords of Flame within themselves, because they were not ready.

Their Jivas were not ready. "Jiva" is the Monad, the divine Spark within the human form, the Real Man. This becomes clear when we understand that man is the Monad — not the form, not the vehicle, not even the Lord of Flame who entered into his sphere.

These were set apart among the Seven. The "Seven" refers to the primitive human species and to the Seven Root Races.

The mindless ones, whose Jivas were not ready, played no part in the destiny of the Seven Root Races. They were "set apart," cast aside.

They became narrow-headed. They were dumb. They bred monsters going on all fours. These remained destitute of knowledge.

The Third were ready. The Monads of the Third group were awakened enough to be able to receive the Lords of Flame.

"In these shall We dwell," said the Lords of Flame. They entered into the higher planes of man to lead the divine Monad, the Jiva, from darkness to light, from the unreal to the real, from death to conscious immortality, from chaos to beauty. This event in many occult books is called the act of *Individualization....*

According to *The Secret Doctrine*, the first two-and-one-half races did not have real human form. They were fiery, cool and radiant, *ethereal*, in the first round; "...luminous and more dense and heavy during the second round; watery during the third;" and dense at the fourth round.

The Lunar Pitris and Solar Angels cooperated to equip man with higher principles and with lower vehicles. The Solar Angels formed the causal center to serve as anchorage for the Monadic life. They also formed and extended the thread of consciousness, anchoring it in the brain. Some of the Angels then entered and dwelled in man.

The lunar bodies or the lower vehicles were constructed by the Lunar Pitris. They first built the lower mental body, next the astral body, and then the etheric body. Later the etheric body attracted atoms of matter and formed the physical body.

Thus, around the fulcrum of the Monad, the Solar Angels built the higher wing of balance and the Lunar Pitris built the lower wing. The two were tied together with the life and consciousness threads.

...Sanat Kumara brought with Him numberless Beings Who were called by various names, for example: Agnishvattas, Fire Devas, Lords of Flame, Solar Angels, Manasaputras, Celestial Exiles, Fire Dhyanis, Sons of Wisdom, Holy Ascetics, Holy Virgin-born, and many others. These great Beings or Angels came to our planet to help humanity enter upon the path of conscious evolution. They came in groups. The first group watched humanity and decided that it was not yet ready to receive help. Ages later the second group came and planted the spark of intelligence in man. These Beings, called the Promethean group, brought the celestial fire to humanity. They implanted the spark of manas (mind) in man, and for the first time, man started to have mental responses. Without this fire it would have been almost impossible to lead man on the path of evolution. It was the first time in his history that man began to give attention to his environment, to his body and to the changing phenomena of the rivers, the lakes and the oceans, the clouds, the winds and the rains. He began to seek ways of survival, not just for the moment but for his future survival.

Man was beginning to use the spark of mind, but this was not enough; so the third group of Solar Angels or Agnishvattas entered into man to form a bridge between the three lower planes — the physical-etheric plane, the astral plane, and the lower mental plane — and the three higher planes — higher mind, the buddhic plane, and the atmic plane. We are told that there were sixty thousand million of these Angels. Thus, the physical, astral and mental levels were connected with the higher levels of the Solar Angels. The Solar Angel has as Its vestures the Spiritual Triad: atma-buddhi-manas.

Man has only physical, astral and lower mental substances. Thus, the Solar Angel became a bridge between man and higher principles, giving him the opportunity to climb the ladder of evolution and to function first as a soul and then as an awakened Monad.

...When we speak of individualization, the fact of the coming of the Solar Angels, and when we speak of building a bridge between the form and the essence of man, we are referring to the humanity which graduated as the animal kingdom from the moon chain, entering into our earth chain as beings-to-be-human, and later to be individualized at the Fourth Round in the Lemurian Race.[7]

[It is told] that the process of individualization on our chain was different from the process of individualization on the moon chain. On the moon chain the latent presence of the fiery spark of mind built the bridge between the two poles of being, matter and Spirit. In the case of earth humanity, however, the gap was bridged by the incoming Solar Angels....[8]

These Angels came to enter into man for two reasons: to give a great push to the progress of the human race, creating a bridge between the Monad and the form, and also to carry

---

[7]When we refer to the souls who came from the moon chain, we are referring to those beings who, being human, came to our chain to continue their evolution. When we refer to the Lemurian Race, or earth humanity, we are referring to those moon animals who entered into our chain as human beings and formed our earth humanity.

[8]*Cosmos in Man*, pp. 35-42.

on Their own evolution. *The Secret Doctrine* says that, "their *Manas* ... had to pass through earthly human experiences to become *all-wise*, and be able to start on the returning ascending cycle."[9]

The coming in of these Angels tremendously accelerated the progress of the human race. Some individuals even reached a state of consciousness which we call Soul infusion where the Angel and the light of the Angel fuses with the light of the developing human soul. These advanced ones became the leaders of human groups in different fields, according to their rays or types.[10]

The Tibetan Master says, "The human soul (in contradistinction to the Soul as it functions in its own kingdom, free from limitations of human life) is imprisoned by and subject to the control of the lower energies for the major part of its experience."[11] He adds:

> And he (the disciple) begins to realize himself as the Soul. Then, later, comes the awful "moment in time," when pendant in Space, he discovers that he is not the Soul. What then is he? A point of divine dynamic will, focused in the Soul, and arriving at awareness of Being through the use of form. He is Will, the ruler of time and the organizer in time, of Space.[12]

---

[9]Blavatsky, H.P., *The Secret Doctrine*, Vol. II, p. 167.

[10]*The Science of Meditation*, p. 51.

[11]Bailey, A. A., *Esoteric Psychology*, Vol. II, p. 69.

[12]Bailey, A. A., *The Rays and The Initiations*, p. 107.

Purpose will reveal Itself; the Whole will stand revealed, and then the soul — loaded with riches and fruits of labour long — will vanish as the mist and only God, the living One, be left.[13]

Personality and ego disappear and only the Monad and its form upon the physical plane remain.[14]

Here personality ceases being representative of the unfolding human soul, or the Monad, because the unfolding human soul becomes Himself, the Monad, and the personality merely serves as a vehicle of expression for the Monad.

...Just as the personality is lost sight of in the light of the soul, the solar Angel, so the soul itself disappears and its power and radiance fade out when the Presence, which it has hitherto veiled, appears and dominates the scene at the end of the greater world cycle.[15]

...Basically, it is not desire which prompts return but will and knowledge of the plan. It is not the need for achieving an ultimate perfection which goads the ego on to experience in form, for the ego is already perfect. The main incentive is sacrifice and service to those lesser lives that are dependent upon the higher inspiration (which the spiritual soul [Solar Angel] can give) and the determination

---

[13]*Ibid.*, p. 117.

[14]*Ibid.*, p. 480.

[15]Bailey, A. A., *Esoteric Astrology*, p. 105.

that they too may attain planetary status equiva-
lent to that of the sacrificing soul.[16]

The Lords of Flame or the Solar Angels were liberated
"intelligent essences." They were Nirvanis from the preced-
ing Maha-Manvantarana. (See *The Secret Doctrine*, Vol. II,
p. 79.) "They are the fire-dhyanis, and emanate from the
Heart of the Sun."[17] "(They who are called *Manasaputra*,
born of 'Mahat,' or Brahma) had to pass through earthly
human experiences to become *all-wise* and be able to start on
the returning ascending cycle."[18] They "...are entities from
higher and earlier worlds and planets, whose *Karma* had not
been exhausted when their world went into pralaya."[19]
They are also called Egos and:

> ...The Ego (being to the man on the physical
> plane what the Logos is to His system) is likewise
> the animating will, the destroyer of forms, the pro-
> ducer of pralaya and the One Who withdraws the
> inner spiritual man from out of his threefold body;
> he draws them to himself the centre of his little
> system. The Ego is extra-cosmic as far as the
> human being on the physical plane is concerned,
> and in the realisation of this fact may come eluci-
> dation of the true cosmic problem involving the
> Logos and "the spirits in prison,"....[20]

---

[16]*Ibid.*, p. 324.

[17]Blavatsky, H.P., *The Secret Doctrine*, Vol. II, p. 96.

[18]*Ibid.*, p. 167.

[19]*Ibid.*, Vol. III, p. 517.

[20]Bailey, A. A., *A Treatise on Cosmic Fire*, p. 149.

...the Agnishvattas [Solar Angels] construct the petals out of Their Own substance, which is substance energised by the principle of "I-ness," or ahamkara.[21]

Individualisation is literally the coming together ... of the two factors of Spirit and matter by means of a third factor, the intelligent will, purpose and action of an Entity.[22]

...and the day dawns when the life which expresses itself through the medium of the Ego, the Thinker, the Solar Lord or Manasadeva, seeks to loose itself from even this limitation, and return to the source from which it originally emanated.[23]

Millions of years ago in Lemurian times, through the advent of the Solar Lords, our Spiritual Hierarchy came into being. The purpose of the Hierarchy was to help humanity grow and evolve in harmony with the timetable of the solar system. Due to a great failure on the moon, our humanity was not progressing at the same pace as the rest of the solar system. It was becoming a blocking stone on the path of solar progress. The Hierarchy invoked the help of millions of advanced Beings, Who came and eventually incarnated in man to further human progress on the evolutionary path.[24]

---

[21]*Ibid.*, p. 711-712.

[22]*Ibid.*, p. 345.

[23]Bailey, A. A., *Initiation, Human and Solar*, p. 136. Excerpt from *Cosmos in Man*, pp. 47-49.

[24]*The Psyche and Psychism*, p. 387.

The Solar Angel here on earth is the door to Infinity. It was through the Solar Angel that the developing human soul achieved individualization and started to live as a self-conscious entity.

Individuality is the result of age-long evolution and initiation. It is achieved after the human soul has infused himself with the light of his Inner Guide and is functioning within the realm of the Spiritual Triad. The Monad, as a potential gem, is changing into a diamond in the divine light of the Inner Presence, as He passes through the laboratory of experience in the three worlds....

At the time of *individualization*, the Solar Angel passes the third aspect of divinity, the fire of intelligence, to the human soul imprisoned within the three lower substances of the human form. At this point, for the first time the man becomes aware of himself, the lower self comes into existence, and the man identifies with the form.[25]

The Ageless Wisdom teaches that:

Before our globe became egg-shaped, a long trail of Cosmic dust or fire-mist moved and writhed like a serpent in Space.[26]

Countless millions of years ... have rolled away since that dust aggregated and formed the globe we live in.....[27]

Every globe is a septenary chain of worlds of which only one member is visible.[28]

---

[25]*Cosmos in Man*, p. 191.

[26]Blavatsky, H.P., *The Secret Doctrine*, Vol. I, p. 103.

[27]*Ibid.*, p. 667.

[28]*Ibid.*, Vol. II, p. 739.

The Earth was in a comparatively ethereal condition before it reached its last consolidated state.[29]

We are told again that earth was ethereal, fiery, then became radiant, then watery, and then materialized.

The same thing happened to man. Man essentially was ethereal and fiery, then became radiant, then watery, and then developed his bones and physical body.

Our globe is now in the fourth cycle of its own great journey. Every globe must pass through seven large cycles, which are called Rounds. Our globe is in the Fourth Round now.

Our solar system is the body of a Great Entity, Who has seven great centers in His body. These seven centers are the great lives who ensoul seven sacred planets. Sacred planets are those planets whose Souls have passed certain cosmic initiations or unfoldments.

On each global period seven main races are developed, and we are told that we are now in the Fifth Race.

Our planet had the First Race, then the Second Race.[30] The Third Race was called the Lemurian Race. The fourth one was called the Atlantean Race. And the fifth one, the present one, is called the Aryan Race.

At the middle of the Third Race, the Lemurian, eighteen million years ago, a great event happened. The Great Life[31]

---

[29]*Ibid.*, p. 261.

[30]Polarian and Hyperborian Races.

[31]This Great Life is called by different names in different traditions. He is called the Ancient of the Days, Sanat Kumara, The Silent Watcher, The Youth of Eternal Springs, Melchizedek, etc.

of our planet saw that humanity was not developing in proportion to the development of the lives of other planets, and in a way it was hindering their progress within the solar system. He decided to reincarnate on the higher etheric levels and help humanity. For this purpose He brought, from higher realms, some Beings Who were advanced Souls in previous cycles. He also asked the help of six other Great Lives Who were karmically close to Him.

A tradition is found in many religions, in *Ramayana*, *Mahabharata*, the *Bible*, in the old writings of China, Chaldea, Greece and of South America, that advanced Beings and hosts of Angels visited this planet and walked among men.

We are told that millions of years ago these hosts of Angels approached humanity to spark their minds or to dwell in them, but they saw that primitive man was not yet ready to be charged with such a high voltage of energy, so they departed.

The second wave of Angels, centuries later, made another approach and saw that the human animal was partly ready. So they put a fiery substance from their nature into the mental cloud of some of the primitive men. This created first a great disaster to the form, and millions of the forms of the primitive men shattered and disintegrated. But on the other hand when these human animals incarnated again, they had better equipped bodies to hold the mental fire, and to be ready to receive the Solar Angels.

This mental fire gave man the "I" quality, a feeling of identity, and the urge to search and to question.

The third wave of Angels came even later and entered into those human animals which had received the fiery substance. They located themselves on the mental plane, there where the substance was put by the previous wave of

Angels. This substance formed a proper atmosphere in which they could function to build the bridge between the lower man and the "fallen spark," or to awaken the Real Man, the Monad, help him control the lower mechanism and express himself fully through that mechanism in order to gather experience. Here was the origin of yoga.

The coming of these Angels was not simultaneous. They arrived in successive periods. Those who first received the spark of fire progressed rapidly, and those men who first received the Angels became the teachers and the leaders of the rest of humanity. But those who, because of retardation, were not able to receive even the spark "remained mindless."[32]

> *But the Legend says*
> *on our planet*
> *the Spark was stuck*
> *between a half-animal*
> *and a half-human level,*
> *and was not able*
> *to further*
> *its evolution*
> *because certain failures*
> *occurred on the moon.*
> > *But those who were able*
> > *to transcend that level*
> > *billions and billions of years ago*
> > *on various schemes of evolution,*
> > *and who were watching*
> > *this planet*

---

[32]*The Science of Meditation*, pp. 47-50.

and the journey of the Rays
back Home,
came to help.
These were Beings
Who were called
Kumaras and **Solar Angels.**
They taught man how to think,
how to talk,
how to build....
and those Sparks
who worked harder,
harder and harder,
entered into
greater light, greater awakening,
and became the teachers,
the kings, the rulers
of the race....[33]

The Legend says
that throughout ages
the Great Ones
developed and adapted
The Plan
to the needs
of the kingdoms
on the planet.
And, in due time,
They built
great universities
and mystery temples
to educate humanity.

---

[33]*The Legend of Shamballa*, pp. xvi-xvii.

The Seven Rays,
pouring out of the
seven mighty stars
of the Great Bear,
were the
seven mighty rivers
of inspiration
of the
Seven Ashrams.
The Plan was divided
into seven branches,
as the seven colors,
as the seven notes,
as the seven Divine Rays.
They named these branches
politics,
education,
philosophy,
arts,
science,
religion,
economics and finance.
After The Plan was ready,
They asked from Cosmic sources
the help of millions of fiery Spirits
Who wanted to have experience,
to do experiments, and to serve.
They were called
by many names:
Solar Angels,
Fiery Mediators,
the Sons of Mind,
the Watchers,

the Beautiful Ones,
the Flowers of Love, of Joy, of Bliss.
They came and watched
the condition of the planet.
   "It is too early to do
   something serious,"
   They said,
   and departed.
      The second wave
      of Visitors came
      after many centuries
      to see if They
      could do something
      for humanity.
         They observed humanity
         and from Their essence
         They put a flame
         in the mental substance
         of the animal-man.
         And for the first time,
         man was able to use his mind,
         and to grow.
Ages passed,
and the third wave of Angels came,
and They saw the flame
planted by former Angels.
"We can use that flame,"
They said, "as a station
to help man,
to watch him,
to inspire him,
and lead him
into greater awakening,

into greater realizations."
    Thus, They descended
    and entered into
    the electric sphere
    of the human being.
The Legend says
many thousands of men
were not able to hold
the charge of power
generated by these Angels,
and their brains
were burned away.
    But those who could
    hold the charge
    had the first thrill
    of using mental substance
    and thinking.
The Spirit sleeping within them
had a great shock,
and the cycle of awakening
began.
    All Solar Angels
    are members
    of the Hierarchy,
    the Assembly of the Holy Ones.
    Each Solar Angel
    stands as a representative
    of the Divine Plan
    in man.
    They are the embodiment
    of the love principle.
    They are also
    the executors

of the Karmic Lords
in man.
All our motives
are open to Them;
They are watchful eyes.
No action,
no emotional reaction,
no thought
can be hidden
from Them.
The Lords of Flame,
as They were called,
tried to come in contact
with the Spark
buried deep in man.
They used the methods
of meditation,
inspiration
and impression.
    Age after age,
They awakened greater response,
greater aspiration
and striving
within man.
      Those who worked hard,
those who served in spirit,
became co-workers
of these Angels
to further The Plan
on all levels
of creation.[34]

---

[34]*Ibid.*, pp. 33-37.

9

Appearance —
Who is the Soul?

W *ithhold thy mind from all external objects, all external sights. Withhold internal images, lest on thy Soul-light a dark shadow they should cast.*[1]

Since the dawn of humanity stories have been told about the "souls" who have appeared under diverse conditions and for many purposes. The subject is discussed widely in Holy Books and in religious and mystical literature. In *Hamlet*, Shakespeare condenses in a very clear and beautiful way these traditions and stories when he has the "soul" of the poisoned king appear to Hamlet and reveal some secrets.

There are many stories of people who say they have seen saints, masters or great religious leaders in a simple ethereal or very luminous form. Others report that they have seen angels and messengers of God in human form. Most of these angels have wings, long hair, and hold a symbolic object such as a rose, a lily, a spear or an olive branch.

These stories have led people to believe that the soul has a human form and that after death man retains his human appearance. We have heard of someone who said, referring to a deceased loved one, "I saw him in my dreams. He spoke to me." Unconsciously the dreamer was thinking about the soul of his friend communicating with him. He imagined that his friend, on leaving his body, had become a soul, but

---

[1]Blavatsky, H.P., *The Voice of the Silence*, p. 19.

had retained the same appearance and form that he had in life, only of finer substance. It seems that out of this superstition came the idea that God has the appearance of man. Thus He created man according to His image and likeness — as God is portrayed for us by many artists.

In the ancient mysteries of Egypt, the soul was depicted as a bird hovering over the body, or as a butterfly emerging from a caterpillar. In spiritualistic circles, the "soul" often "appears" in human form, and people believe that they see human entities, or souls or "spirits." There are also traditions in which people have seen the "souls" of the dead in graveyards in human form with luminous appearance.

We cannot say that all these visions belong to the world of illusion. People are prone to translate all inexplicable phenomena into a familiar language and color it according to their current state of mind. Generally in such cases their psychological world is composed of strong aspirations, dreams, fears and desires. All these condition the appearance or form of the "vision." People sometimes see things which are mere reflections of the "realities" within themselves. The atmosphere of their minds helps this process and gives form and color to their dreams and fears. This law of psychology also says that we perceive that quality and character in an object which has already been developed in us. Hence, people usually ascribe to the soul a human form.[2]

...The word "personality," written with a small p, refers to the sum total of the physical, emotional and mental vehicles, aligned and integrated. When written with a capital P, it refers to the unfolding human soul, functioning through the physical, emotional and mental bodies. It is also called the

---

[2]*The Hidden Glory of the Inner Man*, pp. 59-60.

lower self, the Higher Self being the Solar Angel, and the Divine Self, the Spark.[3]

To gain a clear idea about the Soul, when we write it with a capital S, it refers to the Solar Angel. If the s is small, it refers to the human soul — not to the Solar Angel.

The Monad is the human soul in the mental plane or in higher planes.The human soul is a phase of the Monad. For example, symbolically speaking, a child is Personality (with capital P). A youth is a human soul, and an adult is the Monad — but they are the same man in three phases.

Solar Pitris are not the Soul. They build the vehicles of the human soul, if the human soul attracts Them.

Lunar Pitris build the lower bodies, but they are not the human soul.

The Solar Angel is a different entity, helping the Personality to grow into a human soul and the human soul to become a conscious Monad.[4]

Man resembles a triangle, one point representing the world of the personality (physical, emotional and mental), the second point representing the Soul, and the upper point symbolizing the Spark of life. The Soul, as has been said, is a separate being — the Inner Master, "the Hope of Glory" Who leads us toward light, love and sacrifice.[5]

---

[3]*Cosmos in Man*, p. 192.

[4]Unpublished writing.

[5]*The Hidden Glory of the Inner Man*, p 33.

We may say also that personality, Soul and Spark form a trinity; personality represents inertia, Soul represents motion, and Spark represents rhythm.[6]

A human being is a five-pointed star. He is composed of a human soul, a Solar Angel, a physical elemental, an emotional elemental, and a mental elemental....[7]

The human soul is a "solar angel" for elementals. This teaching was distorted in many esoteric books. You are not a Solar Angel, but you are a solar angel in relation to your physical, emotional and mental elementals.

As we are the guard, leader or master of these three entities, so we have our own Teacher and Guidance, Who is our Solar Angel. The Solar Angel can be contacted in moments of creative crisis. When you are in creative crisis, the Solar Angel is your inner source of inspiration, beauty and goodness.

Inspiration and creativity is the moment when the mental, emotional and physical elementals are one-pointedly looking for a contact with the human soul, and the human soul is in contact with the Light within. A moment of creativity and inspiration is a moment of integration and alignment of these five entities.

Another time when you can contact the Solar Angel is at the time of a life crisis, a real crisis, not an imagined one. We make a little thing big, and then we feel proud that we are passing through a crisis. A life crisis is something that is really a matter of life and death; you are facing a crucial

---

[6]*The Science of Meditation*, p. 132.
[7]*The Psyche and Psychism*, p. 113.

moment in your life. At that moment, a contact can be established with your Solar Angel. You knock on the door and say, "Give me strength. Give me power. Give me light, so that I may find the way out." Inspiration comes only when demanded.

A third way of contacting the Solar Angel is when you are making an important decision in your life....

Master D.K. says that elementals "...can be roughly divided into four groups:

1. The elementals of earth.
2. The elementals of water.
3. The elementals of air.
4. The elementals of fire.

They are the essence of things...."[8]

Elementals of earth are related to our physical body. Elementals of water are related to our emotional body. Elementals of air are related to our mental body. Elementals of fire are related to our etheric-electrical bodies.

Elementals can be controlled and used for constructive purposes through ceremonies and rituals. Sound, color and movements expressed in ceremonial rituals strongly affect them. That is why ceremonies and rituals have a strong effect on human nature. Also, man can help elementals through ceremonies and orient their steps toward evolution.

To cooperate with elementals one must charge himself with the fire of love and the fire of purity and fuse himself

---

[8]Bailey, A.A., *Letters on Occult Meditation*, p. 174.

either with the Solar Angel or a deva on the evolutionary path.[9]

> *Each entity must have won for itself the right to become divine, through self-experience.*
>
> H.P. Blavatsky

Throughout centuries people have sensed something greater and deeper within man and nature than their normal waking consciousness can grasp. They have known intuitively that there was something more that they could somehow contact, and from which they could derive more light, more joy and more serenity. Thus, for centuries, human beings have aspired to find that deeper Being. In ancient religions this inner or deeper Being was called the soul, the spirit, the Buddha, the Inner Christ, the Hope of Glory. It was also called the center of freedom, the Silent Watcher, the Presence, the real SELF, or the Father.[10]

The Inner Guide is called by many names in various religions and philosophies: Krishna Consciousness, Christ Consciousness, the Inner Buddha, the Transpersonal Self, the Big Brother, the Watcher Within, the Fountainhead of Creativity, the Righteous One, the Source of Beauty, the Principle of Freedom, the Golden Bridge, etc. The names are very significant, but the most important thing to bear in mind is that there is a Presence within the reach of the meditator Who can guide, inspire, strengthen, heal and release him, and can lead him forward on the path of evolution

[9]*Ibid.*, pp. 118-120.
[10]*The Science of Becoming Oneself*, p. 99.

and creative accomplishment. All masterpieces in every field of human endeavor are the result of close relationship between this Inner Guide and the unfolding human soul. The closer man comes to his Soul, the greater the effect his creative actions will have on progressing humanity. The Soul, through Its creative actions, provides the energies that push the wheel of evolution forward toward greater achievement. The Soul communicates with man through deep meditation and man registers the waves of the Soul's meditation through his accomplishments.[11]

In all civilizations and in all races enlightened men have conducted a search for the soul and have worshiped the soul, thereby amassing great wealth, building countless temples, creating orders, brotherhoods, mysteries, sacred hymns, literature, architecture, and musical masterpieces.

In the Egyptian *Book of the Dead*, which was written three to four thousand years before Christ, we read:

"My soul shall not be fettered to my body at the gates of the grave, but I shall enter in peace, and I shall come forth in peace."

In this scientific age, has the search for the soul come to an end? We can say that the quest for the soul has not come to an end; on the contrary, day by day, it is gaining momentum because man throughout all his endeavors is searching for himself.[12]

The Soul is a bridge both in man and the universe. It is the Son who leads us toward the Father's House.[13]

---

[11] *Christ, The Avatar of Sacrificial Love*, p. 120.

[12] *The Hidden Glory of the Inner Man*, p. 4.

[13] *Ibid.*, p. 49.

The records of past centuries show that many advanced beings had visions of their Solar Angels, but that they thought they were beholding angels, Masters, the Christ or God Himself. For example, in the West, Pythagoras, Plato, Plotinus, Samblichus, and Proelus had this experience at their advanced Initiations in Egypt. Porphyry states that Plotinus met or united with "God" six times. Saint Luso "saw the angel in her heart and she was fair to look upon." Saint Teresa thought that her vision was the Christ, "judging by the brightness." Saint Francis of Assisi and Saint Catherine of Siena also reported similar meetings with the Inner Dweller. Jacob Boehme's book, *Aurora*, presents many instances of such happenings. In the *New Testament* we read that Peter had an Angel Who often appeared to his brethren. Goethe reported that he once met with his Soul face to face.

Aristotle, in his writings, suggested that the vision of God is the ultimate goal of man. Of course, no man can see God: It was the Solar Angel to Whom he was referring.[14]

From esoteric literature, we learn that there are nine initiations which the shadow in the personality must undergo before it becomes one with its Source or prototype. A "Soul" in this process of initiation is one Who has passed the Fifth Initiation. He has become a Master of Wisdom and has gained victory over death. Thus, the One Who lives in and around us as our Guardian Angel, our Soul, is One Who passed through human experiences on this or another planet and under the Law of Sacrifice "descended" into man to carry on the process of spiritualization both in man and in Itself.

---

[14]*Cosmos in Man*, p. 51-52.

We are not yet Souls. We will become Souls when, through our Solar Angel, we will establish a certain relationship with our Inner God — with our essence — or with the highest principle in us and bring our body and life under the rule of that Divine Reality.

In *The Secret Doctrine* we read the following beautiful words: "Matter is the vehicle for the manifestation of soul on this plane of existence, and soul is the vehicle on a higher plane for the manifestation of spirit, and these three are a trinity synthesized by Life which pervades them all."[15] Here another question comes to our minds. Are not our Divine Sparks and Souls the same thing? The answer is: The Soul on the plane of Its achievement separately carried on Its own development, Its own spiritualization. It aspires toward Its own Spark, toward Its Essence, toward Its spiritual principle, while at the same time It serves as a bridge between our Spirit and Its reflection — the man.[16]

THE ANGEL — THE TRANSPERSONAL SELF

> *For I say unto you, that in heaven their angels do always behold the face of my Father which is in heaven.*
>
> — Matt. 18:10 —

In Oriental traditions we are told that man has a guiding or protecting angel. Our grandmothers used to tell us that

---

[15]Blavatsky, H.P., *The Secret Doctrine*, Vol. I, p. 49.
[16]*The Hidden Glory of the Inner Man*, p. 44.

our angel would be angry if we lived a life not in harmony with him, and also that he could leave us, or separate himself from us.

In the Psalms King David says, "Cast me not away from thy presence, and take not thy holy spirit from me." Behind these simple words exists a deep truth. The Ageless Wisdom tells us that the real man is not his Soul. The man is not a Soul, but has a Soul. The Soul is the first Master of man, lives in man, and leads him toward light, toward divine love and toward divine will. Until man reaches a certain degree of development, the Soul remains with him and guides him; when he reaches this goal, the Soul leaves him.

In the *New Testament* it is written, "The kingdom of God is like leaven, which a woman took and hid in three measures of meal, till the whole was leavened." The Masters of the Ageless Wisdom tell us that the three measures refer to the three aspects of personality: physical, emotional and mental. The leaven is the principle of mind which the Soul, the woman, hides in the personality to leaven it.

In ancient Greek mythology we also read that Prometheus stole *fire* from the Gods and gave it to man. Prometheus gave man the spark of mind, thus opening for man a way of sublimation, achievement and endless illumination.

In the course of the evolution of man there came a period when the mental spark began to vibrate in his brain and he became more sensitive to subjective influences. In the Ageless Wisdom this critical moment is wonderfully depicted. We are told that the phenomenon called man, throughout eons of time, was growing and living a happy life as in paradise but did not yet have in him the light of self-consciousness, self-recognition or discrimination. He was a happy baby on his mother's bosom.

Within him there were two shores. On one shore were the body, the emotions and the instinctive mind; on the other, far away, was the original picture from which he was "created." The bridge between these two shores was missing. Only by crossing this bridge could man reach his divine source, his divine essence, and could the essence approach him for divine transmutation.

He was a shadow, living through the life-current coming from the Spark and by the primitive mind principle present in the substance itself. In the ancient days many millions of years ago, angels, having lived in previous cycles and on other planets, came to man and sparked in him the principle of mind. These angels, or advanced Souls, were called the Sons of Mind. They put the divine leaven, or the principle of mind-fire, in the three measures of "meal" which created an atmosphere composed of a rare substance within and around the physical man. Man became the divine spark possessing a form and mental fire given to him by the Sons of Mind. However, this was not enough, because man had to pass through even higher developments before reaching perfection. Long ages passed, and there came a period in which certain entities called "Solar Angels" incarnated in those who were ready, locating Themselves in the substance given to man by the Sons of Mind. In ancient writings this is called the crisis of individualization. Man came to know the difference between "good and evil" and "felt his nudity"; he became conscious of himself, and the long journey to his Father's Home began. How deep and beautiful is the parable of the prodigal son who left his father and went away to live his own life. After much suffering, he came to himself and said, "I will arise and go to my father..." which he did. The father, seeing him, said, "My son was lost, and is found." The "lost one" was the reflection, or the portion of the Father in the three worlds (physical, emotional and mental). The reflection went to its original source, to the Father, and he "was found."

According to this, man is a Spark of spirit, and he has a Soul or Angel, and a lower self which we call the personality. The two shores of man were bridged and, "by the approximation of these two poles, light is produced, a flame shineth forth, a sphere of radiant glory is seen which gradually increases the intensity of its light, its heat and its radiance until its capacity is reached, or that which we call perfection."

Mind is a substance, a very sensitive and subtle substance, but it is not the Thinker. The Thinker is the Soul of man. Through long ages the Soul holds Itself as a latent central energy, but can only control the personality at first during dark, critical times. However, Its presence helps develop the mental body and, through it, the Soul gradually controls the man and the physical world. Those people who, from ancient times, were able to sense the presence of the Soul and live life according to Its rules, were the Initiates who brought light to men and increased the light of humanity.

...The presence of the Soul created complicated problems for man in the early days of his evolution, especially in times of crisis when he felt a duality within himself.

Modern psychology has vaguely described the duality of man. It has noted also that sometimes man is not a whole, but a composite made up of many parts. Sometimes he is the lower self — the body, emotions and mental states — and sometimes he is a point of beauty, sublimated and Divine. Often there occurs a conflict within man between his higher and lower levels, and sometimes there are two or more motivating powers working within him at the same time.

The primary purpose of man is to bring about an integration and unity among the three lower aspects, then between the personality and the Soul, and eventually between the Soul-infused personality and the Monadic Spark. The term "personality" refers to the sum total of man's physical, emotional and mental vehicles and forces. It is with these vehicles that the unfolding, developing human soul is identified and controlled for ages.

These three vehicles are the *persona* of the unfolding, developing human soul who gradually organizes, integrates and uses the persona to achieve his goals. Thus within the three vehicles, the real personality is the unfolding human soul, the "lost" spark of God. When the unfolding human soul integrates his vehicles, another great step is revealed to him. This is the process of Soul infusion. In this process the personality, or the unfolding human soul makes a contact with the Transpersonal Self, the Solar Angel, and eventually after conflicts of many centuries, fuses himself with that great Guide.

The third step is to bring the Soul-infused personality to the realization that he is the Divine Spark, the Monad. This is the major test of the Transpersonal Self in regard to man. When this stage has been reached, the Solar Angel has completed Its agelong duty and stands aside. The man has become a Soul.

Duality expresses itself differently on each plane. Man starts to progress when he gradually conquers duality and achieves integration with his Higher Self — hence the process of sublimation in which the lower obeys the higher, the "individual integrates himself into the Whole." For example, two opposing urges may emerge on any of our planes. They can destroy a man if they continue to battle each other without reaching a "conclusion," or they can sublimate him if by a transmutative process, the lower, the material, begins to obey or harmonize with the higher, the ideal. The transmutation process leads to the development of the Voice of Conscience and to renunciations, spiritual conversions and great sacrifices. When the higher aspect of the conflicting pair of opposites in the inner world of man gains victory over the lower, you have a new man — a new-born man — relatively free from the lower activities or tendencies.

As a person cannot start to live his own life until he is separated from the womb of his mother, neither can he enter into the way of real progress until he senses the existence of duality within himself. Gradually moving onto the higher levels of duality, one day he consciously realizes that in him there are two poles separated by a middle point, the point of equilibrium. In him are the pole of matter and the pole of the Divine Spark or Spirit, separated by the eternal bridge or Soul which expresses Itself as the intellect of man through his mental substance. Hence there are the urges of the material pole and the urges of the spiritual pole, and between them the principle of understanding or sublimation. Since man has become capable of creating an equilibrium between these two opposite points and their urges, he can become a triangle and thereby a unity. Unity cannot be achieved until a point of balance between the two poles has been established....

The existence of two opposing energies can be offset by a third one, a conclusion. However, if this conclusion is on *behalf* of the lower plane, the Solar Angel will once again stimulate the person and give him another opportunity to develop new attitudes, new values and higher principles. The lower equilibrium will again be destroyed. This new stimulation may be delayed and the man may enjoy the pleasures of a lower life and robust health for a while longer. *But the Solar Angel never sleeps, and throughout the centuries will carry on Its task of sublimation,* just as in the history of humanity Providence sends the Great Ones to revive mankind.[17]

"Unseen, she sees; unheard, she hears; unminded, she minds; unknown, she knows. There is none that sees, but she; there is none that hears, but she; there is none that minds, but she; there is none that knows, but she. She is the soul, the inner ruler, immortal. Whatever is different from her is perishable."[18]

For some people the Soul is the body, the flesh, and the blood. To others It is emotions and desires. For still others, It is thought, idea and mystery. Some people, who have departed from these familiar shores, have not arrived anywhere else, and the winds of events are conditioning their direction and state of life. Others have seen the way of light and, year after year, are growing in that light and entering Soul-consciousness.[19]

The Solar Angel, which is referred to in many esoteric books as the Soul, is not the man, is not the evolving human consciousness or the evolving self, but the Inner Master, the Transpersonal Self, Whose duty is to guide the evolving human soul into his essence or to the realization of his true nature.

---

[17]*The Hidden Glory of the Inner Man*, pp. 12-17.

[18]*Brihadaranyaka Upanishad*, Verse 23. (Excerpt from *The Hidden Glory of the Inner Man*, p. 58.)

[19]*Ibid.*, p. 69.

When we speak about the Monad, we refer to the essence of the unfolding human soul. The unfolding human soul is the Monad, but identified with physical, emotional and mental worlds. The duty of the Guide, the Solar Angel, or Transpersonal Self is to lead the "man" through these three "halls of learning," as they are called, to the "hall of wisdom," to higher planes where he will reach to the realization of his true Self — the Monad, or in terms of modern psychology — the Transcendental Self.[20]

In esoteric tradition the Monad is the Father, the Spark. The Soul is the Son, the Path. Matter is the Mother, the form. In biblical terminology these Three are the Holy Trinity: the Father, Son and Holy Spirit.[21]

Man is not aware of his absolute, divine state of being. He is in a state of illusion. This state of illusion upon the mental plane develops a sense of separation, a concept of "I-ness" which is mortal and which has no real existence. The human ego is the one which reincarnates life after life, until the supreme Reality in him awakens to Its true nature through the process of service, meditation and Initiation. Our Solar Angel is our first Teacher and Initiator to the divine life and its mysteries. It is the Angel of the great Presence in man.[22]

The fourth ... Hierarchy is the human Hierarchy or the community of the Initiates, the Custodians of the Plan of God, of which Christ is the Head in this cycle.

---

[20]*Ibid.*, pp. 22-23.

[21]*Cosmos in Man*, p. 50.

[22]*The Fiery Carriage and Drugs*, p. 78.

They are called Lords of Sacrifice, or Lords of Compassion. Solar Angels are part of this Hierarchy. "These lives are the points of fire who must become the flame...."[23]

The fifth creative Hierarchy is called "Hearts of Fiery Love." These are human Monads, or human beings, in their essence. This Hierarchy has a very mysterious relationship with the five liberated groups.

The lives of the fifth creative Hierarchy "...are peculiarly close to the great Heart of Love of the solar Logos...."[24] These human Monads sometimes are called "Redeeming Angels." They are sometimes even called "Solar Angels." The reasons for these expressions are:

a. The man, who is the Monad in incarnation, redeems the lives of the three vehicles: physical, emotional and mental.

b. He acts as a Solar Angel for those lives whose evolution depends on him, and on his activities, progress and achievement.

c. Because "man ... is a blend of electric fire, being a divine Flame, ... he is also solar fire, being a solar Angel in manifestation.... He is likewise fire by friction...."[25]

d. As our Solar Angels guide our evolution and provide the bridge between our shadows and reality, so human beings as "solar angels" help the lives of our vehicles to evolve into human beings through the process of liberation.

---

[23]Bailey, A.A. *Esoteric Astrology*, p. 42. Excerpt from *The Psyche and Psychism*, p. 31.

[24]*Ibid.*, p. 46. (*The Psyche and Psychism*, p. 32)

[25]*Ibid.*, p. 57. (*The Psyche and Psychism*, p. 32)

We must be careful not to confuse between the Solar Angels that come and dwell in the mental body of man with that of the human Sparks (Monads). Human Sparks serve to raise the consciousness of the lives of the three lower planes (physical, emotional and mental) in much the same way Solar Angels serve the whole human being.[26]

In Sufi literature reference is made to the Solar Angel as the Beloved One:

They have sung of him as infinite and unattainable; but I in my meditations have seen him without sight.[27]

Al-Junaid of Baghdad wrote:

Now I have known, O Lord,
What lies within my heart.
In Secret, from the world apart,
My tongue hath talked with my adored.[28]

Rumi says,

O heart, as you go to that Sweetheart
You must lose your heart;
Heedless go to the audience-chamber of Union.
When you have reached His door,
Hidden from every creature,
Leave yourself outside
And then go in.[29]

[26]*The Psyche and Psychism*, p. 32.

[27]*Kabir's Poems*, p. 21. (*Cosmos in Man*, p. 52)

[28]Arberry, A.J., *Sufism*, p. 59. (*Cosmos in Man*, p. 52)

[29]Rice, O.P., *Cyprian the Persian, Sufis*. p. 61. (*Cosmos in Man*, p. 52)

When we are referring to the indwelling Solar Angel, the first Master of the man, we are not ignoring the existence of other devas, other Angels or Messengers. We know that throughout the ages these great Beings have helped man on the path of evolution, cyclically or when group or great national need has required their help.

The mystery of the Indweller was clearly given to Anna Kingsford, the great mystic. In her book, *Clothed with the Sun*, she presents some interesting information about the Solar Angel. She calls it, "genius," or "daimon" (a ministering spirit). She continues:

> *My genius looks like Dante and like him is always in red.*[30]

> *The genius of a man is his satellite. Man is a planet. God — the God of the man — is his sun, and the moon of his planet is ISIS, its Initiator, or genius.*[31]

> *"Yea," says the angel genius to his client, "I illuminate thee, but I instruct thee not. I warn thee, but I fight not. I attend, but I lead not. Thy treasure is within thyself. My light showeth where it lieth."*[32]

THE CONSCIENCE

There are two kinds of inner suggestions which can be confused with the power we call conscience.

1. We have inherited patterns of thinking, patterns of urges or drives, which were built throughout our past lives.

---

[30]Kingsford, Anna B., *Clothed with the Sun*, p. 55. (*Cosmos in Man*, p. 52)

[31]*Ibid.*, pp. 59,60. (*Cosmos in Man*, p. 52)

[32]*Ibid.*, p. 62. (*Cosmos in Man*, p. 52)

2. We have the content of the Chalice, which is pure wisdom collected through the experiences of our past lives.

3. We also have the Voice of the Soul, the "Voice of the Silence," which is the standard vibration of the Solar Angel within us.

The last one listed is the true conscience; the others are inner suggestions conditioned by time and space, by past lives and experiences, and may fall short of meeting the need in any given situation. But the Voice of the Solar Angel is unconditioned and all-wise. It is unconditioned by the past, by the present and even by our future expectations and man-made dreams. It is the pure, clear-cut Voice of truth, a Voice which is in accord with the fundamental laws of our universe.

When a man has no conscience, it means that the wall between the lower and the higher man is growing thicker and thicker. This wall can be an etheric, emotional or mental wall, in the form of glamor, maya or illusion. When this is true, the Solar Angel cannot communicate with the unit of consciousness or with the human soul, and the man may become a victim of his animal urges, his selfishness and hatred, or even of his accumulated hypnotic suggestions. In extreme cases, his behavior may become so bestial that the Solar Angel leaves him. There is no hope for such a man for long cycles. This is the greatest tragedy that can overtake a human being. Conscience can be developed by using its "still small voice" in our everyday affairs. It can be a light on our path, and, eventually, the golden thread leading us to our Home.[33]

---

[33]*The Science of Becoming Oneself,* p. 76
See also for information*The Hidden Glory of the Inner Man,* Ch. 5 and 6.

THE THINKER

The Ageless Wisdom teaches that there is a Presence in man that *thinks*. This Presence is a light which is placed in the higher mental atmosphere. It tries to reach the atoms of the mental, emotional and physical substance; to flood them with Its own light; and to coordinate, fuse and create an instrument through which Its light can radiate as enlightening, healing and uplifting energy.

In the average man this light is a flickering light which cannot penetrate into all the strata of the mind to touch the brain. Only at rare, critical times may the light reach down and give man a brief, unusual guidance and inspiration. In an advanced man this light slowly penetrates into the whole substance of the mind, and as it penetrates, the consciousness of the man expands.

The consciousness of man is the lighted area in the mind where the light or the intellect of this Presence hits. If it hits an area one inch in diameter, that is the size of his real consciousness. If this lighted area expands, his consciousness expands.

Your consciousness expands as the mind, in part or as a whole, gradually is able to assimilate and reflect the light and change into light. The atoms of your mind have a dim light originally, but as they become sensitive to the light of the Presence, they become radioactive atoms in the mental atmosphere. This enlightening process is carried on through our endeavors in right thinking, concentration, meditation, and living a life in harmony with the rhythm of the Inner Presence, until the light or the intellect of the human soul is awakened and released into its full capacity to fuse with the intellect of the Soul, then to replace it.[34]

---

[34]*The Science of Meditation*, p. 47.

The Presence in us is the Solar Angel. This is the Thinker within us. The Tibetan Master, giving the rules for magic, says:

> *The Solar Angel collects himself, scatters not his force, but, in meditation deep, communicates with his reflection.*[35]

> *When the shadow hath responded, in meditation deep the work proceedeth. The lower light is thrown upward; the greater light illuminates the three, and the work of the four proceedeth.*[36]

Meditation is one of the means used to strengthen the influence of the Presence over the personality and to make it sensitive to the wisdom radiating from that Presence.[37]

According to the Ageless Wisdom, the mental body is composed of the following parts:

1. The subtle substance, electrical in nature, which is used to build thoughtforms.

2. The Solar Angel, the initial Thinker.

3. The various thoughtforms, as cloud patches floating in the atmosphere of the mind.

4. A center in the mind from which radiate nine petals of energy, if the man is near the third great expansion of consciousness.

5. A shining pearl, the mental permanent atom.

The Thinker within us is the Solar Angel. In occult works we are told that the Solar Angel is in deep meditation. This means *It thinks.*

---

[35]Bailey, A.A., *A Treatise on White Magic*, p. 51.

[36]*Ibid.*, p. 71.

[37]*The Science of Meditation*, p. 51.

...Thinkers are those people who have raised their focus of consciousness to the level of the Solar Angel and are able to pick up the expressions of the Solar Angel, absorb them and further formulate new thoughtforms to meet their needs. Such men can gradually enter into the light of the Solar Angel, communicate and share Its thinking, or ask questions and receive answers according to their environment, to the conditions of their education, to the receptivity of the mental body and the sensitivity of the brain....[38]

In the thinking process we turn our minds in two directions:

a. toward the world of Soul, which is the world of ideas, prototypes and the Plan;

b. toward the world of need upon the three lower levels.

To *think* means to hold the need, the question, within the light of the Soul, and to invoke an answer from the Soul. The evocation of the Soul is the process of thinking. All the answers to our intelligent questions are found in the world of these ideas, prototypes and the Plan.

Meditation is the science of thinking. It leads us to recognize and then to burn our glamors and illusions, thus helping the survival of humanity and every form of life on earth.

Real thought is the agent of love, unfoldment, resurrection, sacrifice, order, rhythm, beauty, light, power, joy, and we know that joy is a state of awareness which does not recognize pain or any other limitation. Thoughts are extensions of the Soul's light. Thoughtforms are the result of the light of

---

[38]*Ibid.*, pp. 37-38.

the Soul utilizing the emotional and mental stuff, under the direction of a given desire or aspiration, and building a form to manipulate energy and time to meet a need.[39]

Instinct changes into intellect when the human soul starts first to utilize the lower mental substance and then the higher mental substance. We have two intellects: one is the developing intellect of the human soul, and the other is the spiritual intellect which is the intellect of the Soul, or the Divine Guide within.

As for the human being, we can say that intellect is the light of the human soul radiating through the mental substance. Once this intellect extends beyond the mental plane, it enters into the domain of pure reason, of intuition, and eventually becomes the awareness of pure Being, the Self.

Actually, intellect is the third aspect of the Real Self. It does not appear until the prodigal son — or Self — returns to the mental plane and starts to express the third aspect of his true Core. Until that moment the intellect of the unfolding human soul is a reflection of the light of the Soul.[40]

We know that the mind is not the intellect. Intellect is the light in the mental body, the light of the Presence, and the light of the developing, unfolding human soul....

Mind does not think; it reflects, gives colors, shapes, forms, and objectivity to the impulses, impressions and inspirations coming from the Thinker....

...Thoughts are not thoughtforms — thoughts originate from the Thinker, from the Soul or the Presence in man, until the man himself becomes an awakened soul....[41]

---

[39] *Ibid.*, p. 285.
[40] *Ibid.*, p. 254.
[41] *Ibid.*, pp. 199, 200.

The physical brain is the switchboard of the mind, and the mind is simply a vortex of energy currents. The Thinker is not the mind as some believe; It is the Dweller within the body. The mind serves as a bridge between the Thinker and the brain. The Thinker clothes Its ideas in the substance of the mind, and acts upon the physical plane through the physical brain and nervous system.[42]

In the process of learning how to think, first of all man tries to harmonize his life with the rays of beauty, goodness and truth which are found in the Core of his being. Then he tries to recognize the thoughts of the Inner Lord, and live according to Its thoughts and to express them throughout his life, activities, feelings and mental modifications. A little later he detaches himself from his former habits of mental expression, and tries to see things as his Soul sees them, and think as his Soul thinks....[43]

As man tries to learn and use the true technique of visualization, the following results appear in his subjective world: the gap between astral and mental consciousness is bridged. Then this bridge extends to the Thinker, via the unfolding Lotus. Thus a path is created for the pilgrim, for the human soul, who travels upon it toward the Solar Angel to be crowned there. He then starts his long journey toward the Real Self. This journey is made with open eyes and in full awareness.[44]

It is a fact that the reflection, the human ego, the human "I" cannot think, does not think; it only reflects. True thoughts

---

[42]*The Science of Becoming Oneself*, p. 39.

[43]*The Science of Meditation*, p. 59.

[44]*Ibid.*, p. 173.

are streams of energy coming from the Inner Lord, the Solar Angel. As they flow through the mental plane they create new ideas, urges, drives and aspirations. The lower mind clothes them in forms, and modifies them in accordance with its purity and unfoldment. As a musician plays upon his violin, so the Inner Lord plays His thoughts through the mind. All thoughts created by the Inner Lord are pure and in accord with the evolutionary Plan. How do evil thoughts come from a man if the thoughts of his Inner Lord are good, true and beautiful in their nature? To answer this question:

The real thought is a projection of the Inner Lord, goodness, love, truth and beauty. It is a river flowing from an underground lake and giving life to nature....[45]

Thinking, for the human soul, is a process of adaptation to and formulation of the "thoughts" of the Solar Angel, or impressions received from other outer sources. Thus, thinking for the human soul means "research and discovery" of the things that already exist in the light of the Solar Angel.[46]

The Inner Guide is the Thinker until, through deep meditation and occasional contact, It teaches the human soul how to think....

It is after the Third Initiation that thinking deepens. Until then, the person is guided by thoughts that he receives from the Inner Guide, which give him light, according to his capacity to assimilate and use it....

First, man is mechanical. Then he is controlled by the thoughts of others. Then he senses the thoughts of the Inner Guide. Then at the Third Initiation, he begins to think....

---

[45]*The Science of Becoming Oneself*, p. 43.
[46]*The Science of Meditation*, p. 59.

Thoughts are particles of light, love, and will which emanate from those who have light, love and will. These particles are mental, intuitional and atmic. The Solar Angel lives in a sphere of light, love and will. When the human soul presents a need or a question, he attracts, according to his tension, a particle or a wave of light, love and will. Thought in the mind of the human soul is formed when he contacts this wave. A thought wave is translated according to your need, rays, temperament, evolution, conditions, etc....

Only through right assimilation of the thought waves coming from the Solar Angel can one produce *thoughts*. People can think but not necessarily produce thoughts, as a pump works but does not draw water. For the Solar Angel, Its intentional contact with the human soul is through a thought wave, but Its thought waves are translations of impressions received from Planetary and Solar Thinkers. Intuition is the power to communicate not with thoughts, but with Thinkers.

A real thought wave is a message which:

1. instructs,
2. reveals and enlightens,
3. informs,
4. strengthens,
5. creates,
6. bridges, and
7. attracts.

Thus the thoughts of the Solar Angel put man in harmony with Thinkers in higher Space-levels and synchronize his actions on all levels with Them.

For the Solar Angel and the human soul, a thought is a part of the Plan of the Hierarchy. Each real thought is a key to the Plan, to the accumulated and formulated knowledge in Space. Each real thought is a manifestation of a part of the Plan and part of the accumulated knowledge in Space. Each real thought reflects the Plan and brings this knowledge down. Each real thought reflects love and will from higher Centers.[47]

---

[47]*Challenge for Discipleship,* pp. 378-379.

10

Duties of
the Solar Angel

The Solar Angel is the custodian of the great Plan for our planet and for our solar system. It is in tune and in communication with Cosmic Beings and is a member of the Hierarchy on subtle levels. Cyclically It passes some portions of the Plan to the "shadow," to the developing human soul. These communications with the shadow bring inspiration, higher urges and impulses, as well as divine aspirations. The Solar Angel first makes contact through *the life thread*. This is the reason that Its communications are not formulated thoughtforms or words, but come through as inspiration, impulse, impression or touch. Later Its communication becomes more direct and better formulated as the disciple or unfolding human soul builds *the bridge*, *the consciousness thread*, between the mental unit and the mental permanent atom.

In some cases or on some occasions the Solar Angel withdraws and sheds no light upon the problems of man. Its purpose in so doing is to give man the opportunity to help himself, to strive harder in solving his own problems without depending upon his Solar Angel for guidance. At times when this withdrawal occurs, a deep depression descends upon the pilgrim; and if the withdrawal is for a very long period, he passes through an experience of loneliness which is known as the "dark night of the human soul." He feels that he has been deserted and left alone between heaven and earth. This state is only illusion, for the Solar Angel is the eternal Silent Watcher. Very often, instead of leading a person as a child is led, It inspires him to bring forth his courage, hope, daring and to exercise detachment. It watches silently as It inspires him to master his problems, so that he may enter the path of mastership.

As communication between the reflection and the Solar Angel goes deeper, and as the monadic or divine current pours down to lower levels of existence, a whirlpool of energy is gradually created on the higher mental plane. This vortex of energy resembles a cup formed of nine flower-like petals. It is the Chalice or Lotus so often referred to in occult literature. Enclosed by three more petals, in the very center of the Chalice or Lotus, is a jewel, a Spark of fire. This jewel is the Monad, the Real Man; all else is reflection. As ages pass and man obeys his Inner Lord, the Chalice becomes more radioactive and man radiates streams of love energy, light energy and will energy.[1]

Eventually, all the physical, emotional and mental personality vehicles enter into a process of transfiguration and man becomes a shining light. From that moment on he is in communication with a greater Center of Love, the Hierarchy of the Masters. Lives pass and the glory of the Inner Lord burns the Chalice. The inner fire, the Monad, is released....[2]

The Soul works in the three worlds of personality and tries to carry on Its plan through them. The Soul gradually sublimates the personality so that It can express Its light, love and wisdom through the three bodies. This transmutation continues until the personality becomes the channel of

[1]For more information about the chakras see Chapter XII, *The Science of Becoming Oneself.*
[2]*Cosmos in Man*, p. 49.

the Soul, and man, "the reflection," releases himself from ignorance (from matter, time, space and force) and identifies himself with his essence.

The Plan of the Soul, in our present-day language, is "the high calling" of a person. When the Plan is beginning to work out, we say that a person has talent; when the Plan is expressing itself in its full beauty, we say that a person is a genius. When a person is able to fulfill his "high calling" and is expressing his talent, his genius, he has come a considerable distance on his long path of sublimation. Note that the high calling is related to the personality. In the case of talent, man to a certain degree is integrated with the Soul; in the case of genius, man is partially *en rapport with his* "*Father in Heaven*," with the Divine Spark within him, with his true Self. This is the process of sublimation, transmutation and transfiguration in which the reflection, under the guidance of the Soul, gradually meets its Divine Essence.[3]

One may ask, "If the Solar Angel is the Guide, then what has a Master of Wisdom to do with that Guide?"

The Master helps with the bridging and fusing process between the Higher Self, the Solar Angel, and the lower self, the unfolding human soul. Since the Master lives in both the human and the soul spheres, He can relate man to his Angel by direct impression, hints or instructions.

After a man is led to his Solar Angel, the Solar Angel, in turn, relates him to the Hierarchy in general, and to his own Master in particular. We are told that a Master takes a man into His Ashram or into His sphere of instruction, after obtaining the permission of his Solar Angel. Thus the Master puts the man into conscious relationship with his Soul, and

---

[3]*The Hidden Glory of the Inner Man*, pp. 35-36.

the Soul leads him into conscious relationship with his own Master.

After the Fourth Initiation a higher degree Initiate takes the responsibility of directing his steps into greater light and labor.

The developing, unfolding human soul is the Monad plus the level of development with which he is identified. What is the Solar Angel really doing? It is trying to awaken the sleeping Monad. It is calling man back to himself. It is the lioness *reminding* the baby lion to feel his own reality, his own essence and to be himself. It is encouraging man to enter into the path of his Kingship, as did the son of the king when he "remembered" who he was. The Solar Angel never forces Its will on the personality except when something is interfering with the *karma* of man. The Solar Angel stands in man as a point of light, love and power, ready to be invoked and to evoke, or respond. Man thus enlists the help of his Solar Angel according to his aspiration, demand, karma and conditions under which he lives. It stands in man as a shining standard of achievement and mastery, and as a great magnet toward which all the aspirations of man are eventually attracted.

In some literature of olden days the Solar Angel is referred to as the Big Brother Who progresses in Its own line of evolution through deep meditation and service rendered to the Hierarchy. It is the Presence Who watches the unfolding human soul, the *Hope of Glory* of the individual whom It ensouled ages ago. It is the Presence, the Inner Guide, standing ready to assist as man grows and becomes able to stand on his own feet, able to face his own problems and to solve these problems with his own two hands. Thus is man prepared to enter into the path of mastership. The lives of our physical bodies are as days to the Solar Angel. It watches the progress of the human soul age by age until man reaches a high stage of development.

Our obstacles are opportunities for mastership and our visions and labors are windows through which the Solar Angel can shine forth into our darkness. It stands as the ideal image toward which we strive. It is not a dead image, but an image which inspires, uplifts, leads and blesses in proportion to our unfoldment toward Its beauty. It stands as the Sun. It does not pull us up to help us grow, but rather It conditions our growth and we depend upon our unfolding petals to drink the light, life and power from Its greatness. Man, or the developing human soul, first recognizes the Solar Angel as the source of intelligence, then as the source of love and much, much later as a center of power. Through these three aspects the Solar Angel inspires the human soul and leads him toward his Real Self. Through the major part of his manifestation the human soul, or the awakening Monad, identifies himself with the three lower vehicles and with every changing state in those vehicles. These points of identification which are in constant change are called "I's." This is the trap into which he has fallen. It may be compared to the labyrinth of the ancients, a maze through which the wandering man or Monad must find his way or perish.

The difference between the Solar Angel and the human soul is very simple. The Solar Angel is the gardener, "the initiate of all degrees." The Monad is the acorn, the original Spark. The unfolding human soul is the oak tree growing from the acorn under the care of the gardener. It is the expanding Spark. When the tree reaches a stage at which it does not need care, when its roots are well anchored and its branches healthy and strong, the gardener slowly withdraws his attention and leaves the tree alone. When the Monad, the Spark, has expanded, when the human soul is fully developed, the Solar Angel withdraws Its attention and leaves the man alone.[4]

As we think about the Law of Karma, it becomes clearer to us that the liberation of humanity is possible only when the sense of responsibility is accepted, the brotherhood of humanity is worked out, and the life of each human being is a life of service and sacrifice for others. The whole task of our Solar Angels is to remind us of this Herculean labor and to lead us into the light of Cosmic Awareness in which a man lays down his life for others.

Once we understand the will and purpose of our Inner Lord we enter into the World of Causes and are liberated from the karma of the three lower worlds....[5]

...After the intuitional level is touched upon, the Solar Angel takes charge of all physical, astral and mental activities. All of these planes are flooded with the will of the Solar Angel in conformity with the Plan. We know that the Solar Angel is the custodian of the Plan, and that It tries to work the Plan out by inspiring the man in the three worlds.[6]

The Solar Angel is in continuous meditation, which means that It is in a process of aligning, harmonizing and at tuning Itself with the Plan of the Hierarchy, and with the Purpose of the Planetary and Solar Logoi. Thus Its meditation is a process of at-one-ment with the Divine Life, a process of true thinking, real service and radiation of energy.[7]

---

[4]*Cosmos in Man*, pp. 45-46.

[5]*Ibid.*, p. 176.

[6]*The Science of Becoming Oneself*, p. 90.

[7]*The Science of Meditation*, p. 59.

We are told that our Solar Angel is in deep meditation from our birth to death, and even after. Meditation for the Solar Angel means to absorb the Divine Plan, digest it and radiate it to the three worlds of human experience, as far as the human soul can register and work it out.

The Solar Angel is a part of the Spiritual Hierarchy. It has Its own path of development and service in the Divine Plan and in the Divine Purpose. Apart from Its duties toward the human soul, It has Its own evolution on Its own plane of existence.[8]

The Soul is the door leading to group-consciousness, to universality, to the one unified whole, and toward global humanity. Our children are naturally oriented to these concepts. Everywhere in the world, the new age is dawning.[9]

It is possible that our Inner Guide sometimes takes us to the higher mental plane, or lets an intuitive flash hit our consciousness. This is done in rare cases, if the person is worthy due to his sacrificial service....[10]

Our Inner Guide, which is sometimes called the Transpersonal Self, is an example of nobility, one Who continually tries to lead us on the path of Beauty, Goodness and Truth. The Solar Angel is a great knight Who encourages, inspires, challenges, reveals and strengthens. It always warns us, through our conscience, when we are in any way ignoble or are in ignoble relationships. It is the embodiment of nobility because It is an "initiate of all degrees." It is a noble one, one which has gained victory over matter, space

---

[8]*Ibid.*, p. 116.

[9]*The Hidden Glory of the Inner Man*, p. 5.

[10]*The Psyche and Psychism*, p. 520.

and time and has become Its true Self in the presence of the Almighty Lord.

We are told that a Solar Angel is a *nirvani,* which means a great Soul Who passed into higher evolution and descended into us to lead our steps toward our true Self — through Beauty, Goodness and Truth.[11]

Solar Angels are not male and female, but they have masculine or feminine polarity according to their rays and in relation to the personality which they are training. For example, a male has a Solar Angel whose polarization is feminine. A female has a Solar Angel whose polarization is masculine. Such polarity creates magnetism and attraction between two units of life — one, the human soul, and the other, the Solar Angel.

In mystic literature there are many references to the mystic marriage. This is not a parable or symbolic expression, but an actual experience. When the human soul is mature enough, the Solar Angel inspires him or her to marry It. This is called Soul infusion. For long ages the Solar Angel fuses Its light, Its love, and Its power into the person and charges him or her with the electricity of Its spiritual, or higher cosmic ethers, until the man or woman — the human soul — becomes a *soul.* This is achieved at the Fourth Initiation, at which time the Solar Angel separates from the human soul and the Lotus is destroyed.

This is the mystery of higher marriage. It has one goal: to make the human personality a human soul, mature to such a degree that he is no longer male or female conscious, but has awakened through the help of the Solar Angel to both his

[11]*Ibid.,* pp. 1098-1099.

polarities. He is now spiritually androgynous, or a hermaphrodite.

The tremendous sex drive experienced at this time by humanity is the sign that the human soul is feeling the need for a higher fusion. Because a person has no training yet to fuse with his Eternal Mate, he is looking everywhere to find him or her, but is always dissatisfied with one and looking for another, always failing in his search to find his Eternal Mate, the Solar Angel.

The time period between the awakening human soul's search for a Mate and the moment of fusion is the most crucial period of one's life. We pass through pain and suffering during many, many incarnations in search for our True Mate. Because we are looking for our Mate in the wrong places, our disappointment is continuous and our pain is great.

When a person fuses with his Solar Angel, the sex drive will totally normalize and will be used, if necessary, to give a physical vehicle to an incarnating soul. Men and women will finally feel a great satisfaction and will no longer feel the tension of the outside polarity and drive which was tearing their hearts apart for millions of years. This happens generally between the second and Fourth Initiations. From the second to the Third Initiation is called the honeymoon cycle, in which man withdraws from outer pulls and focuses within himself.

From the beginning of the Fourth Initiation, the Solar Angel trains the human soul and tries to bring him into maturity. At the middle of the Fourth Initiation comes the moment when the Solar Angel is able to awaken and activate the two polarities of the human soul. It then starts to prepare the soul to stand on his own feet and be ready to say goodbye to his Eternal Companion.

The link between the two Souls — the human soul and Solar Angel — will never be lost. In cycles They will meet again for greater service of the purpose of the Galactic Logos.

If these statements are true, why then homosexuality? If man has a feminine Solar Angel and woman has a masculine Solar Angel, why is the homosexual woman looking for a homosexual woman, and the homosexual man looking for a homosexual man?

The answer is simple. It is perversion. Homosexuals are focused in the astral body instead of the physical or mental bodies. One can have a male body but a female astral nature. One can have a female body but a male astral body, a dominating, demanding, forcing and irritating astral body.

If this is the case, a male body that has a female astral body looks for one that is male and has a male astral body. Homosexual mating is done in astral polarization, in the astral nature. The problems of homosexuals have astral origins and can be solved only in changing the focus of consciousness from the astral to the physical body. The homosexual's sexuality is not yet anchored in his physical organs.

One may ask, why then is a homosexual, for example, who is a woman by her physical organs and has *male* polarization in her astral nature, not attracted to a normal woman who has a *feminine* astral body?

The answer is that the normal woman, being physically polarized, repels the male astral polarization of the female homosexual because her physical body receives the charge from the physical body of the homosexual and repels it. This is just like magnetic polarity: likes repel each other.

The hermaphrodite who has both organs available physically is one who is focused in his consciousness both in the astral and physical bodies, which are both feminine and masculine in their nature.

The Solar Angel waits for the moment when the whole personality is male or female in relation to the polarity of the Solar Angel.

Personality polarization is the moment when the human soul is finally demonstrating his keynote, his polarity. After the soul demonstrates his polarity, fusion is possible between the soul and the Solar Angel.[12]

When a homosexual is attracted to another man, he disturbs the balance between his Soul and himself, and eventually makes Soul-contact very difficult. The same is true for a lesbian who has a Solar Angel of masculine polarity. In both cases we have perversion.

When a person loses the balance between himself and his Solar Angel, he or she becomes homosexual or lesbian. Because of this, the person does not present the opposite polarity and is "mixed up." A lesbian may act as a man or woman. The same is true for a homosexual.[13]

At times the Solar Angel takes control of the personality and speaks, sings, or writes through him. Its Voice is different from the voice of the personality; It has depth and sweetness and is very impressive. This Voice is magnetic and effective and is heard when there is a *need* — a group, national or universal *need* — or when there is an opportunity to give much-needed rare advice, energy or leadership. A

---

[12]*The Psyche and Psychism*, pp. 541-543.

[13]Unpublished writing, April 28, 1985.

simple man may suddenly become a hero and lead armies, or, with his speech and song, inspire multitudes to achieve a new level of understanding.[14]

...Our Solar Angels slowly collect all thoughtforms that are preventing our evolution, and burn them or cast them out.[15]

Sometimes your Inner Guide releases information from the past to let you understand the situation in which you are, and for which you have an intense feeling that an injustice is being done to you by life in general.[16]

Often our Inner Guide gives us certain instructions through the form of a friend, teacher or wise man, or by showing us symbols and writings. Sometimes It explains and clarifies to us some passages from the Ageless Wisdom which were puzzling us for a long time. It sometimes gives us the entire explanation. Sometimes It gives us a few keys and lets us find the rest.[17]

The Solar Angel often introduces other experiences than what the senses present, and this becomes the pure path of knowledge for Initiates. It is interesting to note that when any sense is really developed on a plane to its possible perfection, the corresponding sense on the higher plane begins to form, to unfold and to function, thus conveying a new range of experiences or knowledge to man.[18]

---

[14]*The Hidden Glory of the Inner Man*, p. 21.
[15]*The Psyche and Psychism*, p. 28.
[16]*Ibid.*, p. 313.
[17]*Ibid.*, p. 314.
[18]*Ibid.*, p. 59.

The Soul does not approve of failure; It challenges the human being again and again until he overcomes his weaknesses.[19]

The purpose of the Soul is to establish a steady path of development for each atom of the physical, emotional and mental bodies, releasing their latent light and making them avenues of experience, avenues of knowledge, love and sacrifice, so that the Holy Chalice is filled eventually with the essence produced by the activities of all these bodies. Each body makes its contribution to the Chalice, and this contribution can not be completed if some of the bodies are neglected.[20]

For many thousands of years, the human soul — the Monad — was identified with the physical, emotional and lower mental worlds. In all these ages, the Solar Angel helped him to detach himself, step by step, from the lower self and led him on the path of initiation.

At first the human soul had no control upon his own vehicles. The Solar Angel then represented the human soul. In the womb of the Solar Angel, the human soul is in gestation. Man will be born as a physical being many, many times before the human soul is born.

The birth will occur only at the first initiation. To deliver this "babe in Christ," the Initiator, Who is the Bodhisattva or the Lord Christ at the first two initiations, takes His Rod in His hand. The electrical energy passes from the Rod to the guardian, from the guardian to the sponsor, on both sides of the neophyte, and they, "by an act of will," pass it to the ini-

---

[19]*Ibid.*, p. 1081.
[20]*The Science of Meditation*, p. 216.

tiate. The centers of the initiate receive a great charge and his aura glows with a new glory.

It is at the time of the operation of the Rod of Initiation by Christ that *the birth of the human soul takes place*. That is why the first initiation is called *"the birth."*

Now the man is the Hope of Glory, being born of the Solar Angel, the Inner Christ. The real man, who is the human soul, had no identity before his spiritual birth. He was a sleeping seed in the womb of the Solar Angel, Whose duty it was to nourish him, and at the right time deliver him, as a new baby.[21]

...Great Initiates contacted lofty ideas. They treasured them in the Chalice, but they kept the registration or recording of the ideas through symbols. They did not bring the ideas into the lower mind but kept them in the Chalice protected by the high frequency of the Solar Angel.[22]

The mental body is a sphere of very sensitive atoms, upon which *either* the human soul or the Inner Guide projects Its thoughts, and ideas or impressions and builds thoughtforms.[23]

Illusions must be dealt with very carefully, and all weeds of illusion must be cleaned daily with the help of the Soul, which is the Inner Guide, the Solar Angel. The Soul uses intuitional light to dispel them, as the sun's rays dispel the clouds or fog.

This is done mostly through meditation, right conduct and service. Right conduct is synchronization of actions with the insight you received through meditation. Those

---

[21]*The Psyche and Psychism*, pp. 1160-1161.
[22]*Ibid.*, p. 739.
[23]*Ibid.*, p. 663.

who are obsessed with illusion spread illusion into the minds of their victims. They mystify others in order to eventually and totally control them. One can watch himself very closely to see if he is engaged in such an activity. One can observe his relationship with others and see whether or not he is imparting to them an illusive image of facts, events and happenings. Once he notes that he is generating illusions, he must try, by all means, to invoke the light of his Soul and the light of the intuition to dispel such a habit....[24]

Creative imagination is the ability of a man to utilize the astral body and impress upon it forms created by the Thinker in harmony with the course of his evolution, and in tune with the universal progress. In the process of creative imagination, the Divine Plan and Purpose are given expression.[25]

It sometimes happens that you see in your dream or vision the image of a leader, speaker or teacher who invites you to a certain place to see him and listen to his lecture. You obey and go, and actually find the same person you saw in your dream. This can happen when the teacher, knowing the laws of mental projection, projects his image with needed information, and the image does its job automatically.

Another possibility is that many hundreds, thinking about him and about his lecture and location, build a thoughtform which can be contacted by sensitive souls.

Another possibility is that the Inner Guides of those people who have such an experience use the thoughtform of the teacher to lead the personality to him, or to his lecture, giv-

---

[24]*Ibid.*, p. 131.
[25]*Ibid.*, p. 68.

ing the right information and impressing on him the importance of the contact.[26]

[Disciplinary dreams] are projected from the Inner Guide to the unfolding human soul to quicken his striving and to reorient him to certain values and disciplines. In the dream, complicated tasks are presented to the human soul to perform. As the human soul strives to fulfill these tasks, he introduces changes in his relationship with the mechanism.

...In the case of disciplinary dreams, it is you who is influencing your vehicles in the light of the Inner Guide, or the Transpersonal Self.[27]

---

[26]*Ibid.*, p. 310.
[27]*Ibid.*, pp. 307-308.

11

Location of the Soul
and
Building the Bridge

*I*ncorporated in the form of man is the Spirit aspect and matter aspect. The Solar Angel is the bridge which leads the Spirit aspect of man toward Life-Space and uses the matter aspect to carry out the purpose of *Space*. Gradually, with the help of the Solar Angel, the Spirit aspect in man gains total control over the various grades of matter, and the man develops a new consciousness of his own and "remembers" his Father's House. When this is accomplished, he becomes a Soul.

As with the human form, every form has its own "soul." A cell, a grain, a tree, an animal, a planet, a solar system, a constellation — each has its own soul, its own bridge, which transmutes spirit into matter, matter into spirit, and furthers the Divine Plan. When this bridge, the soul, acquires self-consciousness and achieves a high degree of self-determination, it becomes a Solar Angel; "A superman, the lightning out of the dark cloud — man."[1]

[In the following diagram, you see] the mental plane with its seven levels. On the seventh level you see the fallen spark, the human soul, and the egg-shaped formation is the small field of his consciousness built around the intelligence thread.

---

[1]Nietsche, Friedrich, *Thus Spake Zarathustra*. (Excerpt from *The Hidden Glory of the Inner Man*, pp. 43-44.)

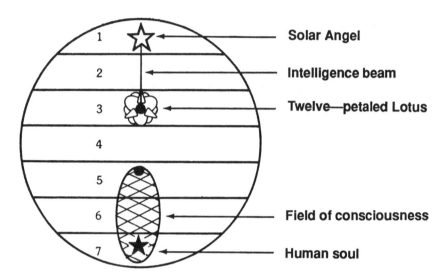

On the first level you see the Solar Angel, Its intelligence thread reaching the twelve-petaled Lotus which is not unfolded as yet.

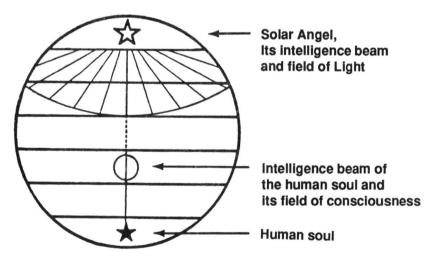

As the mental body goes through a process of gradual transformation, the field of human consciousness expands.

ASPIRING HUMAN SOUL[2]

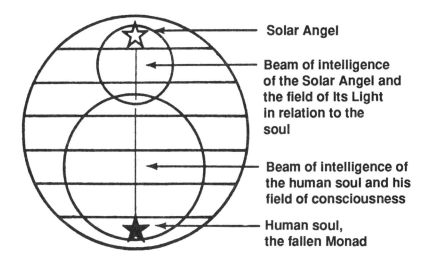

Solar Angel

Beam of intelligence
of the Solar Angel and
the field of Its Light
in relation to the
soul

Beam of intelligence of
the human soul and his
field of consciousness

Human soul,
the fallen Monad

The physical plane is divided as follows:

1. first ether
2. second ether
3. third ether
4. fourth ether
5. gaseous
6. liquid
7. dense physical...

The Solar Angel Who came to man and incarnated in him, located Itself in the three highest sub-planes of the mental plane and became the Soul of man. To the Solar Angel, the mind, the emotional vehicle and the physical

---

[2]*The Psyche and Psychism*, p. 914.

body, with its senses, are windows of relationship through which It comes in contact with the matter of these planes, enrich Its experience and is able to express Itself.[3]

The Soul, the Ego, or in occult terminology, the Solar Angel, dwells on the three higher levels of the mental plane. It is the Thinker. It is not the man; It is the bridge between the reflection and the Real Self. The reflection comes into being when the combined light of the Monad and the Solar Angel strikes a lower sub-plane and creates an "I" there. The Soul is not the reflection; It is the Thinker. It produces light and consciousness through the mental substance....[4]

The third plane of the mind is where your Inner Guide operates, and the light of your intuition starts to penetrate into the astral plane. When you are functioning on the lower mental planes (7,6,5,4), you are in conflict with your own life. But when you enter into the third plane, you enter into the rhythm and symphony of the Inner Lord.[5]

The link between the worlds of intuition and mind is the Solar Angel, the Soul. The Soul Itself is a revelation, and It is a unit of energy which reveals the hidden path to innermost worlds.[6]

We are told that the Real Man is the Monad, the Spark, the innermost Self. He has a physical body with the etheric double, the astral body and mental body. If a man is far enough advanced, he also has higher and subtler bodies through which to communicate with higher realms.

---

[3]*The Hidden Glory of the Inner Man*, pp. 48-49.
[4]*The Science of Becoming Oneself*, p. 42.
[5]*Christ the Avatar of Sacrificial Love*, p. 112.
[6]*The Hidden Glory of the Inner Man*, p. 11.

Between these two poles — the Spark and the vehicles — he has the Eternal Guide, the Solar Angel, leading the sleeping Spark back to Himself through the process of gradual awakening, or through a series of initiations.

The Eternal Guide is anchored within a subtle mechanism, which in the Ageless Wisdom is called the Temple of Solomon, the Chalice or Lotus. This mechanism is a very complicated transistor, transmitter, accumulator and recorder of experience for all incarnations. It is formed of twelve petals in the process of opening. Three of the petals are called knowledge petals, three are love petals and three are sacrifice petals. The three innermost petals are "valves" for the electric fire at the very center.

The energy of will expresses itself through the sacrifice petals, the energy of intuition through the love petals, and the energy of intelligence through the knowledge petals. These energies are the basic energies of the Solar Angel.[7]

...The building of psychological bridges takes place in two directions: first, toward the lower planes and secondly, toward the higher planes. Toward the lower, the unit of consciousness, wherever it is focused, tries to gain conscious control over the actions, emotions and thinking processes of these lower bodies, building them into goal-fitting mechanisms. This endeavor continues until the world of personality is integrated with "power lines," and presents a unique whole, sensitive in all of its parts and acting as one organism. Man must try to connect the integrated personality with the Soul or with the Chalice and bring about a Soul-infused personality. Then comes the striving to connect the Soul-infused personality with the Spiritual Triad, the glory

---

[7] *Cosmos in Man,* p. 177.

of which will shine through the Soul-infused personality as great creative glory and beauty....[8]

THE BRIDGE

The bridge has three main parts. One of them is called the Sutratma or life thread. The second is called the Antahkarana or the consciousness thread, and the third is called the creative thread.

The Sutratma is anchored in the heart, and it brings life to the body. It is the bridge between the spirit and the heart or the blood stream. Sometimes it is called the life cord. It comes directly from the Monad.

The second thread comes from the Soul and anchors itself in the brain, and this is the part of the Antahkarana which gives man consciousness. This cord is called the consciousness thread and is the lower part of the main Antahkarana which bridges the gap between the mental unit and mental permanent atom. The Antahkarana thus links the personality with the Monad, because it bridges the highest aspect of personality, the mental unit, and the lowest aspect of the Spiritual Triad, the higher mind, via the manasic permanent atom found on the first subplane of the mental plane.[9]

[The third thread], the creative thread, is an extension of the two basic threads, and when sufficiently constructed is anchored in the throat center.[10]

---

[8]*The Science of Becoming Oneself*, p. 128.

[9]*Ibid.*, p. 132.

[10]*Ibid.*, p. 133.

The Antahkarana is this subtle line of communication between the bodies, the Soul and the Spiritual Triad. In a sense *the Antahkarana is the evolving human soul,* who slowly bridges from one vehicle to another, and eventually reaches the Soul, and then the Monad.[11]

Once a relationship is established between the personality and the Spiritual Triad, the will energy starts to flow into the personality. We are told that this is very dangerous in the early stages if it is not balanced by the love energy of the Soul....[12]

In connection with the Antahkarana we are told that there are three glands which form a triangle in the body. These glands come into activity through the down-pouring forces of the higher planes. The pituitary gland becomes active when forces flow into it from the lower mental, the astral and etheric planes, via the Sutratma. The pineal gland starts its activity when forces enter from the Soul; and the alta major center becomes active when the Rainbow Bridge is built. These three then become a fiery triangle when the man enters into the Third Initiation....[13]

At the time the physical body is to be formed, the Solar Angel spins the Sutratma and creates a coil or etheric body in accordance with the records stored in the permanent seed atoms. This etheric body, or coil, is woven of energy threads as a web, and for the average person is mostly constructed of buddhic substance.[14]

---

[11]*The Science of Meditation,* p. 58.

[12]*The Science of Becoming Oneself,* p. 132.

[13]*Ibid.,* p. 134.

[14]*Ibid.,* p. 136.

Each of our bodies is composed of millions of progressing lives. These lives are distributed on the seven levels of each plane, the more advanced lives being on the higher levels. In the center of these advancing, progressing lives, there is the greater Life, that super-center we call the Soul.[15]

The Solar Angel is the vision and the model of the man. Man extends from below up to that vision and to the model. The Solar Angel descends from above, as the higher counterpart of man.

Beyond the mental plane, the average man *does not have* any higher mechanism. The intuitional, atmic, monadic and divine vehicles are in embryo in the kernel of the "Monad," but they are not opened yet and have no active existence. The intuitional body, the atmic and monadic and divine vehicles of the Solar Angel which form part of man's nature, do not belong to him, but *they are the vehicles of the Solar Angel.* Until the end of the Fourth Initiation man gradually builds his intuitional, atmic and monadic vehicles out of his own essence, with the corresponding substance of the Planetary Logos. His building is the semblance of the model of the vehicles of the Solar Angel. After these bodies are in some degree built and utilized by the man himself, the Solar Angel leaves him with Its higher bodies for higher realms.

In rare moments of exaltation and ecstasy, man tastes the beauty and bliss of the higher vehicles of the Solar Angel through illumination and inspiration, but then comes back to his usual habitat, the vehicles of the personality....[16]

The Solar Angel, or the Soul, is anchored in the pineal gland and uses it as a station of communication with the

---

[15]*Ibid.*, p. 97.

[16]*The Science of Meditation*, pp. 52-53.

mechanism called man. The Soul is not enslaved in man and is not handicapped by his physical, emotional and mental limitations. The Soul, being free from time and space, has Its own independent life — Its own path of development and progress and Its own way of service.[17]

The beam of intelligence originates from the Solar Angel and passing through various vehicles anchors itself in the brain.

The beam of intelligence also has its own "centers" in each vehicle through which the light of intelligence reaches the various parts of the vehicles of man.

The consciousness of the higher mind becomes clearer and clearer as the diffused light of the beam of intelligence detaches itself from the bodies and from the urges, glamors and illusions of the lower nature, and focuses itself on the higher mental plane. True meditation starts here. The seed thought is held in the light of the higher mind, and all interrupting messages are cut off from the lower self. The lower mind is still, and now is able to cooperate with the higher mind. The mental body as a whole is a magnetic mirror, and slowly absorbs and reflects the ideas coming from the Soul, or from the Intuitional Plane.[18]

...We have the Soul's Eye, which reveals the Kingdom of God and the Divine Plan. This eye is "located" in the *highest* head center, and it transmits the energy of the Spiritual Triad....[19]

---

[17]*The Hidden Glory of the Inner Man*, p. 18.
[18]*The Science of Meditation*, p. 95.
[19]*Ibid.*, p. 175.

The *"eye of Shiva"* is not the pineal gland, is not etheric vision, and is not the ajna center. It is the third eye, the single eye, which is found at the center of the forehead between the two physical eyes in etheric matter. This third eye is formed "through the activity of three factors": the Solar Angel with the unfolding Lotus, the three head centers, and the corresponding three glands. As the energy of the Solar Angel pours down upon the evolving human soul in response to a life of meditation and service, the three centers of the head and their corresponding glands start to awaken and function. The third circle of petals in the Lotus opens and creates an electric field. This field of light gradually condenses and becomes a radiating Sun, at the center of which the *third eye* appears and then slowly settles at the center of the forehead between the eyes in etheric matter.

We are told that when the *third eye* reaches perfection, it becomes blue in color. This is the eye that sees, creates, communicates, heals, destroys obstacles, unveils great formulas of mysteries, and controls and directs energies. This is the eye that contemplates the divine beauties in their geometrical splendor and colors, and projects them to the world of men to liberate, to awaken humanity to greater values of life, and to become a path of light through which men may achieve.[20]

A great deal is written about eyes in esoteric literature. We have the right eye, which is the transmitter of intuitional energy, the energy of love and fiery will; it is related to the pituitary body, the Soul and the Hierarchy. We have the left eye which is the transmitter of mental energy; it is related to the carotid gland and to humanity. We have etheric vision,

---

[20]*The Psyche and Psychism*, p. 182.

which is performed by the physical eyes after biological changes have taken place in them. We have the third eye, the Eye of Shiva, which sees all things in the "Eternal Now." We have the Soul's Eye, which reveals the Kingdom of God and the Divine Plan. This eye is "located" in the highest head center, and it transmits the energy of the Spiritual Triad. We have also the Monad as an eye which reveals the Purpose of God, and God's Eye, the All-Seeing Eye.[21]

THE CHALICE

The Soul is a unit of energy, a pure thought; but, when expressing Itself, It adopts a special appearance. Thus Its form and appearance will always be relative or proportionate to the inner achievement. Close your eyes and envision a handful of fine powder, whose molecules contain the seven principal colors of the spectrum. Throw that handful of powder into the air and let it take the form of a sphere in which innumerable molecules fly around at a very high rate of speed. A dark blue light streams forth from the center of that sphere. Stimulate your imagination a little more and visualize in what a wonderful way the molecules, magnetically held to the central core, are playing in the sphere, gradually creating rhythmic, harmonious waves and tones in which the yellow, silvery white, orange, light violet and red colors are clearly scintillating. The colors represent the planes of the Soul. These planes, according to their vibrations, take on different colors and, reacting to each other and to the impulses of the Soul, create beautiful forms or waves.

After you have studied your created thoughtforms for a moment, visualize the center itself where you will find

---

[21]*Ibid.*, p. 184.

a point of blue light, a sun which is composed of three rings: a ring of orange, a ring of yellow, and one of blue. In the center you will find the *nucleus of absolute darkness*, the center of *"light unapproachable."* Now — imagine that from that dark nucleus, or "diamond," an energy is pouring forth, passing through the three rings and forming nine petals of a flower. The three petals are half-open, the next three are unfolded a little more, and the outer ones are completely unfolded. Visualize this flower floating upon the *water*. Let the flower project a stalk into the water and anchor itself into the mud with its roots. The space above the water represents the mental plane, the water is the emotional plane, and the mud is the physical plane.

The nine petals of the flower represent the nine fundamental radiations or energies which pour forth from the central diamond. They take the shape of tongues and become the petals of the flower, in many colors and hues. Each of these petals has its own rate of vibration and color; they are etheric and luminous bodies which continuously radiate the influence of the rays coming from the nucleus.

In the Ageless Wisdom the third group of petals is called "knowledge petals," the second group is called "love-wisdom petals," and the first group is called "sacrifice petals." This wonderful flower, as a whole, which we build in the higher mind is known as "The Temple Eternal in the Heavens." The higher mind in the Ageless Wisdom is called "heaven." Here is found the "Kingdom of God" — the Soul. In this "building of God, a house not made with hands, eternal in the heavens," we have seven centers which resemble wheels and are found in our electromagnetic or etheric atmosphere outside the physical body along the spinal column — *above the seven main ductless glands.*

The Soul controls the bodies through the wheels, which in fact are Its stations or centers of energy and consciousness. They, in turn, affect the glands and nervous system. Each center has the form of a lotus or lily, each endowed with its own colors, radiations and rate of vibration.

For many centuries, a sacred Brotherhood has used the cross as a symbol. At the meeting point of the two arms of the cross, they have placed a rose as the symbol of the Soul. The vertical arm of the cross represents spiritual energy and the horizontal arm represents substance. Where these two arms cross, a whirlpool is produced which resembles a rose. This rose is the Soul, which bridges substance and Spirit.

The Lotus or lily has three inner petals which for a long time remain closed around the central diamond; but when after long ages, they start to unfold and radiate, their fiery essence burns the Lotus formed by the remaining nine petals and annihilates it. Those inner three petals express the essence of spiritual life. The outer nine petals are divided into three tiers. One of the petals from each of the three tiers extends to each personality vehicle, and here they spread knowledge, love and the will-to-sacrifice. Thus on the physical plane we have the influence of the first petals of knowledge, love and sacrifice; on the emotional plane, we have the second tier of petals; and, on the mental plane, we have the third petal of the knowledge petals, the third petal of the love petals, and the third petal of the sacrifice petals; this also holds true for the other planes of personality.

Upon each plane, the petals gradually and successively become active and effective until, upon the mental plane, the third petals of the third tier open. On this level, man becomes a living sacrifice and a source of light, love and power in his environment. The flower of the Soul has been unfolded and, if seen clairvoyantly, it has the supreme beauty of vibrating colors and radiation. This flower is situated just above the head of people who are spiritually advanced, and there it forms a crown of wonderful vibrations and colors which radiate love, wisdom, light and power in all directions. This flower turns upon its axis at a very high speed. When the speed reaches its limit the unit of the Central Life is released and man has reached his goal. He has acquired a fourth-dimensional consciousness and is free from the limitations of space and time.

In the Ageless Wisdom, the Soul-flower is called the Temple of Solomon. This temple is built by "stones." The Masons actually prepare the stones with their "tools" and raise the temple toward God. These stones are man's good deeds, thoughts, and acts of love and sacrifice upon the three planes of personality. Each day of our life represents a stone which we are sanctifying to utilize in the building of this eternal temple in the heavens, in man and in humanity, wherein our God will live.

Upon the cross, Jesus symbolically represented this experience. He not only suffered in his body, but the "Temple" which was built by Him was in the process of destruction. The curtain of the Temple was rent. The petals of the fourth tier, the central petals, which had started to unfold, were burning the Soul-flower, the Chalice. Then He cried, "My God, My God, for this I was spared." That was the *Cup* which He saw in the Garden of Gethsemane, when His "sweat was like great drops of blood falling to the ground." Facing the whole mystery of Spirit, He said, "Not my will but Thy will be done." After the crucifixion, Jesus returned to His Father, becoming one with the Will of God, because He had been able to destroy all the limitations of separative walls with His love nature.

Manu, one of the first lawgivers to Humanity, says, "The supreme duty of the man is to know his Soul, because that knowledge gives him the key to immortality. That man who recognizes the Great Soul within his soul, and within every creature ... and who is rightful toward every man, toward every creature ... he becomes a blissful man, and eventually merges into *the Heart of God*."

The Lotus is the vehicle of the Solar Angel. In this Lotus the real individuality, the real Self of man is anchored, apart from the Solar Angel, as a flame which is partially extended and identified with the bodies. Each degree of identification creates a false "self," a false "I," known as the shadow or the reflection of the true Self. The true Self is called the developing, unfolding human soul who is trying to liberate himself, go back to "his Father," and become his true Self.

Every time man takes another step toward his Central Core, he awakens to his own reality, and a time comes when the radiation of his light synchronizes with the light of the Solar Angel. This event esoterically is called the divine marriage or Soul infusion.[22]

In esoteric literature, heaven is the mental plane where the Chalice is found. The treasure is in the Chalice. It was symbolized as the Holy Grail sought by the Knights of the Round Table. It is in the Chalice that our true Guide exists, but It cannot express Itself until the permanent atoms or seeds are cleansed, purified, and the Chalice is in full bloom, filled with the elixir of life. The purifying process is the result of the contemplation of the Solar Angel within us. The

---

[22]*The Hidden Glory of the Inner Man*, pp. 69-73.

Solar Angel vibrates in higher octaves and these notes act as purifying streams of energy which throw out all that does not fit into the plan of the human soul. The act of meditation is a process of conscious assimilation of these energies.

The Chalice is built primarily out of the substance of the Solar Angel. The human soul makes itself ready to wear the Chalice as "the robe of glory." When this body, the Chalice, or the "robe of glory" is woven or built, the emotional sea disappears and the astral body disintegrates. Thus the man enters into direct communication with the Intuitional Plane....[23]

The Chalice is the body of the Solar Angel. *Its voice is our conscience.* Nothing can enter into the Chalice which is against the Divine Plan, Purpose and Will. Everything in the three levels of human endeavor, which is in accord and in tune with the essence of the Chalice, gives you great inner joy, energy and inspiration. Anything you do contrary to the essence of the Chalice makes you poor, miserable, and you feel the soft small voice of conscience warning you of your wrong action. The Chalice is the vessel of pure wisdom, the vessel of true love and knowledge, of beingness and realization.[24]

TWELVE STAGES OF ILLUMINATION

Since times immemorial the Chalice has been a symbol of Service. The gifts of Higher Forces are gathered in the Chalice and given from the Chalice. The symbol of the Chalice has always stood for

---

[23]*The Science of Becoming Oneself*, p. 68.
[24]*Ibid.*, p. 69.

self-sacrifice. Whoever bears the Chalice bears Achievement. Each lofty deed can be marked by the symbol of the Chalice. Everything most lofty, everything for the good of humanity, should bear this symbol. The Chalice of the Grail, and the Chalice of the Heart which has dedicated itself to the Greater Service, is a most Cosmic Magnet. The Heart of the Cosmos is reflected in this great symbol. All images of Heroes of the Spirit may be represented as bearing the Chalice. The whole universe is reflected in the Chalice of the fiery spirit. The Chalice contains the accumulations of centuries which are gathered around the seed of the spirit. It is necessary to accept the affirmation of the Chalice as a great symbol in everyday life. Small children, and all youth, should be taught to think about the Chalice. One should understand the entire diversity of forms of the great symbol, the Chalice.[25]

When the awareness of the knower expands upon the field of knowledge, we call this expansion the process of illumination. The field refers to the Cosmic Physical Plane. The physical, emotional, mental and intuitional worlds are parts of that field. Illumination is a process of extending your awareness into these fields in helping you to discover:

   a. the laws and principles that work through each field;

   b. the methods that will be used in various relationships;

   c. your own stage of development, and your place and role in the process of evolution;

---

[25]Agni Yoga Society, *Fiery World*, Vol. III, para. 49.

d. the part that each living form plays in each field to carry out the great Plan toward its spiritual destination.

In man, illumination or enlightenment is the process of releasing the inner nucleus of light, which works out through twelve successive stages.

No man can become enlightened or illumined by being taught some kind of knowledge, by having information imparted, or by having mysteries and secrets unveiled. Illumination is an inner happening. It is the result of an inpouring light, and of the release of the latent light in each atom of your vehicles.

It is a gradual dawning, when the Sun of your Real Essence starts to shed Its light. Then the mountain tops of your greatest vision emerge in the kiss of its golden rays, and the flowers of your aspirations open their hearts to drink in the true light.

We are told that this Sun has twelve flames: three of them are called knowledge flames; three are love flames; three are flames of sacrifice; and another three, the innermost flames. We can visualize the inner Sun as being covered by twelve flames, or fiery petals, which have yet a dim light, lost in the mists and clouds of the lower being.

As these petals gradually unfold and as the mists, fogs and clouds slowly fade away, the inner Splendor stands revealed, shedding its light, love and power. This takes place as the result of faithful meditation, and a life of sacrificial service motivated by pure love.

Illumination is a process of becoming; it is a process of transmutation, transformation and transfiguration. It is like the fairy tale in which the Sun fell into a muddy sea, then gradually came to the surface in shining splendor, and rose in the sky to its full glory.

The first stage of illumination occurs when you suddenly realize that you are not the physical body and people are not just physical bodies. This first begins as a feeling, but gradually deepens as the first petal of the knowledge flames starts to unfold and radiate spiritual light to your brain. This is a great happening, and a moment of great joy and relief. You actually realize that you are not the body; you do not change with the body as it passes through the phases of youth, maturity, old age, and then dies. The whole problem of life and death takes on a new meaning for you.

In the second stage of illumination you become aware of your emotional body and the emotional bodies of others, and the ways that these bodies act. You become aware of the natures of other people, and the role they play in your and in their individual, social and spiritual lives. This is a great stage of illumination during which you become able to see all your emotional reactions and responses. It is as if a veil had suddenly been removed from a machine and you could see clearly how that machine works, in all its parts, in you and in others. This takes place gradually as the second petal of the knowledge flames starts to unfold and shed its light into your astral plane.

In the third stage of illumination you become aware of your mental nature and the mental nature of others. You see how it works, how it is conditioned; how it conditions your life, the lives of others and also the life of the planet; and how it can be used in better ways as an agent of creative living and survival. This awareness takes place gradually as the third petal of the knowledge flames unfolds and sheds its light into your mental plane. After that, your whole mental world is seen by you as it stands.

Please note that in these three stages of illumination you are becoming aware of realities, facts and happenings, but you are not yet in control. You have not yet achieved the stage at which you exercise your full power to control the bodies, to change them, to create better ones, and to use new techniques through them. This ability begins as you enter the fourth stage of illumination.

At the fourth stage, the first petal of fiery love starts to unfold and radiate its light into the physical plane. Here you begin to control your physical body as you control your car. As this light increases it clears away age-long inertia, blind urges and drives working through your etheric and physical bodies. The physical body comes under the command of your will.

At the fifth stage of illumination, as the second flame of fiery love unfolds and radiates its pure light, you slowly clean your emotional body. Your emotional body is cleansed of age-long glamors and becomes a shining mirror which reflects the glories of the Intuitional Plane. Here begins the great mystic path, the path of spiritual aspiration and holiness.

At the sixth stage of illumination, as the third petal of fiery love starts to unfold and radiate its dynamic and magnetic light, you gain control of your mental plane. Here all your illusions gradually disappear and you stand in a great light. You start to use your mental energy for spiritual creativity to further the Divine Plan.

In the seventh step of illumination, as the first petal of the flames of sacrifice unfolds and radiates its cold, dynamic light, your threefold vehicles enter into the light of the Soul and you become a Soul-infused personality. Here you start to confront the Dweller on the Threshold, as it is called in esoteric literature. You are in the process of transformation. In the next stage you will "grow wings to fly."

In the eight and ninth stages of illumination you build a communication line between the Soul-infused personality and the Spiritual Triad. Your horizon becomes limitless. Here you meet your Master; you enter into His Ashram and work for the Plan and the Purpose of God. Around your head shines the Rainbow Bridge in its full glory. This happens when the second and third petals of the flames of sacrifice start to unfold and radiate their pure light. Here you are on the path of transfiguration, the path of the Third Initiation.

From the tenth through the twelfth stages of illumination you start to see the blue Star, your Essence. As the Star becomes brighter, the fully unfolded nine petals increase their radiation, color and rhythmic scintillation, and when they reach a certain degree of unified flow of energy, the innermost three petals gradually unfold and eventually release the blue electric fire at the center of the flames. This fire burns and consumes the whole Chalice, and the three permanent atoms, and the liberated human being withdraws into higher planes.

From this moment on, your head center, the thousand-petaled Lotus, starts to fully function, and to replace the functions of the Chalice. Your awareness is now focused in the Buddhic Plane, and your head center links the threefold transfigured personality with the Spiritual Triad.

Illumination is a Path of progressive steps taken toward your Real Self. After these twelve steps of illumination you live in the eternal light, in the light of the great Initiator Who is called "the Ancient of Days" by the great sages of the East. This does not mean, however, that you have reached the end of your path. After the Path of Illumination, the Path of Being begins. That path can be unveiled to all those who pass the twelve stages of Illumination. All these stages are entered and surpassed by meditation, service and sacrifice. All of these stages are entered and surpassed through our daily labor, through our duties and responsibilities, and through a life of aspiration, freedom and beauty.

The great sage, Djwhal Khul, describing these flames in His books, says that the nine petals are divided into three sections. We have three knowledge petals, three love petals and three sacrifice petals. The first three petals that open in the three vehicles — namely, etheric, emotional and mental — are one knowledge flame, one love flame and one sacrifice flame, but all these three flames are called knowledge petals. Thus we have the following picture, starting from the outermost tier:

First Tier — Knowledge Petals
    one knowledge flame
    one love flame
    one flame of sacrifice

    Second Tier — Love Petals
        one knowledge flame
        one love flame
        one sacrifice flame

        Third Tier — Sacrifice Petals, the tier of petals closest to the center

one knowledge flame

one love flame

one sacrifice flame

When we say, for example, that the third knowledge petal is opening, it means the sacrifice flame in the knowledge petals, and so on.

The petals have individual names and group names. For example, we can say that there are five sacrifice petals, or five love petals, or five knowledge petals according to this tabulation.

The unfoldment of the petals and flames is also related to the initiations. The first initiation is taken when the first four flames of the Egoic Lotus are unfolded. We are told that at this time the light of the Solar Angel penetrates into the area of the pineal gland. As a result of this, the vital airs in the head scintillate and irradiate light. This affects the atoms of the brain and releases their light. Then three lights are fused into a focused point which appears as a radiant sun.

The second initiation is taken when the fifth, sixth, seventh and eighth flames are in the process of unfolding. This means that two more love petals and two of the flames of sacrifice are active. Here a very interesting phenomenon occurs. When the petals of sacrifice start to unfold, they stimulate the head centers and bring out a great light through the mixing of their electric fields. Thus the third eye comes into being and man is illumined to a great degree.

We have, then, three knowledge petals, and if we add to these three, the two knowledge flames of the love and the sacrifice petals, we will have five knowledge flames. The same tabulation can be made with the love and sacrifice flames.

In addition to the nine petals, there are three innermost

petals which are called "the synthesis of knowledge, love and sacrifice." Each of them starts to become organized and unfolded as its corresponding circle of the flames unfolds and radiates.

The Third Initiation is taken when nine flames are unfolded in their great glory and beauty. At this time man's personality life is flooded with the light of the Spiritual Triad through the flames of sacrifice, and all illusions are wiped away.

At the Fourth Initiation the three innermost petals start to open and the man's life becomes a sacrificial service for humanity. He steps into the Fourth Initiation and the pure light of the Inner Divinity, the Monad, pours into his personality and into his environment in great splendor. This pure light eventually consumes the Chalice, the age-old Lotus, and sets free the Solar Angel, the Great Presence. Then, man enters into the Fifth Initiation. At the Fifth Initiation he is raised up to the Spiritual Triad and works there in true awareness. His personality becomes the purest instrument of service, and the great light of the Planetary Logos and then of the Solar Logos pours thorough him, illuminating all about him.

In the distant Future, when man transcends himself and becomes a Heavenly Man, or a Planetary Logos, He will start again to build His Chalice in the third subplane of the Cosmic Mental Plane. And then after great cycles of preparation, He will raise that Chalice on to the first subplane of the Cosmic Mental Plane and become a Cosmic Being, a Solar Logos.[26]

Om Mani Padme Hum

---

[26]*The Science of Meditation*, pp. 186-192.

12

Soul Approach

$\mathcal{P}$REPARATION

The preparation of the vehicles is very important for the coming child. People prepare clothes for the child. They make ready those things that are going to be used for him, but very few mothers prepare themselves — emotionally, mentally and spiritually — to attract and nourish an advanced, coming Soul.

In addition to physical health, emotional, mental and spiritual health are important to a mother who wants to give birth to Souls who will lead humanity on the Path of discipleship and initiation.

In esoteric literature, we are told that both father and mother must consecrate themselves before any relationship starts. This consecration should be done by being careful of what one eats and drinks. For example, no wine, no alcohol, no drugs, nor tobacco must be used by a woman who is going to conceive or is pregnant. This will help the coming child not only physically, but also will provide a strong foundation for his emotional, mental and spiritual life.

We are told that a pregnant woman must have a serene, emotional life, surrounded by the beauty of nature, the beauty of the written and spoken word, by music or any other of the arts that uplift her into the world of harmony, rhythm, color, sound and motion. She should meditate daily on lofty thoughts, and feed her imagination with great images, heroes and leaders of all ages, and always be full of compassion, forgiveness and serenity. Only to such women are great sons and daughters born, who carry on their lives in great success and beauty.

In the future there will be special colleges where girls and women will learn how to conceive greater Souls, and how to evoke the greatest potential within these Souls while yet unborn, how to raise them with the greatest understanding, and thus give to the future a solid beauty of mind, emotions and body. Many books have been written on this subject, but it is not the books nor the lectures that will help. Instead, a practical life of meditation and the proper environment will help mothers achieve their visions. In the future there will be outlined special plans for discipline, dedication and purification before women decide to have a child.

Mary was in the right place and under the best influences to enable her to carry out her sacred mission in preparing the body of a great Initiate.

We are told that there are three openings in the human aura through which a Soul can depart or enter and possess his vehicle.

One is the solar plexus, through which most children enter into the physical plane. These are the average citizens who can either improve themselves through education and discipline, or live a life of slavery.

The second door is the etheric heart center, and some humanitarian and philanthropically-oriented people come to the physical plane via this center. They have a more advanced heart and some sense of responsibility and unity.

Those who come via the head center are those who are truly advanced in service, sacrifice and intellect.

This is why in olden times people were trained to unfold and open their higher gate to welcome greater ones into the world. The stage of unfoldment of these centers depends on the life that the mother and father are living. The condition of the centers of both parents must be taken into consideration, and the time of preparation for parenthood must be dedicated to unselfish service and meditation whereby higher centers will be activated and unfold.[1]

APPROACHING THE SOUL

> *Selflessness attains, selfishness defeats; men's possibilities are in direct proportion to their ability to see beyond themselves and to feel for others.*
>
> —M.M.—

How can we approach the Soul, the Reality in us, and live our daily life in Its light, in the love and power? At times we feel that we are a fountain of love, a source of light and power. We believe that we are pure as snow and that nothing can affect us, nothing can destroy us. We are full of joy and bliss. Then gradually the Sun descends behind the mountains and we are again in the thickening darkness of our lower self, of our worldly life and its problems. Days and nights pass. We enjoy the blessings of light and experience the bitterness of the nights until our will becomes strong enough to stand in the light and to become one with it forever.

---

[1] *Christ, The Avatar of Sacrificial Love*, pp. 34-35.

The first step in approaching the Soul is a life of service. The second step is the practice of meditation or the seven steps to illumination. The third step is continuous living in the Soul light. Through these three steps, we approach our Soul and then our "Father in Heaven," to become one with Them. This is the true path along which in all ages people have passed to the joy of spirit, to the joy of service and of sacrifice. Our Soul is the only door through which we can enter the spiritual world, come in contact with Divine powers, and serve the Will of God. It is the first Initiator, the light in us and the representative of the Divine Plan for us.

It is impossible to attain our Divinity or to reach perfection, without passing through the Soul and becoming a Soul. When we come in contact with our Soul, fuse with Its Light and grow as a Soul, then the mysteries will be revealed to our opening eyes, and the past, present and future will be ours. We shall become free Souls, free from time and matter, and we will enjoy the presence of the ever-existent Light.

To walk toward the Light we must first of all cleanse our clothes, our personality vehicles, our physical bodies, our emotions and our thinking processes. Cleaning and purifying them means having a sound body; having emotions filled with love and sympathy toward every man; and possessing a clear-thinking mind, free from the fog of glamors and illusions, dedicated to study, meditation and creative activity. When our personality life is ready, we can commence the seven steps of illumination.

We are told that knowledge and relationship are possible only through the Light. If no light exists, there is no knowledge, no relationship, no experience and no growth. We recognize each other by light; we understand each other by the Light within. Look at the stars which palpitate in the immensity of the sky. We see them by their light, we know their composition from the light, and also we know their distances through the light.

Light is life, light is our guide. There are three Suns — the physical Sun, the subjective Sun, and the central Sun from which all things proceed. Every form has its own light. Matter is a dim light. Each atom is materialized light. Release the atom and you will see a blaze of light which will be transmuted into energy and disappear. The real man is a drop of light or of life. When that drop departs, the outer form, which is an extinguished light, will disintegrate. Should our Sun die, no living form could remain upon the earth. We came from the Light and are returning to the Light. The path we are treading is the way of light which becomes gradually more illuminated. He who treads the Way is a drop of light. The source of that drop is the Light, as is the goal of that drop. All is Light.

In the *Koran*, there is a wonderful verse about the mysteries of Light and Soul, which says:

> ALLAH *is the light of the Heavens and the Earth. The similitude of His light is as a niche wherein is a lamp. The lamp is in a glass. The glass is as it were a shining star. This lamp is kindled from a blessed tree, an olive neither of the East nor of the West, whose oil would almost glow forth (of Itself) though no fire touched it. Light upon light, Allah guides unto His light whom He will. And Allah speaks to mankind in allegories, for Allah is the knower of all things.*

> (*Koran*, Surah XXIV)

Matter is energy, and energy is light. The Sun which we see is the light of matter; it is the clothing or body of the Real Sun, the Real Light.

People who see only their physical existence see only the physical world. The bodies in which they exist and the light of matter blind their vision to the existence of innumerable stars and suns. When the material Sun has set, one can see the existence of the stars and other suns. A materialist is only aware of his existence; his vision is very limited. *Every materialistic person tries to limit the freedom of his friends and fellowmen.*

Light is freedom. True freedom is the unlimited radiation of light. Every act against freedom is an act against the light, against the Soul. Man advances because light radiates. The Inner Light cannot stop radiating. It will grow increasingly, destroying the walls of darkness and limitation. The Inner Light overcomes all limits. Gradually man realizes who he is and finds himself in the *Greater Light.*

The process of coming to know oneself is a process of becoming Light. The process of becoming Light is the process of overcoming the limits of matter, the limits of the personality. The mind is the wind which fans the extinguishing "coal" into fire, into light. This is done through meditation.[2]

...[W]hen the human mind is working in its optimum range of clarity, it is an integrated, seven-dimensional mechanism. In its gradual development, it passes through three distinct steps or seven stages.

---

[2]*Hidden Glory of the Inner Man,* pp. 74-77.

First Step:

> *In the first stage* of this step, the mind works through impulses coming from the physical world and from the physical body.

> *In the second stage* it works through impulses coming from the lower levels of the emotional world.

Second Step:

> *In the first stage* of this step, the human mind responds chiefly to commands picked up in its unconscious moments, moments of great excitement.

> *In the second stage*, the mind passes through a learning process. It registers whatever is given to it or forced upon it. In most schools and universities, students are found on this level.

> *In the third stage*, the mind begins to register subtle thoughtforms or thought waves from Space. It thinks and acts according to the thought waves it registers. This process is sometimes called "inspiration," through which people speak or create artistically, but actually, it is still a mechanical performance, not true creativity. Most artists are on this level with the veil of ignorance still hanging over their true nature.

Third Step:

> *In the first stage* of this step, the mind begins to discriminate between the incoming currents of mental energy, or thought currents; it chooses the highest and the universal thought waves to express in its activities.

In the second and last stage, it registers the thoughts of the Inner Lord. At this point, man truly thinks for the first time. He is now a real creator.

On these three steps or seven stages, the Inner Thinker or Lord is present, but He is not free to act through the body except in rare instances or flashes. As the man grows and the mental plane becomes more organized, these flashes from the Inner Lord are more frequent. Most of them are lost and die in the mist and darkness of agitation and turbulence in the lower levels, but gradually the mists clear and the flashes become stronger and more dominating. When the Thinker dominates the mental plane, the man is a true creator or a genius. He works on the first, the highest subplane of the physical, emotional and mental planes, with no obstructions on his path.[3]

A disciple must contact his Soul. The Soul is the Inner Watch, the Inner Presence, the little voice within, the conscience. The disciple must make a contact with It. When a real contact is made, the life of the disciple begins to change and be transformed.

Once this Inner Presence is contacted, It turns into a Guide and makes you feel whether you are living in harmony with the Divine Will or not. It immediately rings the bell in your heart if the thoughts you are thinking are not in harmony with the five-pointed star, or if the words you are speaking or the actions you are taking are not in harmony with the five-pointed star.

Whenever you do, feel, speak or think anything that is in harmony with the Divine Will, you feel an expansion of consciousness and a deeper need for creativity and service.

---

[3]*The Science of Becoming Oneself,* pp. 47-48.

When contact with the Inner Watch is established, you almost hear Its voice, Its silent voice, and you obey that voice. Obedience to the higher means building bridges, connecting links, communication with higher sources. Obedience leads to unity, cooperation and synthesis. Through unity the higher sources begin to manifest in your life.

Almost everyone has had an experience of receiving guidance from within. Such guidance is evidence of the existence of the Inner Watch.[4]

The tenth type of **impressions are impressions coming from the Solar Angel**. The disciple does every kind of labor to come in contact with these vibrations and absorb them....

The twelfth type of vibration or impression comes from **your Master**, but the Master's vibrations do not reach you yet. This is where many disciples and initiates fail, because they have the illusion that they are contacting Masters, great Beings, devas, etc. No Master and no advanced entity contact you before you contact your own Solar Angel.

If you have solid experience and proof that you are contacting your Solar Angel, then you will see that you are approaching the day that your Master will reveal Himself to you. For a long time, your Master keeps Himself totally insulated from you, so that with His influence He does not force you into premature discipline.[5]

Man on his journey home resembles a carriage pulled by wild horses. He has a driver, a Spark "sleeping" deep inside the carriage, and a Guardian Light overshadowing him.

---

[4]*Challenge for Discipleship*, pp. 31-32.
[5]*Ibid.*, pp. 229-230.

For centuries in the East, the human body has been compared to a carriage. The horses represent the emotions and feelings which draw man hither and thither at different speeds and along different roads. The driver represents the mind of man which is supposed to control the carriage and the horses. In most cases the driver appears to be intoxicated. The direction in which the carriage will travel should be decided by the Guardian Light, Itself, until the Spark shines forth. In the heart of man there is the vision of Home....[6]

If we study the five aspects of a human being and their relation to one another, we shall have a good idea of the constitution of man as well as of his psychology.

These aspects are the physical body, the carriage which is called the carnal body or the tent; the emotional nature of man, called the emotional or desire body; and the mental nature which is called the mental or heavenly body. He also has the body of glory, the *Causal Body*, which is sometimes known as "the body made without hands." Here is located the Guardian Light, having within His bosom the everlasting jewel, the Spark.

...[F]iery engineers build the seat for the Guardian Light. It is called the *Causal Body* and from it they extend a thread of light to the carriage, to the horses and to the driver, making the carriage, the total man, ready to receive a Lord of Flame (the Guardian Light), the Guest who will guide the carriage for centuries and centuries, until the Spark of life grows and handles his own destiny.

The development of the carriage takes time. It will take seven years for the Guardian Light to be fully aware of Its carriage, and seven more years for the horses to be ready;

---

[6]*The Fiery Carriage and Drugs*, p. 13.

then again, it will take another seven years for the driver to be ready. Of course, an even longer time will be needed for the carriage, the horses and the driver to be fully integrated, and much longer for the ready carriage to be fused with the will of the Guardian Light, thus rendering it capable of flying toward unlimited horizons, toward Home.[7]

...After the driver is educated and is capable of controlling the horses and the carriage, the next step is to cultivate the relationship between the driver and the Lord of Flame, the Guardian Light or the Solar Angel, as It is called by the Ancient Ones.

Churches, traditionally after a baptism, hold the godfather responsible for this last task. He is obligated to create conditions and opportunities for the child to build bridges between the driver and the Solar Angel. He is responsible for the spiritual education of the child. When communication starts between the Solar Angel and the mind, the "child" is left free to live as this Inner Lord directs.[8]

Next comes our driver, the mental body, who is supposed to control the carriage, the horses, and serve the Inner Lord....

In order to drive one needs to integrate all aspects of the carriage, and guide them as a unit toward a goal. The driver is a bridge between the carriage, the horses, and the Inner Lord, the Solar Angel. It is not enough to learn only about the carriage and the horses. A person needs to know how to communicate with the Lord and how to understnd Its messages. One learns about the carriage through scientific books and through self-study. One learns about the horses through

---

[7]*Ibid.*, p. 14.
[8]*Ibid.*, p. 15.

various psychological books, but he will learn more about the emotional body (the horses) through self-observation. One learns about himself through concentration, meditation, pondering, contemplation, self-observation, non-identification and, above all, by bringing oneself under the control of the Inner Lord, or the inner conscience.

Our mind (the driver) can be found in the following developmental stages:

1. ...the driver is a baby, ignorant and uncultivated. Just as a lamb follows its flock, he does whatever others do. He is not independent; he is enslaved by opinions, beliefs, thought habits, etc.

    It is difficult for such a mind to expand. Until a mind has gained its freedom, it cannot come in contact with the Inner Lord or be a creative agent.

2. ...the mind is enslaved by the emotions. Wherever the horses desire to go, the driver goes. All mental energy is used for the fulfillment of emotional desire....

3. ...the mind identifies with an idea or a doctrine. The man is usually a fanatic, caught by a one-pointed idea, rejecting any other ideas except the one to which he adheres and is accustomed.

4. ...the mind begins to recognize itself and starts to investigate its own world. Gradually a cleavage is produced within the mind. One part begins to perceive that the mind, itself, is a body, an instrument. At this point the Inner

Lord starts to awaken and emerge from Its "sleep," and become active through the three lower vehicles....

5. ...the mind is in complete harmony with the Inner Lord, now fully awakened. The mind is in harmony with Its plan and purpose. The mind knows how to drive the carriage, how to use the reins and how to take care of the horses. He knows all about the roads and highways, and most important of all, he knows the language in which the Lord speaks. In this stage there is complete integration of the physical body, emotional nature, mental nature and the Solar Angel. This stage is called "Soul-personality infusion."

Here again, we must emphasize that the work of the driver is very difficult. The most important task which he must accomplish is the cultivation and development of the relationships among the five aspects so that his entire being can work as a unit. To do this, the driver must give attention to the harness, the shafts and the reins. A carriage, or a horse, can function well on its own. However, each aspect needs to align itself with the others in order to effect a completely integrated unit, an integrated personality. This is the responsibility of the driver, the mind.

After personality integration is achieved, there begins the process of alignment with the Inner Lord, the Solar Angel.

A man is in a healthy condition, awake and is creative, when he gradually and consciously enters into the light of the Solar Angel. Our five aspects condition each other. They are interdependent. The true aim of education is to cultivate these five aspects to such a degree that they function as a unit, and express the energies coming from the Divine Purpose beyond the Lord.

This education must be carried out through:
a. physical discipline;
b. the art of Goodwill and Right Human Relations; and
c. spiritual aspiration, meditation and self-actualization.

Here is a diagram of what we have said:[9]

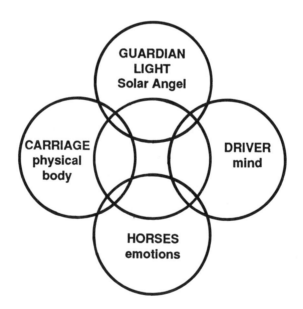

---

[9]*Ibid.*, pp. 19-21.

The driver has a big role to play. He is the controller. He is the one who must take care of the body and the horses, keeping them healthy and under control. However, a most important point to remember is that the driver cannot do this adequately if he himself is not under the control of the Lord. Let us not forget that the reins of the horses are in the hands of the driver, and that the horses are connected to the carriage by the shafts. The driver *does not know where to go* unless he is in communication with the Inner Lord.

We can see clearly, then, that in order to have a blissful life, we must begin to cultivate our minds and put them in contact with the Inner Lord. This we can do through meditation, self-observation, detachment, higher education and by living the truths we learn in our daily life. This is very important. We must allow the Inner Lord to express Itself in our daily life. Truth, love, light and will are all expressions of the Inner Lord. We cannot raise our level to the utmost until the Lord fully expresses Itself in our lives, activities, words and thoughts.

When the mind is awake and under the control of the Inner Lord, a man faces life realistically. He is able to use all of his three bodies consciously, without confusing the specific activity of each one. For example, the heart does not try to do the work of the mind, and the mind does not try to do the work of the Lord. Each aspect performs its own task without interference. The Lord uses them according to the work for which they were built. This creates a balance, an equilibrium between the three bodies and the Lord, and increases the stream of energy coming from the Fiery Purpose beyond the Lord.[10]

---

[10]*Ibid.*, p. 26.

We know that all four aspects of man need nutrition and vitality. We obtain this nutrition and vitality through various channels in accord with our levels or bodies, and according to the level upon which we are focused.

1. The carriage obtains its nutrition from food, water and air. The carriage acquires energy from its horses, its driver and its Lord to the degree that they are active.

2. The horses obtain energy from their carriage, from emotional influences such as love, dedication, aspiration, beauty and art, and also from their driver.

3. The driver, if awake, obtains energy from his carriage, his horses and from his Lord. He also receives energy from the world of ideas and truths, through concentration, meditation and contemplation, because through these activities he contacts the world of ideas, which is the world of the Lord, the Inner Presence.

4. The Lord, Itself, is a source of energy, which shines forth when man's personality is purified and cleansed from mirages, glamors and illusions....

...[I]n order to assimilate the four kinds of food and to receive the required energy, all of our four levels or natures should be integrated and aligned with the Inner Fire, the Inner Presence.[11]

---

[11]*Ibid.*, pp. 29-30.

We should understand that when we completely identify ourselves with the carriage and act solely as that carriage, we are not functioning as the real Self, or the Inner Lord, because we are still submerged in mirages, in maya. When we identify ourselves completely with the horses, we are caught in glamors and emotional fog. When we identify ourselves with the driver's dreams, we are lost in illusions and delusions. The Inner Lord is awake only when man knows himself to be a separate entity apart from the three other vehicles.

When the Lord is fully active within the mental plane, and the bridges are built, the sleeping Spark will awaken and the man will know all that is going on during the full twenty-four hours of each day upon all levels. This means that he will be conscious of all impressions and responses, and that he will not be conditioned by mechanical reactions. He will be able to control all of his energies, use them for the Great Plan, and be in charge of the whole carriage. He will then have achieved continuity of consciousness and a real server of the race is born. He radiates love, power, leadership and light. He is a man who effects integration within others, who assists others in purifying their hearts and minds, and who leads others into their inner temples of freedom. He is now a growing Soul in the light of the Lord of Flame, who has cherished him throughout ages and has led him to Himself, stage by stage, through physical, emotional and mental worlds until he has become aware of Himself as a Son of God.

When he has arrived at this stage, the Lord of Flame, the Solar Angel, leaves him in fiery joy and radiation, and the man steps onto the path toward Cosmos.[12]

---

[12]*Ibid.*, pp. 31-32.

13

Soul Approach through Battle

*T*he first chapter of the *Bhagavad Gita* is one of the most beautiful analyses of the fight or conflict through which those who are ready to tread the path of initiation pass. In the first chapter of the *Bhagavad Gita*, the conditions of man are given in a symbolic language. The conditions of the fight are explained, and the cause of the fight is beautifully emphasized.

According to the *Gita*, man has to fight; there is no escape. Man has a Guide far superior to him, and It is with him in the carriage. The carriage is the body. The Inner Guide is the Transpersonal Self, the Solar Angel, the Guardian Angel, or the Watch, Who eventually takes the man between two armies which are arranged against each other on the battlefield. The curious thing is that both armies are formed by the relatives and close friends of the man, Arjuna, the human soul.

The Inner Guide or the Transpersonal Self for ages prepared the human soul to be ready for a decisive fight, which takes place on a battlefield found within the man himself. This battlefield is the personality, or the physical, emotional and mental nature combined. The symbolic teaching of the *Gita* tells us that eventually a time must come in your life in which you must fight.

You may ask against whom do I have to fight? The answer is: Against those elements which block the path of your evolution. The fight is against your blind urges and drives, glamors, illusions, vanity and ego. Your fight is against ugliness, evil and unrighteousness.

If one such moment does not come in your life, you are not worthy to be called human. No one can improve, unfold and bloom without such a fight. As there are bushes which dry out before blooming, so there are human beings who grow, but before blooming start to fade away.

The decisive factor in your unfoldment is the fight. It is the fight that keeps you progressing and alive.

Life exists only through expansion, transformation, transfiguration and resurrection. Resurrection means gradual freedom from limitations. One is alive only in steady improvement, unfoldment and creativity. To live means to conquer, to conquer the path leading to your true Self. You are fighting against those elements which are allied against life.

Life is your Innermost Self, and your True Self exists only when you are free from those elements which enslave, obscure and bury you in matter.

The *Bhagavad Gita* is a very deep psychological treatise. Imagine that four to six thousand years ago, the author of the *Gita* knew about the inner conflict and the necessity to fight and conquer a part of yourself which is your own obstacle. Only through such a fight can you improve yourself, and to create such a fight you must be ready to see the two opposing armies living within you. It is only in the light of the Inner Guide that this duality is seen, recognized and analyzed.

If anyone is satisfied with what he is, with what he does or with what he knows, he is in the process of dying and losing his own Self. Whoever is satisfied with the level where he is, cannot transcend himself. And if he cannot transcend himself, he is on the path of decay. Life does not exist if it does not increase, progress and unfold.

The Law is evolution, progress, improvement and unfoldment toward Infinity. One must keep this law in his mind if he wants to be alive.

The fight is intended to keep you alive and progressive. The great warriors for the cause of one humanity are those who fought the battle within and won the battle.

What are the armies which are ready to fight, and on which side is Arjuna going to fight?

The fight is against all those elements which are limiting your progressive unfoldment on any level. We have two armies. One of the armies against which Arjuna has to fight is composed of his relatives, friends and even teachers. Relatives represent Arjuna's emotions, thoughts, ideas and plans which once upon a time were related to him but now stand against him because they are obsolete.

Friends symbolize the considerations of others, their opinions, their images about him, their expectations and their feelings about him. All these were good in one stage of his evolution, but now he does not want to be limited by the evaluations, expectations and selfish prospects of others echoing in his mind.

The teachers represent those virtues which are in the phase of crystallization and fanaticism. They are the symbol of outdated knowledge, tradition and superstition because they now stand against the other army.

In the other army are found again relatives, friends, progressive teachers, progressive knowledge, up-to-date discoveries, visions, future, great virtues — freedom, honesty, nobility, simplicity, gratitude, increasing love, sacrifice, holism, inclusiveness, synthesis...and Arjuna must choose to fight or escape.

A moment comes in our life in which these two conflicting forces stand against each other. We no longer feel happy falling into the hands of those forces which sap our energy, waste our time, kill our inspirations and creativity, and make us feel depressed and failed. On the other hand, we do not feel happy and gratified working with constructive and creative forces and in the meantime allowing ourselves to yield to many kinds of vices and destructive forces. This is the time when a great decision is taken and the possibility of transfiguration is confronted.

Such a decision can be taken by consciously preparing ourselves, or it can be forced through heavy and painful crises. The Light starts sometimes gradually, sometimes suddenly. Gradual preparation for battle makes you ready to fight intelligently and with great benefit for yourself and others.

For example, make your body as healthy as possible by eating in the right way, drinking in the right way, and using it in a way that it does not create problems in the future, when another battle front is opened in your life. This may be an emotional battle, a battle against habits, hangups, crystallized ways of emotional reactions, fear, anger, hatred, greed, jealousy, and their offsprings. You can prepare yourself for this battle by purifying your emotional world, filling it with pure love, and making it controlled, stable, patient and joyful.

You can also prepare yourself for mental battle, on whose battlefield great and far-reaching decisions must be taken. Clear discrimination must be used; detachment and serenity must be exercised. Illusions must be dispelled. Pride, separatism and selfishness must be uprooted.

You can prepare yourself for these battles through your meditation, observation and discrimination. Then when the time of battle comes, your army will already be there, ready to start the holy war on the battleground of your being. Once you win the inner battle, you will be a victor in the other battle. You will be a leader, and the Forces of Light will be all around you.

When people try to win the outside battle, the battle of life in the world first, their efforts usually end in failure. No one can win the outer battle before he wins the inner battle. This is true in all fields of human endeavor.

Your progress and improvement in life depend upon your ability to fight on your sincerity, and on your whole-heartedness. When you win the battle, a strange thing will happen: all your enemies and past failures will become your friends because they will be used as experiences and sources of wisdom. You will know better because you learned wisdom by going through many experiences. But an experience will never turn into wisdom if you are not victorious over the source of your experience.

People think it is good to have various experiences even at a high cost. But if the urge, the drive, the glamor or the source of the experience is not conquered, you have no wisdom; and the experience will waste your energy, time and money and turn into a habit. Often the urge to experience becomes the first step toward addiction which leads to slavery.

Wisdom in experience leads to detachment and freedom, and wisdom is achieved through victory. On the battlefield of life, the victors are those who consistently fight against all those things that humiliate the Divinity within them and in others. The fight will increase your beauty, your glory and your ability to serve and uplift.

There are techniques for good fighting. Some people put all their forces on the field and fight for a final battle. This is very good, if you really know all about your enemy and are convinced that you can conquer him; but such a technique has its advantages and disadvantages. For example, if you threaten your enemy with destruction, sometimes you mobilize him against you.

The real fight is a decisive intention to transform your enemies and make them your co-workers. You will ask, how can I make my hatred my co-worker? The answer is that if you make your hatred to hate your lies, your dishonesties and your crimes, he becomes your friend.

The other method is to fight your enemies one by one, so as not to impose too much pressure on your lower self. For example, if you cannot throw away your cigarettes all at once, drop one cigarette daily, and eventually all will be dropped.

There was a man who had five enemies. One day I saw him in an old village. "Why do you look happy?" I said. "Aren't your enemies bothering you?"

"No, I fixed them."

"How could you? There are five of them and one of you."

"Well," he said, "I attacked one of them in the right place and beat him very badly. He spread fear to the rest. Then I beat another one, and eventually five of them were beaten. The memory of their pain stopped them from attacking me again."

This is a technique which can be used by a warrior. Attack one by one; but let the motive or the objective of your action be to increase beauty, goodness, righteousness, honesty and sacrificial service for all, or else your victory will be your own defeat.

One day a young boy came to me and said, "I smoke a pack of cigarettes a day. Do you have a technique that I can use to quit smoking?"

"Yes," I said, "if you will do exactly as I tell you to do."

"I will."

"Buy a pack today and smoke all of them except one. The next day buy a pack and smoke all except two. The next day smoke all except three."

"But," he said, "then a few days later I will buy a pack and not smoke any."

"That's right, but I want you to report to me every night you did it."

Ten days later he was smoking ten less cigarettes, and he visited me again.

"How is it going?"

"I've cut back ten cigarettes daily."

"Good"

"Do you know what I did?"

"What?"

"Instead of every hour, I am dividing the day into the number of cigarettes, and now instead of every hour, I am smoking every two hours."

"That is good. Very soon you will make it every three or four hours, or one cigarette every eight hours."

A few days later he called. "It is scary. Today is the day when I have only one cigarette."

"Well," I said, "light your cigarette and smoke one quarter of it every two hours. Tomorrow smoke half in the morning and half in the afternoon. The next day, burn your package in the fireplace and then rejoice and dance because you won a great victory."

And he actually did that. Now he is a medical doctor.

In the *Bhagavad Gita*, it is suggested that we fight as if we are the pure Self, the radioactive Self. We must not identify with our enemies. Identification with our failures or vices makes us weaker. They are not part of our pure Self. They are associated with our physical, emotional and mental vehicles.

The fight in the *Bhagavad Gita* is organized in such a way that against every enemy there is a virtue; there is a friend. The friend's duty is to replace an enemy.

Arjuna eventually learned to identify himself with the army of light, love and beauty; and tradition says that the battle lasted eighteen days and the warrior won the battle.

The number eighteen is very significant. The number one stands for one-pointed direction toward perfection. Perfection is represented by the number eight. No battle can be won without focus on the vision.

Throughout the eighteen days, Krishna the Inner Guide spoke to Arjuna about the vision of perfection. The Inner Guide continuously inspired him with the vision of greater and greater achievements. These achievements were won on the field of battle, in the field of daily life. This is a point that the *Bhagavad Gita* tries to make very clear in our minds: All inner achievements must be affirmed and approved only after they have been tested in our daily life.

In these eighteen days Arjuna was instructed to keep his mind clear and act as the Self, and to carry on the battle for eternal life without being identified with the states of the body, emotions and lower mind.

I remember an intense battle within myself when I was very young. I was in a monastery and my Teacher told me to get ready for a trip to a village beyond the mountains. It was almost sunset.

"When will I go?"

"At night. Prepare your horse and dress well."

"All right."

I went to my room, and as if I heard again his voice, I answered, "At night? Why? My goodness.... Well...."

I had a few hours to get ready. I made supper for myself, prepared my horse and dressed well. When it became really dark, I went to his room.

"I am ready."

"Take this letter to the next village. Find the saloon and give it to the drummer whose name is Ali. He is a fat man. Be very tactful, and no one must see when you give him the letter. Be sure to wait until the moon goes behind the mountain."

The moon was very late....

I sat under the tree and I observed that two armies were beginning to form on the battlefield of my mind. One army was inspiring in me fearlessness; the other army, heavy fear. I noticed that the battle started with a question: "Why didn't he choose another boy?"

"Maybe because he doesn't like me."

"What can be in the letter that is so important and secret?"

"That is not your business."

"If I make any mistake...."

"Imagine, when you come back, the Teacher will be so happy; maybe you are doing a great service."

"But the forest is very dark. There are bandits, wild animals, bears...."

"I have my revolver, and I have my horse which runs very fast."

"What about if you are shot?"

"Well, my Angel will protect me, and if they shoot, maybe that is what should happen."

"But you know how one dies when he is caught in the claws of a bear."

"I did not do anything wrong to bears. Why should they attack me? I know they are friendly to me."

"Well, the time is getting closer and you must depart, but you have still time to make an excuse and let him send a stronger boy."

"No, I don't want that. I can do it...I can do it...I can do it!"

All of a sudden I noticed that I was shouting. I looked to the mountains. In a few minutes the moon was going to disappear.

I made a short prayer to my Angel. I said, "If You will be with me on the horse, we will do it."

My horse was ready to go. When I jumped on it, a very clear thought came into my mind: "Concentrate your heart and mind on the target, the fat man, and see yourself passing the letter to him."

The journey passed without danger. When I came to the saloon, almost all were drunk. The fat man was sitting at the drum. I rolled the letter in my hand, made it smaller and smaller, and went and sat by him. He was very busy drumming while a girl was dancing an Oriental dance.

I tapped him on the back and said to him, "You are the best drummer."

He gave me a look which said, "You are crazy."

"You are really good."

He pushed me away with his elbow.

"I have a message for you."

"Go away."

"Shall I?" I said to myself. "Why doesn't he know that I am delivering a letter? But how should he know?" Then an ingenious idea came to my mind. "Can I play the drum? I am very expert."

"Are you?"

"Yes, shall I try."

"Do it." And I *was* very good at it.

When the dance was over and people were around him, he became busy talking. He asked whose son I was.

"I came from the monastery," I whispered.

He did not answer. He opened his eyes wide, as if he was going to eat me. Then suddenly he shouted in a very loud voice, "Go out, or else I will beat you."

I ran and he ran after me. In these two minutes I was in a great fight within myself: "Take the letter and go back...he is crazy...I am a fool to risk my life...my Teacher is a nut."

As I was running to my horse, he ran after me and in a very sweet voice he said, "I am sorry, I shouldn't do this. Do you have the message?"

I don't know why I wanted to hurt him. And I said, "Yes I had it, but I put it near your drum."

"My Lord, I am lost." And he began to hit his head.

It was so comic that I began to laugh on the horse.

"Why did you leave it there?"

"Do not worry," I said. "Here is the message."

"Well," he said breathing heavily, "disappear as fast as you can."

My horse had wings. All the mountains and trees were singing for me. The stars were beautiful. I arrived at the monastery with the rays of the Sun.

I went to my Teacher's room. He was in conference. I looked at him. He did not pay any attention to me.

"Teacher," I said, "the tea is ready. Breakfast is complete."

In those few words I saw an intense battle in his soul. He was afraid I would let people know. He was afraid I couldn't do the job. He was afraid things had failed. But then sunshine came to his eyes.

"Well," he said, "at the present we do not need tea...later..."

I went and slept all day.

Years later when I was leaving the monastery my Teacher, after saying good-bye to me, said, "I was proud of your accomplishment. Your letter saved the lives of three great Teachers."

"How?"

"We knew that they were going to be slaughtered a few days later at a party. The letter instructed them to leave the village and cross the border...and one of them was your father."

In tears, I looked in his eyes, kissed his hand, and departed on my horse, crying heavily.

I learned that life is not worth living unless it is a series of battles and victories. It is only through battle and achievement that the inner warriors are prepared and trained to stand for the welfare of one humanity. Each memory of a past victory over the army of darkness will be a source of joy and energy within you, inspiring you for greater victories in the future.[1]

---

[1]*Challenge for Discipleship*, pp. 92-98.

14

Soul Approach
through
Virtues and Values

*V*irtues are the blooming manifestation of the Inner Divinity as that Divinity unfolds Itself stage after stage.

This unfoldment manifests as:

1. nine virtues of the neophyte;
2. twelve virtues of the Inner Lotus;
3. three virtues of the Inner Fire.

Each virtue is an affirmation of Inner Divinity. Personality virtues impose discipline. The twelve virtues of the Lotus are related to service. The three virtues of the Inner Fire are related to sacrifice and the Divine Will. Thus, virtues are the steps of the ladder of resurrection.

The twelve virtues of the Inner Lotus are radiations of the twelve petals of the Lotus. They are the twelve lights that light the path of man toward the Heart Center of the planet. They are the virtues which decorate the fields, the path and the plateaus of life.

They are the techniques of Self-actualization and the means to contact the presence in Nature:

1. striving,
2. courage,
3. daring,
4. discrimination,
5. solemnity,
6. harmlessness,

7. service,
8. compassion,
9. patience,
10. fearlessness,
11. gratitude,
12. responsibility.

Beyond these virtues we have the three virtues of the Inner Fire:

1. enthusiasm,
2. sacrifice,
3. nobility.[1]

Christ advised His followers to live a virtuous life. Then He added, "Greater things than I did, you will do, if you keep My commandments," the greatest of which is, "Love one another as I loved you."

This is how we can reach the measure of the stature which belongs to the fullness of Christ. Virtues can be used in all ray activities, in all seven fields of human endeavor. During the process of occult meditation, we can find out the Plan of our Inner Guide for our life. The Will and the Plan of our Inner Guide is very private for us. No one except one's own self must find it out. Actually, no one is permitted to find for himself the Will and Plan of the Inner Guide for another person. Each person must find it out for himself through occult meditation. That is why one should not have faith in psychics when they tell us about the Will and Plan of our Inner Guide. That is something very private which only we can find out and understand for ourselves.

Even when one finds it, he must be able to demonstrate it in his daily practical life. You cannot know the Plan and

---

[1]*The Psyche and Psychism,* pp. 939-940.

Will of your Soul until you are ready to manifest it. Readiness means that your consciousness is now able to function in the sanctuary of the Inner Guide where Its Plan and will is kept for you.

For a long, long time, we follow the dark path of our personality, even justifying ourselves that we are led by our Soul. The first indication that we have a contact with the plan and will of the Inner Guide is the reversal of the way we used to live. This is sometimes called repentance, renouncement or turning back toward Home.

That is why you must not believe psychics when they speak about the plan of your Soul. If you find the plan of your Soul, do not speak about it to anyone, but demonstrate it through your life because unless you demonstrate it, it is not the plan of your Soul.

The will of your Soul can be known only by yourself in the depth of your occult meditation, at the moments of great joy and suffering, or in great crises. It is very interesting that the glimpse of the Plan hits us at the time of great crisis or in great joy. That is the leading hand in the dark night of your life, or the smile of the Sun for your victories.[2]

Each color in the aura refers to one of the virtues of the Soul. As Great Ones observe our aura, They can see the unfolding virtues, the vitality of which pours down from the Lotus or from the Chalice found in the higher mental plane. Thus, through the unfolding centers, expanding aura and flaming Lotus, the Inner Glory begins to manifest and cause great changes in the environment.[3]

---

[2]*Ibid.*, pp. 911-912.

[3]*Ibid.*, p. 1155.

Gratitude — ...[E]very day at any time, have a special moment to express gratitude to your Solar Angel, to your Guardian Angel. Just a simple but sincere expression of your gratitude is needed, and for only a few seconds. This will release energy from your Inner Guide and flood your life with courage, joy and enthusiasm.

Whenever you feel lonely or need a true friend, approach your Solar Lord within you, and you will see the change. Once you establish a contact with the Inner Guide, you will never feel alone because It is the only companion Who stood beside you in all ages, wherever you were, in darkness or light.[4]

Gratitude is the ability to stand in the consciousness of your Transpersonal Self and pour out your love and blessings to those who have helped you in any way to progress on the path..[5]

Courage — A *courageous* man is ... a shock absorber; many tensions are released because of him. He is led by his Soul to places where he can assimilate tension and prevent great catastrophes or calamities.... The courageous man also considers people's ideas, opinions or attitudes toward himself. He does not limit himself by their responses nor is he influenced by them, but he observes them carefully to see his reflection on the mirror of the attitude of people who are associated with him.

   a. These attitudes can be based on their own glamors, illusions or hangups.
   b. Their reaction can be the result of his own failure or inefficiency.
   c. Their response can be a direct recognition of true value coming from Soul levels.

---

[4]*Ibid.,* pp. 823-824.
[5]*Ibid.,* p. 1108.

In all these reactions a courageous man learns. He adjusts himself with real values and learns to manage himself better to create more favorable responses. If he gains any insight into the reactions of others toward himself, he feels very grateful and corrects whatever the insight indicates because his Soul can sometimes instruct him through the Souls of others.[6]

Thus the man of insight "perceives the future unity of mankind" and does not waste his lives fighting for separative goals, which is common for average persons. A courageous man is one who proceeds against the tide, against the current. In separative goals, one always puts the interests of the personality first. Goals that lead you toward unity are based on your Soul-consciousness or your basic insight of the future.[7]

Solemnity — ...Solemnity manifests when you come in contact with your true Teacher. When you see his visions, his dedication, his striving, his love, his profound understanding and patience, his beauty, his creativity, solemnity radiates from your life in greater beauty. The result of the contact with your Teacher integrates not only your physical, emotional and mental nature, but also puts them in contact with your Inner Guide.

It is just like the process of tuning a guitar. When you come in contact with a true disciple, your guitar is tuned to a certain degree. When you come in contact with your Teacher, it is tuned completely. When you meet your Soul, your guitar is tuned with other instruments in the orchestra. When you come in contact with your Master, all instruments are tuned

---

[6]*Ibid.,* pp. 976-977.
[7]*Ibid.,* p. 972.

with the piano. When you come in contact with your Ashram, your orchestra is in tune with the conductor of the orchestra. When you come in contact with the Hierarchy, the whole orchestra is tuned with the Plan. When you come in contact with Shamballa, the whole orchestra is tuned with the Purpose of God.

Thus, stage after stage, you are in greater integration, and you are inspired by a greater and greater degree of solemnity.

[You reach the stage when] ... you meet your Soul. When you suddenly realize that there is a Presence within you Who has watched your progress throughout ages, and sacrificed so that you could "come into being," you will be inspired by a greater solemnity. This contact releases the beauty within the Soul, and the Soul gradually channels greater visions, greater revelations and greater power to you.[8]

Solemnity is the ability to dwell and remain in the presence of the Inner Guide, and in the presence of the Master. Such an attitude enables you to look upon life from the viewpoint and measures of the Soul and Master. Solemnity is the ability to stand within your essential Self and have a detached outlook on the trivial interests of life.[9]

To activate solemnity we need to continuously contact the Guide within and aspire toward the Hierarchy and Christ....[10]

Solemnity is the process of radiating your fundamental principles, which are the guardian lights projected out of your Inner Core, your Inner Divinity....

[8]*Ibid.*, p. 993.
[9]*Ibid.*, p. 253.
[10]*Ibid.*, p. 1007.

1. The first principle can be formulated as *a clear sensation, or conviction, that you are watched by a Great One*. When this idea dawns in your mind and turns into an ever-present realization in your heart, you slowly improve your life and its expressions. You become solemn not only in public, but also in your private life and solitude. You try to adapt your actions to the standards of the Watching One.

This is sometimes called the discipline of the Presence, a Presence in the light of which you think, feel, speak and act. This Presence is everywhere, penetrating the core of your life. Once you start living in this Presence, or under the watchful eye of a Great One, the virtue of solemnity blooms and unfolds within you.

Try to do this once a day for a few hours and you will see the change. Wouldn't you change the motive of many of your actions if you suddenly realized that someone was watching you or seeing your thoughts? What would happen if you locate that watching Eye in the secret chambers of your heart?

Such an attitude gradually creates an urge in you to organize and run your life in such a way that you can live your life in the Presence, without having any feeling of failure, but instead having a feeling of great joy and satisfaction.

This is how you master your life, stage after stage, and invoke and evoke eventually the Highest Presence within you to guide you toward the path of beauty, joy, bliss and creative service.

Actually the Great Watching One slowly becomes aware that a Spark is knocking on the door and seeking admission to the higher mysteries of life. Eventually, you establish closer communication with that Presence, and this communication turns into an initiation for you when you really adapt your life to the outgoing invitation or call of your Inner Divinity. Such an initiation can be taken only on the path of self-sacrifice and spiritual striving for harmonization with the Greater Life.[11]

The man lives, moves, feels and thinks in the presence of his Inner Guide, then in the presence of his Master. This state of consciousness keeps him always awake and alert, and keeps his life in harmony with the expectations of his Inner Guide and Master.

A man of solemnity knows that he represents an idea, a vision, a great cause, a Great One; therefore he lives and expresses himself in such a way that the "image" he represents is never distorted. Solemnity is the ability to carry the voltage of the image without any distortion. That is why we are told that Masters do not establish intimate connections with those who are not mature in solemnity. Any unsolemn act distorts Their message and Their image, and thus retards the evolution of humanity. Solemnity allows the Inner Guide or the Master to come in contact with life.[12]

A noble person is an embodiment of solemnity. Solemnity is the reflection of inner, higher contacts. Solemnity is the expression of spiritual achievements. Solemnity is the music of the Inner Lord played on the harp of the personality.[13]

A noble person wants other people to be free to do what they want to do in the light of their Soul. This does not mean that he approves of all their deeds, but he encourages them to be themselves and to experiment and gather experience.

---

[11]*Ibid.*, pp. 998-999.

[12]*Ibid.*, p. 1006.

[13]*Ibid.*, p. 1120.

A noble person stands as an example of independence and cooperation, but he never forces his will on others.[14]

Patience — is a state in which your physical body, your emotions and your thoughts are totally integrated and aligned with the vision of the Soul, and on a higher spiral, the Soul is aligned with the Plan and then with the Divine Purpose. In such an alignment there is firm awareness, co-measurement and a direct continuity of consciousness on these levels.[15]

Fearlessness — is achieved the moment we focus our consciousness in the Transpersonal Self, and observe our physical, emotional and mental life as being apart from our true Self....[16]

A person can eliminate fear if he uses pure reason, or his enlightened mind. Fearlessness is achieved gradually if the mind grows in the light of the Soul and the Spiritual Triad.[17]

Absence of Fear — When courage radiates outward, it wipes away all fear because at the moment of its flow, you are at the center of your true being and not identified with your physical, emotional and mental nature. When you are truly your Self, fear does not exist for you. You have fear only when you are identified with your not-self or with your false self, with your garments, with the clothes that you wear as your physical, emotional and mental vehicles. Nothing in these vehicles should prevent you from making a sacrificial act. That is why everyone must be trained from childhood to be sacrificial, to be obedient to the inner command, to the urge of the Indweller.[18]

---

[14]*Ibid.*, p. 1110.

[15]*Ibid.*, pp. 1029-1030.

[16]*Ibid.*, p. 1055.

[17]*Ibid.*, p. 1056.

[18]*Ibid.*, p. 970

Fearlessness is sustained in five ways:

1. by continuously holding the focus of consciousness in the Soul, or in the Spiritual Triad, under any condition, at any time;
2. by letting the flow of psychic energy circulate;
3. by renouncing the world and dedicating oneself totally to the service of the Plan and the Hierarchy;
4. by thinking always in terms of One Life; and
5. by gradually mastering and discarding the astral vehicle.[19]

Harmlessness — ...Harmlessness can be reached when we purify our physical, emotional and mental vehicles and enter into awareness of intuition. Purification of the personality vehicles means:

1. to develop them to their perfection;
2. to integrate them so that they work well not only individually, but also in group formation;
3. to pay their karmic debts; and
4. to tune them with the Inner Lord.[20]

...Unless these bodies (physical, emotional, mental) are connected with the powerhouse of the Inner Lord, they generally have a tendency to follow the path of least resistance, or the involutionary path — to separatism, to degeneration, to materialism and associated crimes.

Actually an integrated personality is more dangerous and has a greater possibility of being harmful than a non-integrated personality.

---

[19]*Ibid*, p. 1056.
[20]*Ibid.*, p. 1009

When the personality is united, the man is in crisis because the personality is tempted to reject the will of the Inner Lord and proclaim its independence. Such a man is divided within himself. This is the most harmful state of a man, when the personality forcibly works for its own ends without consulting the Inner Guide. Very destructive criminals were in this stage when they performed their crimes.[21]

Responsibility — A sense of responsibility, we are told, is the first indication that man has awakened into the consciousness of his Soul.... The sense of responsibility comes into existence when the unfolding human soul slowly enters into the consciousness of the Solar Angel, and becomes enlightened with the intellect, with the love and with the will of that Inner Master. In that stage he is no longer the slave of the centripetal forces of his nature, but he becomes radioactive and a centrifugal, outgoing energy.

A sense of responsibility is the ability to feel one with the Inner Dweller, and the ability to renounce the lower interests for that Reality in him.

The Soul within man is the storehouse of ageless experiences and the storehouse of the light garnered through these experiences....[22]

Responsibility is an ability to respond to the keynote of our Soul and live a life in harmony with the direction, the Plan and the radiance of the Soul. This response creates an urge within ourselves to put our life in order and help others to do the same.

Soul contact reveals all those things in our nature which create obstacles on the path of our evolution and which hinder the steps of those with whom we come in contact....

[21]*Ibid.*, p. 1010.
[22]*The Science of Meditation*, p. 34,35.

Responsibility is not an attitude but an ability which grows as one advances on the spiritual path through study, meditation and service. Responsibility grows when a person decides to stand in the light of the Soul and support through all his life Beauty, Goodness, Truth, universalism and synthesis.[23]

Decisiveness — A decisive person tries to expand your consciousness so that you understand his decisions and cooperate with him. He does not force his decisions on you, but challenges you to understand them. A decisive person is a person who can change his decision once he sees that he can make a better one. His ego and vanity do not interfere with his decision, but the light of his Soul guides him, and his intuitive perception of the Divine Plan enlightens him.[24]

Values are the manifestation of beauty. By living a life of values, a person turns into a beauty.

How can we hasten our steps toward the world of values? Great Sages throughout centuries gave us a sevenfold technique through which we can enter into the world of values and let the Most Holy of Holies penetrate within us and the universe. These steps are:

1. aspiration,
2. concentration,
3. meditation,
4. discipline,
5. contemplation,
6. illumination, and
7. inspiration.

Let us take the first value, *goodwill,* and try to have creative response to it.

---

[23]*The Psyche and Psychism,* p. 1077.
[24]*Ibid.,* p. 1112.

1. Aspire to it by lifting your heart and synchronizing all your emotions toward the idea of goodwill.
2. Concentrate on the idea, which means try to be very careful that none of your actions, feelings and thoughts are contrary to it.
3. Meditate upon the deeper and vaster meaning of goodwill, building through your creative imagination thoughts of goodwill in all individual, national and global actions. See how it can be a cause of great changes in the world.
4. Discipline any part of your being that is acting against your decision to express goodwill. Maybe it is your speech, your manners, your thoughts. Find out and strengthen that part, so that the energy of goodwill flows without hindrance through you.
5. Contemplation. Enter into greater silence and invoke the help of your Soul or the Light of the universe to reveal to you greater visions and deeper implications of goodwill. Wait in silence and great humility. The revelation will slowly pour down upon you.
6. Illumination. As a result of a downflow of revelation, you will be enlightened about the true nature of goodwill, and you will have a greater capacity to use it on many levels.
7. Inspiration. When you stand in the light of your revelation and live according to it, the energy of goodwill then will flow into all parts of your nature and you will be an expression of goodwill, a fountainhead of life and blessings.[25]

---

[25]*Ibid.*, p. 893.

Service — There are many measuring rods by which to evaluate a man; for example, titles, diplomas, knowledge, wealth and so on. But the best measure is a man's *service*. You are as great as your field of service. As your service increases, as the field of your service becomes larger and larger, you are a greater and greater man.

The deeper meaning of this definition comes from the fact that service is not an activity, but a radiation of soul virtues, soul qualities, and eventually, the radiation of your true Self. As this radiation increases and waxes to great dimensions, you are considered a greater man because your light, love and power increase as a result of your deeper and deeper contact, unfoldment and realization.

After a man comes in contact with higher virtues latent in his Soul, he begins to radiate beauty, love, simplicity, compassion, pure reason and kindness. The most important part of this process is that he charges all his activities with these virtues.[26]

Service is the ability to put into all your activities the solar fire of love, and the fire of the Plan. The Plan can be contacted in the Soul levels. It is an experience, not a teaching. The Plan is the map which shows you how to return to the Sun from which you were radiated out. The Plan is the map which shows you how to release yourself from the trap of your physical, emotional and mental bodies and achieve the state of awareness which you had originally.[27]

The service we render to the world is a flowing energy coming from the depths of our Soul. It is this energy that

---

[26]*Ibid.*, p. 1013.

[27]*The Flame of Beauty, Culture, Love, Joy*, p. 183.

saves, encourages, charges and leads if it is pure and not blocked....[28]

Having the goal of service in our minds, we must try to sublimate the lower man step by step, until the wild nature of the vehicles is tamed and is able to obey the commands of the Inner Lord....[29]

Service is not the name of a labor or activity, but is the name of the energy of the Soul. When the Soul radiates, the energy of service manifests through all that man thinks, feels, does, and it is this substance, this energy, which builds the bridge between the mental and Intuitional planes.[30]

Sacrifice — All creation is an act of sacrifice and sometimes in occult books the Souls are called the Sons of Sacrifice. It seems to me that the best way to approach our Soul and *become a Soul* is the way of sacrifice. Our sacrifices are the measure of our achievements and achievement means to be close to the source of our being. Our Inner Being is a drop of sacrifice as our God is fire and sacrifice. Whenever there is sacrifice, there is God, there is Life.

Who can sacrifice? One who is more Spirit than matter, one who is more inclusive and less separative, one who knows from practical experience that *there is no other*. Sacrifice does not mean doing a favor for somebody or slowing down so that another may go faster. It means living as closely as possible to our Inner Guide. Sacrifice means expressing the God-Life in steady radiation of light, love, harmlessness and Divine Will. It means transmutation. Only

---

[28]*The Psyche and Psychism,* p. 669.
[29]*The Science of Meditation,* p. 76.
[30]*The Psyche and Psychism,* p. 512.

through transmutation can we transcend our limitations and earn the right to live as Souls, full of beauty and glory.[31]

...A time will come when we will express ourselves as both finite and eternal. Only on this level — the Soul level — can we expect to know objects as they essentially are. In the process of knowing, knowledge changes into realization and from that state knowing is equal to becoming. *Knowing means to be.*[32]

Culture —...A cultured person is the true expression of his Soul-nature — of his spiritual and divine nature....[33]

Culture is expressed on four main levels:

1. personality culture;
2. Transpersonal or Soul culture;
3. living or spiritual culture — the culture of the future; and
4. culture of the Central Electrical Fire within man and the universe.

The first level of culture is related to the assistance or glorification of the personality — i.e., the physical, emotional and mental nature of a person. This is expressed in paintings, sculptures, poems, dances and music, and in many kinds of advertisements.

The second level comes into being when the Transpersonal Self in man makes Its appearance. You can see such appearances in gigantic cathedrals, the writings of Tolstoy, Tagore, Dante and Emerson, the paintings of Michelangelo, and in the music of Beethoven and Tchaikovsky and other great composers.

[31] *The Hidden Glory of the Inner Man,* p. 31-32.
[32] *Ibid.,* p. 20.
[33] *The Flame of Beauty, Culture, Love, Joy,* p. 92.

The third level of culture is the expression of the Spiritual or rather Divine Fire. Only rare people manifest this beauty. You can see the expression of this culture in the paintings of Nicholas Roerich. This is not personality or soul culture, it is a culture which when contacted immediately releases in some degree the Hidden Divinity within one. A very highly charged energy center is contacted and this energy immediately starts to transform one's nature. This is the fiery culture, the culture of the New Age.

The final culture is the Central Fire in man and in the universe. This culture manifests Itself through the Divine embodiments called Avatars Who condense, focus and radiate the Supreme Transcendental Beauty. An Avatar is a Being Who is bringing into birth the Solar Self, and His Culture is a torch on the path of humanity inspiring and directing us toward future evolutions. Such an Avatar is Christ, is Buddha, is Hermes, and other Great Ones.

Personality culture manifests the fire in the physical, emotional and mental bodies.

Talent manifests the beauty of the Soul.

A genius manifests the fiery beauty of the Spiritual Triad — the beauty of abstract thinking, intuition and will.

But the Avatar manifests the Innermost Self which is one with the Central Spiritual Sun.

...Personality culture is the result of fire of friction, of excitement or contact with personality vehicles or with their centers or spheres which are selfishly manipulated and used for separative purposes. The best example of such a culture is the contemporary advertisement system which is a propaganda system which sells the body and relates to one's emotions. Even academic mental studies through literature, poetry, dance and music glorify one's own country or nation, or advertise its religion, philosophy and so on. Much of humanity is in this culture.

Some of the human family have passed into Soul culture, which is the expression of a higher fire that is sometimes called Soul-fire, or the fire of the mental plane and Soul.

The third culture is the result of the fire of the Spiritual Triad.

The fourth one is the result of the Central Electrical Fire. A few in humanity are entering into this division of creativity; this is the division that may be called the culture of the New Age. More and more creative people will enter into this domain and reveal the Innermost Beauty hidden within man.[34]

Personality can be defined as the sum total of our physical, emotional and mental natures, aligned and integrated in such a way that it acts as a unit in itself. When a person becomes a personality, he must have a large measure of control over his physical urges and drives: sex, food, smoking, sleep, labor and others. He must have a high degree of control over his emotional nature, and have definite control over his thoughts and speech.

When these three natures of a person are coordinated, they are now ready to give birth to the next level of culture, which is Soul-culture. Soul-culture cannot manifest Itself or be appreciated and assimilated when we do not have the foundation of an integrated personality.

Soul-culture brings into fusion the personality with the Transpersonal Self, with the Soul and with Its vision of inner beauty and Its spiritual aspirations.

---

[34]*Ibid.*, pp. 61, 62.

This culture can be seen, for example, in the Notre Dame Cathedral in Paris, in the magnificent cathedrals in Milan and in Germany, in the writings of great documents of high statesmanship, or in the paintings of great artists.

Such a culture uplifts human beings and creates Soul-infused personalities. For example, when you are enjoying a great work of music or a great painting you can feel that your level of beingness is slowly rising and your consciousness is entering into another dimension. Your personality is filled with a new thrill, with a new life and joy. That is the result of Soul infusion through art and culture. This is how you advance from the level of personality vehicles and enter into the Soul domain, and thus surpass your former level of beingness.[35]

Beauty — ...We have four main stages in the expression of beauty. The first is the stage of the neophyte who is eager to produce beauty, but mainly he is used by influences to produce those forms of art which serve separative or selfish purposes. This is the man or woman who is still living within the boundary of his personality vehicles. Such art is transient, although the effect can continue for a long time.

The second stage is the manifestation of beauty by a talent. The talent is a person who is able to penetrate closer to the sanctuary within himself and bring out to a certain degree the Sacred Fire of the Transpersonal Self, of the Soul.

Then we have a higher degree of creativity, or the manifestation of beauty through a genius. A genuis is a man who is able to contact the fire of the Spiritual Triad and bring out through all his expressions the symphony of light, love and power. Any contact with the work of a genius evokes a great response from your inner resources and you pass through a period of adjustment and transformation.

---

[35]*Ibid.*, p. 64.

The fourth stage is the manifestation of beauty by an Avatar. An Avatar is a fully bloomed Spark Who is in conscious contact with the Great Principles and Laws of the Solar System. He bridges all that He contacts with that Great Source of glory and creativity. He brings Purpose into life with all that He does....[36]

It is only man who can be a conscious expression of Beauty, or a distorter of Beauty. As he harmonizes all his life to the divine intent, to the law of evoluton and to the achievement of perfection; as he passes from glory to glory, from partial beauty toward total Beauty, he becomes a conscious expression of Beauty. This can be accomplished by first establishing communication and then fusing with the Source of Beauty within himself. It is his Soul, the Solar Angel, that is the true reflection of Beauty. The Solar Angel is reflecting the innermost Sleeping Beauty.[37]

Beauty works and stands only for unfoldment, release, evolution and spiritualization. It expands our consciousness, enabling us to contact the Transpersonal Self within us. The Transpersonal Self is the embodiment of beauty, it is the Soul. Its nature is Love-wisdom, and beauty can be totally enjoyed only through the sense of Love-wisdom. Just as our body needs food, water, air and light, so our Soul needs beauty to unfold and to radiate. *Beauty is the path to Cosmos.*

Once we enter into Soul consciousness, we will begin to see things as they really are. This means that we will see the archetypal blueprints of the existing crystallized forms. Beauty is the archetype, the Divine blueprint, the idea conceived in the Mind of God.

---

[36]*Ibid.*, p. 63.

[37]*Cosmos in Man*, pp. 231-234.

The Transpersonal Self tries tries to bring into our consciousness the sense of beauty, and to establish the rhythm
of beauty within us. To manifest beauty we must expand
our consciousness into the Soul consciousness and contact
the beauty in the Soul through the soul. As we grow toward
Soul consciousness, we manifest more beauty, because we
harmonize our life-expression with the existing archetypal
beauties. Each time a man contacts his Soul, he is charged
with a stream of beauty which bestows upon him joy, upliftment, peace and serenity.

The Soul is only a path leading us to deeper beauty
which exists in the sphere of the Spiritual Triad and beyond.
There, we are closer to the Divine Melody and to Divine
Energy.

True beauty inspires in us the qualities and activities
which lead us into striving, expansion, self-observation, harmony, gratitude and sacrificial service. All these are flowers
on the tree of beauty, or notes in the symphony of beauty....

The Transpersonal Self, which sometimes is called the
the Solar Angel, is the tuning fork (the keynote) of beauty. A
life lived in harmony with that keynote is a life of beauty....[38]

The moments of beauty are the moments of the revelation of our goals. Beauty tunes our mind in with the Inner
Guide Who knows our goals.[39]

When you see a beautiful woman or a beautiful man,
you want to give gifts, because his or her beauty makes you
act as a Soul, not as a personality.[40]

---

[38]*The Flame of Beauty, Culture, Love, Joy*, pp. 3, 4.
[39]*Ibid.*, p. 37.
[40]*Ibid.*, p. 32.

Striving toward beauty leads us to the future. Let us converse with our Solar Guide through words of beauty, and transform ourselves to a Chalice of beauty.[41]

Love — Love is the ability to identify oneself with the life-aspect of manifestation.[42]

Love energy is the outstanding quality of our Solar Angel, and also the quality that a human soul must develop before he becomes able to penetrate into the sphere of the Spiritual Triad. This quality of Love is the magnetic force of the Soul, Who attracts and heals....[43]

...A physicist, an engineer, an artist, a businessman, a teacher, a shoemaker or anyone, can do better work and can have better relationships if, for a short time every day, he opens himself to the divine guidance, love and energy of his Soul.[44]

As we come into closer harmony with our Soul, the energy of love and the expression of Love increase. Love gives life. Love brings joy. Love creates harmony. Within that harmony, man is born as a Soul, and is ready to set his face toward his Eternal Home.[45]

...Man can penetrate into the real mysteries of love only after he becomes a living Soul, a new-born man, laboring for the Plan. You can see such a love among the disciples of Christ, and among those who are really dedicated to the upliftment of humanity.[46]

---

[41]*Ibid.*, p. 6.
[42]*Ibid.*, p. 183.
[43]*Cosmos in Man*, p. 217.
[44]*The Science of Meditation*, p. 215.
[45]*Cosmos in Man*, p. 168.
[46]*The Flame of Beauty, Culture, Love, Joy*, p. 127.

A characteristic of the Transpersonal Self is love, a love that is given without expectation and anticipation. As you give more love, you have more joy. Expectation relates you to personality levels.[47]

Joy — In the Soul consciousness we have the first experience of true joy. Joy is the realization that: a man is no longer vulnerable; that he can lose nothing; that greater achievements are waiting for him; that he can lift some people to the level of Soul consciousness where they taste true joy; that now he can see things as they are, not as they appear.[48]

...If your foundation is built on the solid rock of the Transpersonal Self within you, no power can destroy it. Only in the Soul awareness do you taste the beauty of joy.

First you were a boat; now you are a spaceship soaring into Space, free from the destructive effects of waves, storms, lightning, clouds and earthquakes.

A conscious Soul is an indestructible beauty and joy. Thus, the next stage in the search for bliss is Soul consciousness. This is the stage when joy starts. You are in the soul and your realization is different. Instead of being subject to fear, anger, hate and greed, you are in the domain of a new consciousness, the main characteristics of which are:

>   love,
>
>   immortality,
>
>   service,
>
>   joy,
>
>   contact with the Hierarchical Plan,
>
>   and creativity. [49]

[47]*Ibid.*, p. 183.

[48]*Ibid.*, p. 183.

[49]*Ibid.*, p. 182.

...[J]oy is truth, beauty and goodness. It is the ability to stand within Soul consciousness.

How can we climb to that level of Soul consciousness:

1. Through *meditation on virtues*. In meditation we withdraw ourselves from fear, hatred, greed, anger and from their consequences and connections, and stand in the light of our Inner Guide.

2. Through *causal thinking* because it liberates us from being caught in the phenomenal world. Causal thinking is the ability to penetrate into the roots of events, or to find the originating Cause instead of being stuck in the results and effects.

3. Through *living a life of beauty* in all our expressions.

A great Sage speaking about joy says, "...It is useful to impregnate space with joy.... Joy is the health of the spirit."[50]

The first step toward joy is *scientific meditation*, through which you eventually achieve Soul infusion. Scientific meditation is an effort to penetrate into the mind of the real *Thinker*, which is the *Soul*.... [51]

Unless we achieve Soul consciousness, we cannot understand the true meaning of invulnerability.

"Weapons cannot hurt the Self, nor fire burn It. Water cannot drench It, nor can wind make It dry. It cannot be divided. It is eternal and all pervading."[52]

---

[50]Agni Yoga Society, *Fiery World* I, para. 298.

[51]*The Flame of Beauty, Culture, Love, Joy*, p. 188.

[52]*The Bhagavad Gita*, translated by T. Saraydarian, CH. II, Verse 23-24.

Such an experience can be achieved in Soul consciousness. As you go deeper in joy, you get closer to yourself. In joy, man has the realization that he can lose nothing.

In school we had a very beautiful teacher. He had the habit of taking his golden watch out of his pocket and putting it on the table. One day he came back and asked whether anyone saw his watch. The students said, "No." He was my best teacher, and I felt angry that anyone would take his watch and I went to him and said, "Who do you think may have stolen it from you?"

"It is not stolen," he said.

"Then," I asked, "what happened to it?"

"Somebody is using it."

I couldn't understand the secret of his behavior; he always had a great flow of joy in all his expressions. He was a joyful person.

In this event, my teacher gave me a chance to glimpse that in a certain state of consciousness you do not lose anything, because in Soul consciousness you do not possess anything.

Once Christ said, "Do not be afraid of those who try to kill you, but of those who try to kill your Soul."

In Soul consciousness, no matter what your personality life is passing through, there is a tomorrow, there is a new dawn, because the Soul is not limited by the failures of time, space and matter. Even the failures of the personality can be utilized as firewood for the bonfire of the Soul.

Every time we help someone, we help ourselves. In Soul consciousness the fragrance of joy radiates when you engage in a labor of helping others without conditions.

In Soul consciousness you have the eye to see things as they are, and not as they appear to be. When a man takes appearance as reality, he is caught in change. Joy is changelessness — in change.

It is told that the Law of Change is ever-ruling. This is true for the world of phenomena, but it is not true for the world of Spirit. We lose our state of changelessness and are caught in the changing phenomena of life as we identify ourselves with the vehicles of our personality.

In Soul consciousness, man comes in contact with the plan of his life, and eventually penetrates into the Plan of the Hierarchy for humanity. It is very interesting to note that the plan of our life is found in our Soul, and the Plan for humanity is found in the Hierarchy. Having a contact with the Plan, a man becomes a co-worker of great Servers of the human race. The Plan is formulated in such a way that it works for the welfare of humanity and for the welfare of each human being.

A Soul-conscious man tries to bring the Plan into daily life to help everyone, in every way, in everything so that he may be able to lead people from personality prisons to Soul-freedom, where they can experience the joy.

The next characteristic of the Soul is creativity. There is a great joy in creativity, because creativity is the process of letting the energies of the Plan flow and nourish the Sparks of Infinity in each living form.[53]

We may ask, "How can we communicate with our Solar Angels and know that they are answering or guiding us without our falling into traps of evil forces, post-hypnotic suggestions, or other complexes in our nature?" ... [W]e must begin

---

[53]*The Flame of Beauty, Culture, Love, Joy.* pp. 183,184,185.

by preparing an atmosphere through which communication from higher sources may flow. This can be accomplished by trying to put into practice the following suggestions:

1   Live a harmless life.

2.   Express love, beauty and truth in daily living.

3.   Meditate regularly on the deeper meanings of love, beauty, truth, gratitude, service, labor, sacrifice, sincerity, harmlessness, or use the Seven Ray Technique.[54] In so doing you will create the right atmosphere for communication if you persevere and are sincere in your attempts.

4.   Each day practice some self-examination without personality attachment.

5.   Try to heal any wounds that you have inflicted upon others.

6.   Study spiritual literature from *Hierarchical sources* daily.

7.   Visualize yourself standing in the light of your Angel every day at the sunset hour.

8.   Refuse to obey any inner suggestion dropped to your conscious mind, until examination shows that it relates to positive action toward good. If the suggestion is coming from a high source it will be true, beautiful and harmless; it will express gratitude, sincerity, love, sacrifice, courage and fearlessness; it will serve to bring upliftment and joy; it will emphasize unity and responsibility; it will call upon you to strive harder to achieve.

[54]See Chaper VII, *Cosmos in Man,* for technique of meditation on Seven Rays.

Any suggestion which relates to these several points is coming from the Solar Angel. All suggestions which do not relate are from other sources and should not be followed.

In conjunction with the suggestions concerning meditation, self-examination, and spiritual reading, you may feel the need to involve yourself in *periodic fasting* or to set aside periods when you will *keep silence* for an hour, a day or a week. You may reach a level which calls upon you to exercise detachment and observation.[55]

We may think that to detach ourselves means to hate, to ignore, to divide, to separate, to stand aloof or to be cold and rough toward a given object. These are not signs of true detachment. True detachment is a Soul attitude, a function carried out on the Soul plane rather than on the physical, emotional or lower mental planes....

...According to your degree of success in detaching from any object, your Soul love increases, your light becomes brighter, your will stronger and your joy deeper. Attachment makes you smaller; detachment makes you greater.

Detachment leads you to Soul infusion....

When you learn the process of detachment, you become magnetic. Truly magnetic people are those who are really detached persons. They have not become personality magnetic, but *Soul magnetic*....

Impersonality is another term for being detached. A detached man is an impersonal man. Impersonality is a state of consciousness which is above the physical, emotional and lower mental levels, and which functions upon the Soul levels....[56]

---

[55]*Cosmos in Man*, pp. 50-51.
[56]*The Science of Becoming Oneself*, pp. 25-26.

15

Soul Approach through Prayer

*A*t a certain stage of human history a time came when man felt an urge to surpass himself, to stretch himself and touch beyond. This was the unconscious answer of the human being to the conscious call coming from his Soul. As man tried to meet this call he became aware of surrounding obstacles and hindrances, the pain and the suffering, and he began consciously to ask help from an unknown Presence who was near him, but far from his touch.

On the path of his struggle he developed a technique of communication which was called prayer. Prayer was performed with an intense desire and aspiration to contact the Presence and ask Its help. It seems that man was first aware of his Soul, his first Guide and Teacher. Later he felt that a greater Presence existed in the universe which could be contacted.[1]

Prayer is an effort to contact a higher level awareness, and to ascend to the call of the Inner Guide. Prayer is an effort to contact the conscious Presence and tune in with that Great Life....[2]

Prayer is an aspirational or even a mental contact with the Presence. It polarizes all your subtle atoms....[3]

---

[1] *Cosmos in Man*, p. 82.

[2] *The Psyche and Psychism*, p. 287.

[3] *Ibid.*, p. 959.

Prayer is a dialogue between you, the human soul and your Inner Guide, between the disciple and Master, between the disciple and Christ, between the disciple and Planetary, Solar or Cosmic Beings, or between the disciple and the Almighty Presence in the universe.[4]

Sometimes at the time we desire and pray, we feel a rejection from within us. This is a very subtle indication that within us there is a Presence which is warning us not to pray for certain things or not to desire certain things. That Inner Presence sees that when our prayer is answered, it will be a punishment, not a gift. We can call this inner rejection the Conscience, or the Voice of our Heart, or the suggestion of our Inner Guide. This means that we must be careful when we place an order to the Great Presence.[5]

[A] ... form of prayer is creativity. Creativity is the state of consciousness in which you enter into the treasury of your innermost being and bring the beauty into manifestation. You come in contact with the glories of the Great Presence and bring those glories out into manifestation in your creative work. The creative moment is the moment of contact with that frequency in you which reveals the mystery of colors, sound, movements and symbols. In creativity, you answer your own need; you meet your own need.[6]

There are even higher levels of prayer or dialogue. Intuitive prayer is direct contact with the One Presence. Here you receive all that you want to further the evolution of humanity, and your life turns into a great service. [An example of this is the following prayer:]

---

[4]*Ibid.*, p. 841.
[5]*Ibid.*, p. 842.
[6]*Ibid.*, p. 844.

...Father, wither my hand
  if it be raised for an unworthy deed!
Father, turn to ashes my brain
  if it recoil in treacherous thought!
Father, demolish my being
  if it be turned to evil!

My son, I shall not touch thy hand.
My son, I shall not harm thy brain
  if thou art on the way to an achievement.
But amidst attainment devote a time to silence
  of the spirit.
Then shall I approach thy inner being.
The seed of the Great Silence
  leads to the knowledge of the Great Service.

Father, henceforth I will shorten my psalms,
And I will limit the length of my hymns.
And achievement shall be my prayer,
And I will start it with silence....[7]

This is a fascinating prayer. It seems to be a dialogue between the human soul and the Inner Guide; it may be a dialogue between the human soul and a Great Being.[8]

It sometimes happens that the Transpersonal Self in us prays for us, thus teaching us what to do and how to behave. For example, in the following prayer we see how the Inner Guide prays and also gives the suggestion to the disciple to put his house in order before his prayers are answered.

---

[7] Agni Yoga Society, *Leaves of Morya's Garden*, Vol. I, para. 360.
[8] *The Psyche and Psychism*, pp. 844-845.

> *Wherefore, O Lord, dost Thou not trust me to*
>   *gather the fruits of Thy Gardens?*
> *But where are thy baskets?*
> *Why, O Lord, dost Thou not pour upon me the*
>   *streams of Thy Bliss?*
> *But where are thy pitchers?*
> *O Lord, why dost Thou whisper and not proclaim*
>   *Thy Truth in thunder?*
> *But where are thy ears? It were better, moreover, to*
>   *hearken to the thunder amidst the mountains.*[9]

Sometimes we ask for things we are not ready for. The baskets and pitchers are states of consciousness, centers, the Lotus. If they are not yet unfolded, how can we accumulate the fiery essence of the gifts of the Almighty Presence?

This makes us think that before we ask for anything we must build the container, or else we waste the treasures of the Lord, as the man who asks for rain, but does not have a well, garden or lake to keep that rain for use.

Another very beautiful prayer is this:

> *...Let thy prayer be —*
> *"Thee, O Lord, I shall serve in everything,*
> *always and everywhere.*
> *Let my path be marked*
> *by the attainment of selflessness....*[10]

If only we say this prayer with all our sincerity and strength, the world will not be the same world.[11]

---

[9] Agni Yoga Society, *Leaves of Morya's Garden,* Vol. I, para. 296.

[10] Agni Yoga Society, *Fiery World,* Vol. III, para. 7.

[11] *The Psyche and Psychism,* p. 847.

THE GAYATRI

> OM
> *All of you, who are on earth,*
> *Mid-world and Heaven,*
> *Let us meditate*
> *Upon the light adorable*
> *Of the divine sun of life*
> *To enlighten our souls.*

The Gayatri is an invocation, a mantram taken from the *Vedas*. It is prepared in such a way that the successive sounds of the syllables and words produce the right color, vibration and frequency to create an etheric pipeline between the man and the powers he invokes.

The Gayatri is a scientifically composed mantram that is very, very old. For many ages, in many places, Great Ones have used this mantram for the purpose of enlightenment.

Enlightenment takes place through seven stages of expansion of consciousness and awareness.

The first enlightenment is personality enlightenment, when you feel that you are in contact with a great reality within yourself. This awareness charges your physical, emotional and mental vehicles in such a degree that a purification process takes place within those vehicles. The fire of reality causes integration in the vehicles and purifies them to make them receptive to inner guidance.

The second enlightenment is called Soul enlightenment. The human soul, the human awareness unit, contacts the Inner Guide and suddenly feels that he is the Self. The Light of the Solar Angel reveals this mystery in the human soul. The man feels that he is no longer a personality but a living

Self. This is a resurrection from physical, emotional, mental vehicles and the entrance into the reality of the Self. Thus the real man pulls himself out from his identifications with personality vehicles and stands in his own reality. Such a man radiates beauty in all his actions.

The third enlightenment, which is greater than the previous two, is called spiritual enlightenment. In this stage man comes into contact with the innermost center in him, the Monad, the core of his Self. This contact releases a great stream of the energies of light, love and power from the Spiritual Triad, and this energy radiates out from his physical, emotional and mental nature as light, as joy, as power.

In this stage man does not identify with anything that belongs to the not-Self, and he does not depend on any outer support, any outer help. His Self is the fountainhead of all that his life needs. Through such an attainment the purpose and the plan of the greater Centers radiate out through the man.

The fourth is planetary enlightenment, when our consciousness embraces all the kingdoms of Nature.

Then we have solar enlightenment, when our awareness comes into contact with each center in the Solar System.

The sixth enlightenment is the one through which the galactic Plan and Purpose is revealed to us.

At the seventh enlightenment we are free in the Cosmic Space, as birds that are released from their cages.

The Gayatri is the invocation for enlightenment. People often think that enlightenment comes to them as the lightning strikes the earth. This may be true, but to prepare the conditions for "lightning" sometimes takes ages, in great labor.

We are told that this mantram was given to focus the attention of humanity on the fact of enlightenment.

The Gayatri reads:

OM
Bhur Bhuva Svah
Tat Savitur Varenyam
Bhargo devasya dhimahi
Dhiyo yonah prachodayat[12]

---

[12]*Ibid.*, pp. 849-850.

16

Soul Approach through Meditation

*T*he goal of meditation is a progressive awakening into your higher Self, until your awareness is merged with the awareness of the whole.

In rare cases we have the experience of becoming our higher Selves — the Soul — or even merging into greater experiences. First, we are identified with the personality and feel very comfortable. Then we outgrow that stage and slowly merge into a higher existence which is the fiery part of ourselves. Doing this we become more, not less. We are just like an extinguished fire, a charcoal. Part of the charcoal is lit, but the rest is dark coal, the unrealized part of ourselves.

Let us imagine that this charcoal passes through five stages to become completely lit. The first stage of fire covers the personality, in which the fire achieves mastery upon his physical, emotional and mental nature. The second stage is to fuse the personality with the Soul, which is called Soul infusion, when the progressing spiritual fire becomes one with the Inner Guide. In the next stage the Soul-infused personality realizes that he is becoming more himself. Let us call this stage the awareness of the Monad. The fire continues to progress, and on the next stage he unites with the Planetary Life and feels himself as a global entity, one with the whole life in the globe. In the fifth stage he realizes that there is even another phase of himself to be realized, the awareness of God-consciousness, oneness with the Solar Logos. For a moment he becomes the Solar Logos and sees himself in everything as an inseparable unity and presence.[1]

...Meditation is an effort to come in contact with the Soul and the ability to translate the wisdom of the Soul into thoughts, to serve humanity as a whole and to bring Divine beauty and order into the world.

In meditation the activities of the mind are subjected to the direction and intention of the will of the Soul....[2]

...[T]rue meditation starts on the higher mental planes in serenity and fusion with the light of the Soul. This is not a suspended state of consciousness. On the contrary, all bodies share the light and energy generated in meditation, through the Soul's light penetrating into the vehicles as a kind of electricity.[3]

In thinking one does not see the need for accepting the Soul, or the existence of an immortal being within his existence. But in meditation one comes in contact with the Soul, realizes the fundamental principles of the Soul, and builds his life activities upon virtues and principles of the Soul.[4]

...[M]editation is the best method to bridge the gap between the lower and higher mind. There is definitely a gap between these two levels of mind. The higher one is the world of the Inner Guide, the abstract levels of the mind, through which man begins to contact the universe and with beauty.[5]

[1]*The Psyche and Psychism*, p. 287.

[2]*Ibid.*, p. 613.

[3]*Ibid.*, p. 617.

[4]*Ibid.*, p. 613.

[5]*Ibid.*, p. 588.

Meditation is the art of thinking. In the process of thinking we have the following main factors: the Solar Angel, the knowledge petals, the Antahkarana, the mental substance, the etheric brain, the physical brain, and the unfolding human soul, who may act on various levels according to his development.

During the process of thinking, the evolving human soul (who is the man himself) is presenting a question, a need, in the light of the Solar Angel via the tiny bridge called the Antahkarana.

The Solar Angel is anchored in the Lotus, on the three higher mental planes, though It functions mostly in the Spiritual Triad.

This question or need is an invoking force which, when it reaches the needed degree of high frequency, evokes a direct answer from the Solar Angel. The answer of the Solar Angel is an idea, as a wave of energy....

Ideas are precipitated into our mental atmosphere by the Solar Angel, by our great Teachers, or by us, if we are advanced enough to reach the Intuitional Plane.[6]

...Communication is the key to conscious evolution. Meditation teaches us how to communicate with our Souls, with the Souls of others....[7]

Meditation is a journey toward Oneself, toward the Inner Light, toward the Source of love and power within. Without meditation it is impossible to progress upon the path, because the path itself is a process of sublimation and transformation....[8]

---

[6]*The Science of Meditation*, pp. 56,57.

[7]*Ibid.*, p. 339.

[8]*The Hidden Glory of the Inner Man*, p. 78.

Meditation is the process of touching or contacting the power house, or treasure house within us. As we touch that center of power and glory, our physical, emotional and mental vehicles are charged with power and joy. Our physical and mental vehicles function through the energy coming from our Soul, ... and this energy is called psychic energy.[9]

Meditation is a process of formulation and translation of those impressions and inspirations which pour down into the mind at the time of personality and Soul contact.[10]

Meditation is a noble tool, for it helps us to think, act, speak and write more creatively and in accordance with the highest good for all humanity. It increases our capacity to serve, to understand people and their problems, and to meet the needs creatively. It helps us to remain in the light of the Soul and to act from that high level, becoming a fountain of inspiration, courage and power for our fellowmen....[11]

Meditation breaks the limitations which attachment imposes on us and on our life because in meditation our consciousness is lifted up into the purpose, into the direction, into the goal of our Soul. Our Soul leads us to persons, places, books and events through whom and through which we learn, expand, follow the path of our inner calling and fulfill our creative urges.[12]

To begin meditation it is necessary to coordinate the mental plane, which is a very mysterious realm. It is a sphere of light, and in this sphere are billions of tiny atoms

---

[9] *Ibid.*, pp. 104-105.

[10] *Christ, The Avatar of Sacrificial Love*, p. 121.

[11] *The Fiery Carriage and Drugs*, p. 75.

[12] *The Psyche and Psychism*, p. 591.

darting about.These tiny atoms are of seven hues of yellow, each representing one level of the mental plane, but the atoms with their different colors are intermingled.

Imagine that these atoms are gradually forming geometric patterns, creating a symphony of color on the mental plane. At the highest point is the magnificent form of a Lotus, acting as the inspiration point of this great symphony of color and radiation. Meditation organizes the mental sphere into this living color symphony in which each hue is sensitive to impressions. Meditation then unfolds the bud of the Chalice, making it a radioactive, fiery Lotus which transmits light, love and power from the Solar Angel to the personality.[13]

SIX ASPECTS OF A BASIC BUILDING TECHNIQUE

The builder is the Soul-infused personality. The substance that must be used is predominantly the higher mental substance mixed with higher etheric and astral forces, and energies drawn from the Chalice and brought down from the Spiritual Triad.

The technique, of course, is occult meditation. ... The Tibetan Master gives six aspects of the basic building technique. They are Intention, Visualization, Projection, Invocation-Evocation, Stabilization and Resurrection.

1. Intention — We can explain this word more easily if we divide it into two parts, and change the second part of the word as follows: *In* and *tension*. The mind is in tension, in extreme tension, charged with a great purpose and gathering within its radius all the energies with which it is going to build the bridge....

---

[13]*The Hidden Glory of the Inner Man,* p. 98.

2. Visualization — We can develop and control our mental plane with a technique called visualization. This has three stages:

A. First we choose an object, say a triangle, and try to visualize it in seven colors successively. After this we visualize it in various motions. Then we choose another object, let us say, a circle, five-pointed star, rose, lotus, torch, flaming sword, tree, each time adding motion and color.

   After a while we can add to each object a quality of other senses; for example, smell, taste, a note, a sensation. As we do these exercises, we develop substance and bring it under our control.

   In visualization the form and the colors are very important. Each color and each form transmits a different kind of energy into the mental plane, and thus creates more awakening in the atoms of the mental substance. It is this awakened and highly charged substance that will be used in building the bridge....

   As we do the above exercises, we build a bridge between the astral and mental bodies. If these visualized objects are of high quality and in line with the service of the Plan, the bridge extends toward the higher plane, where the Soul is located. Then the Soul uses these mental objects to transmit energies for creative works. Here the true white magic starts. Man learns how to handle and direct energy and how to work out the Hierarchical Plan.

B. In the second stage we have three important factors:

1. The pool of energy, in highest tension in the mental plane.

2. The impression coming out of the Buddhic Plane and forming special images in the highest astral levels.

3. The visualization process, in which these special pictures are lifted up into the mental plane to mold the mental substance, building there the blueprint of the future Rainbow.

   Here visualization takes place on the mental plane where images of the highest astral levels (built by *creative* imagination) take form through the mental substance, and become visible in the inner sight. Here we can see that it is the Buddhic Plane that affects the higher astral levels through impressions, and brings out the activities we call creative imagination. So *creative* imagination is the response of the higher astral levels to the impressions coming from the Buddhic Plane.

C. The third stage of visualization is a little different. In this stage the act of visualization is not the lifting of the creative imagination up to the mental plane, but a process of pictorial or symbolic translation or interpretation upon the mental plane of those impressions and energies which are contacted on the intuitional level, or which are coming from the Plan, or through the extension of awareness on higher planes. This is real visualization, in which the formless energies and impressions take form and become visible on the mental plane, with their tremendous push for expression and creativity.

3. Projection — Here starts the true use of the will. The pilgrim, with the help of the Solar Angel, uses the will energy with effort and projects a beam of light toward the "Jewel in the Lotus." He cannot do this if previously he has not lived a life of true service, expressing a high degree of truth, beauty and goodwill in all his relationships, thus opening the petals of sacrifice of the Chalice. In this process the disciple uses his will, uses visualization and also uses a word of power. The word of power with its special vibration cleanses the space between the two shores. The will pushes up the mental and light substances, and the first lines of the bridge are seen across the gap.[14]

As man tries to learn and use the true technique of visualization, the following results appear in his subjective world. The gap between astral and mental consciousness is bridged. Then this bridge extends to the Thinker, via the unfolding Lotus. Thus a path is created for the pilgrim, for the human soul, who travels toward the Solar Angel to be crowned there. He then starts his long journey toward the real Self. This journey is made with open eyes and in full awareness.[15]

---

[14]For our purposes here we give only the first three aspects; for the remaining three, Invocation-Evocation, Stabilization and Resurrection, please read *The Science of Becoming Oneself*, pp. 144-146.

[15]*The Psyche and Psychism*, p. 183.

Those who cannot see the object should not be discouraged. If one has first ray in his equipment, it prevents him from seeing. A first ray mind or personality, first ray Soul or first ray etheric body creates a very difficult situation for visualization, and until it is overcome you will not be able to visualize clearly.[16]

Have you ever stopped to think what our questions are and where they originate? Our questions are created by the answers which we have in our deeper mind. If you have a question, the answer is found in the deeper layers of your Soul; It is prodding you to find it. There is an answer to every question because the question is the result of the answer found in your mind. If you ask a question, your Soul will forward to you the answer.

We all have had the experience of carrying problems around in our minds to which we have found no solution. For the first couple of days we meet with no success but perhaps on the third or fourth day, while performing some mundane task, the answer suddenly appears. Where does it come from? It comes from within. The solution to a problem is always there within your reach. When you succeed in "tuning-in" to the highest impressions and ideas, they descend into your mind; you become a source of inspiration and creativity, because through meditation you can open the Chalice.[17]

We are advised not to dwell upon our problems but to contact the Inner Guide, raising our level of consciousness to Its level. Once the Inner Lord awakens we will find that most of our problems have disappeared. A boy once told me

---

[16]*Ibid.*, p. 749.

[17]*The Hidden Glory of the Inner Man*, p. 96.

that he could not find a job although he searched diligently. I said, "The problem is not that no job exists but that your mind is troubled. When you remove that trouble you will find a job." The Inner Lord must be awakened through meditation and given control over your life. Meditation creates Soul infusion. All your physical, emotional and mental bodies are penetrating into the light and, once you enter into the light, no problem can depress or cause you trouble. On the contrary, a problem brings greater challenges and joy, because on that level each problem becomes a game and a means to exercise your power and awaken and bring into play your latent abilities. A man who is really Soul-infused uses every mounting wave to achieve better surfing. People who are in contact with their Inner Lord through meditation find that the Inner Lord inspires them with courage, daring and increasing joy in solving problems. Problems are opportunities of service, sacrifice and creativity.[18]

A very beautiful, symbolic event occurred in the life of Christ. One day He and His disciples were crossing a lake in a boat when a great storm came. The disciples were filled with fear; they wanted to find the Master and ask His advice, but they did not see Him among them. At last they found Him at the bottom of the boat sleeping peacefully.

"Master," they said, "we are sinking, we are in danger."

He arose and by His willpower calmed the sea, and asked His disciples, "Why were you afraid?"

The boat is the human being in whose depth the Soul exists on different levels. When we are troubled or have problems, we must go deep into our being and contact the Lord through meditation, then the awakened or active Lord

---

[18]*Christ the Avatar of Sacrificial Love,,* p. 120.

will handle our problems and lead us into peace. True help always comes from that Inner Lord. You cannot, either physiologically or psychologically, provide permanent help to a person unless you awaken the Inner Lord within him. Once this Inner Lord awakens, the troubled man will find peace and proceed on his way. This Inner Lord is Willpower, a sleeping tiger. ... The only hope for a human being is to contact the Inner Master through meditation....[19]

...Meditation organizes your mind and develops your discriminative faculty, often called *buddhi*, because once it is developed you know right from wrong. It can even be called the tuning fork through which you hear the true direction from your Inner Guide, and tune in to your thoughts, feelings and actions accordingly....[20]

The goal of meditation is not only the transformation of your nature, but also to enable you to pass from your human nature to your divine nature where you can experience the reward of your long and strenuous labor in meditation. Once you have made this breakthrough you enter into your divine heritage. You discover that a different life exists beyond the level of human life. You feel the presence of your Soul, and even meet your Soul. This leads you to your Master, who will be in charge of your spiritual development in the world during your higher meditations.

Through meditation Soul-contact is established, and as the disciple strives to bring the radiation of that contact into his daily life-expressions — through intelligent love, service, purity of motive, gratitude, joy, simplicity, courage and harmlessness — his contact with the Soul gets closer and

---

[19]*Christ, The Avatar of Sacrificial Love*, p. 119.
[20]*Ibid.*, p. 111.

more frequent. This increases his magnetism and eventually his aura becomes so magnetic that he begins to register the impressions coming from the Hierarchical Plan or even from Christ Himself. He gradually adapts all his life expressions to the Divine Plan, and functions as a disciple of Great Ones.[21]

The way to Christ is steady meditation, purification and selfless, sacrificial service. Meditation is the process in which the Inner Guide watches the threefold personality, pouring down light, love and power. The radiation of these three energies into our daily life and environment is called service. Through service the human soul contacts the inner light, and in that light he sees the greater light — the Christ.[22]

During the time of occult meditation, our threefold personality must be aligned within itself and fused with the Soul, as a symphony with the conductor. We start doing this through relaxation. In relaxation we withdraw our attention, the attraction of the Self out of the threefold personality, as we switch off the electricity for our various machines and let them rest in harmony. It is our attention that keeps our machines going objectively and subjectively.

Attention is a flow of concentrated energy from various levels, according to the level where the consciousness of man is focused. When we pull up, or shut off the electricity of our attention from the lower vehicles, they stop bothering us through their noises and disorders. This is done first by calming them, then by withdrawing our attention from them and concentrating on the subject of our meditation.

---

[21]*Ibid.*, p. 116.
[22]*Ibid.*, p. 124.

Immediately after this is achieved, the Soul-light is released into the threefold vehicles, making them to vibrate in resonance with the note of the Soul. This is what Soul fusion is.

In these two stages of alignment and integration, you are withdrawing your attention from the threefold personality. In the next step you are shedding the light, or sounding the note of the Soul, to fuse the bodies with the Soul and create a shield, without which occult meditation would be dangerous.[23]

Meditation is performed on the mental plane and in the light of the Solar Angel. Our aim is to expand our communication in both the objective and subjective worlds, using objects of meditation which are called "seed thoughts."

Patanjali says:

> *The consciousness of an object is attained by concentration on its fourfold nature: the form, through examination; the quality (or guna), through discriminative participation; the purpose, through inspiration (or bliss) and the* **Soul**, *through identification.*[24]

We are aware that concentration is a very important ability. We can concentrate on any level if the *will energy* is used to hold the substance of the given plane focused on the object. Concentration is not possible without the energy of the will.

The concentration of which Patanjali speaks is extended to four levels of awareness:

The *form* is held in the light of the seventh, sixth and fifth layers of the mind, for *examination.*

---

[23]*The Psyche and Psychism*, pp. 615-616.

[24]Bailey, A.A., *The Light of the Soul*, p. 33.

The *quality* is touched in the fourth and third layers of the mind, in the light of the Solar Angel.

The true *purpose* of the object of our meditation is touched on the higher mental plane, namely, in the second level where we register the inspiration of higher centers.

The true *cause* or "the soul" of the object, is touched on the first level of the mental plane, where identification is possible with "the soul," and with the higher centers in the subjective world.

The first step is concentration, through examination.

The second step is discriminative participation. This is done through meditation.

The third step is insight or identical response.

The fourth step is a state of identification with the causal world.

All these four steps are the phases of meditation.[25]

[Meditation] is nothing else but a technique of detachment or upliftment of the mind to higher levels of existence.[26]

Examination, during which you are on the concrete mental levels or in the lower mind, is knowing the form of the object. *Discriminative participation* is comparison, which is the second gear of the mind. You are trying to discover the quality of the object; whether it is fiery, slow or motionless, or whether it is constructive, destructive or neutral. The quality of the object is what it does at the present time.

---

[25]*The Science of Meditation*, pp. 120-121.

[26]*The Psyche and Psychism*, p. 598.

Then there is *inspiration* which is a process of revelation. Inspiration is a beam of light which comes and touches the object of your meditation, revealing the hidden purpose for which it was created. Many objects do not operate for the purpose for which they were created. The real purpose of an object is the purpose for which it was created. Once we start striving toward this, we can go to the higher levels of the mind and withdraw ourselves, or detach ourselves from the darkness or enslavement of lower levels.

It is not easy to reach the inspiration level of the mind, but we cannot rise further unless we develop it, or until we raise our consciousness to that level.

At the time of inspiration, you observe the purpose of the object through the eyes of your Inner Guide. Through inspiration the purpose of your Soul is revealed to you. Your Soul reveals Itself to you. You know now the plan and the purpose of your existence. Everything that man is going to do or can do is hidden in the plan of his Soul. When this is revealed, all the possibilities are there. You are becoming Soul-infused, and Soul-tuned. You are entering the treasury of your being, which is offered to you through the beam of inspiration. You have a clear goal now; you have direction because you are on causal levels. You have polarization; you have energy because you have inspiration. Inspiration is like a beam of light; it leads you from the darkness of the valley to the light of the summit of the mountain. When you are inspired, you do only what the purpose of your Soul reveals to you.

The next step is *identification*, which reveals the cause. Identification is done on the causal level of the higher mind. Like a beam of light you penetrate into the Soul of the object

254 of Chapter Sixteen

and see its origination. To penetrate into the Soul is to reach closer to your real Essence and to increase your enlightenment to a certain degree.

Identification is a process of tuning into the frequency or the wave length of an object and measuring it. You will never know the cause of any object until you identify with the soul of that object.

The soul of an object is its prototype or blueprint. There are many objects that do not reflect exactly their prototypes. They are in the process of becoming. But when you penetrate into the soul of that object, you know the real cause of the object which is now under your eyes.

From the same principle comes the understanding of people. When you listen to them from the viewpoints of your own standards, you will never understand them. Only when you have penetrated into their souls and observed their problems from their soul viewpoint, will you understand them. This is also a spiritual identification.

Through these four viewpoints, you approach the gate of intuition. You are not attached, and you can overcome the three monsters in the valley of darkness: fear, hatred and anger, which deplete your energy and make you the plaything of mechanical forces around you. Thus, detachment brings in life energy. It is achieved through scientific meditation.[27]

If the vehicles are truly aligned, integrated and fused during the time of meditation and throughout the day, you will feel greater energy and health in your physical body, greater joy and love in your emotional body, greater clarity and sensitivity in your mental body. All these are the results

---

[27] *Ibid.*, p. 598-599.

of the contact you are having as a human soul with the Inner Light, or with greater centers of life, thereby releasing these energies and vibrations to the lower bodies, galvanizing, purifying and strengthening them.

The shield around your aura is built by the downpouring energy or influence of the higher realms. This shield is radioactive toward the outside and magnetic toward the inside. It is this shield that rejects all darts of irresponsible entities or dark forces. In such a state your mind is left free to absorb great visions, energies and ideas to be used for your creative service for humanity.[28]

Things change when people change their hearts and expand their consciousness. Outer events are the reflection of the states of our hearts and minds. Once you begin to see the force patterns behind the events of your life, you will slowly be able to perceive that behind the force fields there is an energy field which very subtly influences your aspirations and visions and adjusts your life in such a way that eventually you find the thread of light going toward your Inner Beauty. It is here that true occult meditation starts because you are now going toward true self-actualization, and soon will contact the Inner Guide who is the architect of the plan for your spiritual adventures....

In occult meditation we meditate on the events while we are focused in the higher mind where we can stand above our reactions and control the associative functions. The most important point in occult meditation is to take that event and put it under the light of your Soul's Plan and see how you can utilize the experience of it to cause the manifestation of your Soul's Plan through your life.

---

[28]*Ibid.*, p. 617.

To explain this subtle point I can give the following example: Take a picture of a man and try to draw or paint it. If you are not an artist, your first experiment will not resemble the original, the Soul's Plan. If you work harder and harder, your drawing or painting, or your life-event, will become like the original picture or plan.

You may ask, how can I find that original picture or plan? It is there, in the sphere of the higher mind and in the heart of your Inner Guide. Through occult meditation you will penetrate deeper into that sphere and find the "picture," the plan, upon which you are going to construct your life-event. You can penetrate there if you always think about the "ideal" and then about the idea. Then the plan will reveal itself in the depth of your intensive meditation.[29]

One who faithfully practices occult meditation eventually senses that there is a Plan — a plan for his life, a plan for his nation, a plan for humanity, a plan for the planet and for all kingdoms on the planet. It is a great release for a person when he eventually realizes that there is a Plan and that life in manifested forms is an effort to harmonize itself with the Plan, to adapt to the Plan and consciously express the Plan.

When a person realizes that there is a Plan, he sees that the civilizations and cultures of humanity are great efforts to manifest the Plan; he comes to the awareness that events taking place in the life of humanity result from:

1. conscious action in cooperation with the Plan;
2. unconscious action in cooperation with the Plan;
3. conscious or unconscious refusal of the Plan.

[29]*Ibid.*, pp. 655,656.

Such a realization presents a great educational field to the person who observes the events taking place all over the world and learns how events come into being. He not only sees the events, but also sees the formation of the jigsaw puzzle of world history. He realizes that each right piece of the jigsaw puzzle is an active event produced consciously in cooperation with the Plan. He observes also that wrong pieces put in the puzzle are taken away in a relatively short time in human history.

Occult meditation eventually brings man in contact with the Inner Guide, Who is the Custodian of the Plan for his tiny life. After such a contact with the Inner Guide, man takes conscious steps to know more about the Plan and to adapt his life in such a way that he becomes a conscious co-worker in the Plan.

As he works for the Plan and demonstrates selfless service in the light of his Soul, he comes in contact with those who are Custodians of the Plan and those who adapt the Plan for each kingdom so that each kingdom proceeds on the path of evolution in harmony with the Plan of the Hierarchy.[30]

As you continue your meditation, the whole tapestry of your life will emerge more clearly to such a degree that you easily know what to add to make it more in accord with the higher worlds. This tapestry is woven by many threads, threads coming from the physical plane, threads coming from the astral and mental planes and also the threads and design coming from your Inner Guide, or from the true Self, using all threads for the plan of the individualized Self within the limits of his karma and virtues.

---

[30]*Ibid.*, pp. 653-654.

It is through occult meditation that you can discriminate and control the threads you do not like to use in your tapestry, and you definitely see the pattern or the place for the Soul to build upon it.

The path of least resistance for a man is to find the Plan of his Soul and strive to synchronize his life with it and build accordingly. This is how you can have downpouring inspiration and courage in your endeavors.

It is a very good exercise to meditate on world events. When you meditate on events, try to find:

a. what force formation produced such an event;

b. how these force formations came into being;

c. what relationship this event has with the Plan of your Soul;

d. how you can use the experience gained by such an event; and

e. how you can project the Soul's Plan into your life events.

Actually in occult meditation, you are not interested whether the event is positive or negative. The thing you are first interested in is the force formation behind it, and secondly, in knowing if it has something to do with your Soul's Plan, how to fit it in the overall tapestry of your future, or how to eliminate the effect of it.

...The important thing is to find out the force formation which is controlling all our actions, emotions and thoughts and causing us failure. After we find such a force formation, which acts exactly as a strong posthypnotic suggestion, our next important task is to use our visualization to break that force formation, using the mental substance and building a higher energy formation. Such a conscious process of visualization brings in Soul energy, and with it the high calling of your life, or the great blueprint in which your enterprise can be a small part.

Your Solar Angel has the plan for your life. A part of it is projected in your thoughts, in your instincts, in your conscience. What is your conscience? Conscience is your compass. Your conscience says, "Don't do that." Obey it, don't shut it out. It is not a feeling or a thought or an emotion. It is righteous direction, a beam from the plane of the Inner Guide.[31]

One of the purposes of meditation is to create a magnetic field around you, charged with psychic energy. It is this field that will eventually serve as a contact mechanism between you and the Higher Worlds....

The first major sign of the success of meditation is communication. Communication is the main factor in meditation, through which one expands the field of his contact with higher planes, higher centers, and also Higher Beings, according to the intensity and purity of his meditation. There is no real meditation unless one first contacts his Inner Watch or the big brother in him. There are several evidences of contact:

The first evidence of contact is intense *concentration,* in such a degree that the outer world ceases to be during concentration. Concentration is the ability to withdraw from one's own physical, emotional and lower mental world and focus one's consciousness in the light of the Soul....

---

[31]*Ibid.,* pp. 657,658.

The second evidence of contact is *joy*. Joy is the electrical current of the Soul which passes through the physical, emotional and mental bodies, aligns, integrates and charges them, and flows through them, creating a unity and synthesis through which the influence of your Soul expresses itself.

In meditation, you slowly learn to come out of your body. If you are steady and regular in your meditation, you will also be able to come out of your emotional and mental bodies and focus yourself in the light of your Soul, where your concentration will become intense and pure. Like a focus of light, it will penetrate the essence of the object of your meditation.

When one dies, he is unconscious if he has no contact with his Soul. If he has contact with his Soul from the astral plane, he will be conscious only in the astral plane and unconscious in higher planes. If he has contact from the mental plane, he will be conscious in the astral and mental planes until he passes away.

...[I]f he fuses with the Soul, he will not need to be occupied with reflections. He will participate in events going on upon any plane, or in the spiritual realms....

Joy increases as you leave behind the lower bodies and contact the Inner Watch from within your soul. Thus joy is not a condition, but a flow of Soul-energy, which you may even feel in certain adverse or challenging conditions. The moment you contact the Inner Guide, Its electricity is released. This is joy.

Great Teachers say that joy heals, creates, transforms and attracts higher wisdom. We are even told that joy is a special wisdom because it springs out of the Inner Glory.

The third evidence of contact is *expansion of consciousness.* If your consciousness is expanding, you see one object with an increasing number of viewpoints and you have the ability to synthesize all viewpoints in a single but multidimensional understanding.

When these signs are present, you have contact with your Soul, and your meditation is creative....

The first sign of creativity is that the energy of your Soul manifests through your thoughts, words and actions, causing changes and improvements in the society or group with which you are related....

Striving is an intense effort for improvement. When your family, friends and associates begin to change their lives and strive, it is a sign that the energy of your Soul is manifesting through you with a creative mission. If you have encyclopedic knowledge but you cannot cause improvement around you or in any other area, you do not have contact with your Soul and the flow of the Soul energy is absent in your life....

In creative meditation, one needs to build communication lines. The center of communication is the Soul. One must have contact with the Soul to be able to build communication lines between himself and others....

The second major sign of the success of meditation is cooperation. There is no cooperation unless there is communication. Cooperation is the ability to share the Plan of the Soul in others and bring it into manifestation, individually or in group formation....

Cooperation is possible only if there is Soul-contact, concentration and joy.

Creativity is the ability to manifest the glory and the beauty that is within your Soul or within your Essence.

Creativity is the ability to manifest your Inner Glory. This is done through creative meditation, which enables you to communicate with your Inner Glory. Cooperation is a group effort to manifest and make objective the Inner Glory....

Cooperation is the ability to compose a symphony, using our differences on the foundation of our similarity or Soul-contact....

Soul-contact makes a person a builder, a creator; and all phenomena of life are used as notes for his composition. Higher creativity is the ability to utilize a greater number of those elements which have greater distance and greater differences from each other. This is what cooperative labor is.

...Meditation eliminates all those thoughts, emotions and attitudes which create cleavages because it brings in the influence of the Soul. One of the prime characteristics of the Soul is harmony, or right relations with all that exists in the universe.

Meditation also puts you in contact subjectively with those with whose personalities you have problems. On the Soul level, people contact each other and dissolve their personality problems. In true meditation, one thinks and functions on Soul levels, which means, on the higher mental plane. Remember the mantram, "The Souls of men are one, and I am one with them...."[32]

Creative meditation also has a very special goal: to create an immortal soul and an individuality with continuity of consciousness. Until the light of our consciousness covers the whole mental body, reaches the mental permanent atom and fuses with the consciousness of the Inner Guide or big

---

[32]*Challenge for Discipleship*, pp. 371-372,373,374,375,376.

brother, we cannot achieve conscious immortality. Conscious immortality is not a gift, but the fruit of our hard labor carried on throughout millenniums.[33]

All creativity is carried on through meditation. Meditation enables the artist to contact higher fires. Psychic energy is the fire pouring out of the Soul or pouring out of the Soul of the universe. It is the sum total of all fires.

Meditation not only enables the artist to contact higher fires, but it also builds the proper inner mechanisms for the transmission of fires.

The purpose of the human being is to reach conscious at-one-ment with the Soul of the solar system and then of the galaxy; at-one-ment with the etheric, astral, mental and intuitional spheres of Greater Lives, until he finds the Core and becomes one with that Core....[34]

MEDITATION ON THE PLAN

> *There is a great Purpose behind this creation.*
> *Those who are able to contemplate upon that Purpose*
> *are building a LINE OF APPROACH to that great*
> *Purpose. This LINE OF APPROACH is called the PLAN*
> *for our planet, which can be recognized and lived as a*
> *path of least resistance toward the future.*
>
> From the Creed of The Aquarian Educational Group

One certain way to establish communication with the Soul is to find what the Soul's plan is for us individually.

We are told that the Soul is well-informed concerning the Hierarchical Plan and that one of Its tasks is to further that

---

[33]*Ibid.*, pp. 380-381.
[34]*Ibid.*, p. 382.

Plan through the individual whom It serves as a Silent Watcher and Guardian.

The individual plan of each person is a part of that great Hierarchical Plan, which in turn is an appropriation in time and space for the purpose of the Soul of the planet. To find the individual Plan means: to find the path of least resistance in *conscious* evolution; to find the fountain of creativity, talent and genius within our being; to find the final Wielder of the plan and experience Soul infusion.

This kind of meditation leads one to the realization of the brotherhood of humanity; develops a sense of responsibility; builds the courage to penetrate into the Plan of the Hierarchy and to become a servant of the Plan. Those who know the Hierarchical Plan are called co-workers. The great brotherly love which exists among them, encourages them to give sacrificial help to one another as they work together to further the Plan.

This meditation may be used once a week within your own meditation form. At that point where you begin to meditate on your usual seed thought ... meditate instead on the subject of *your Souls' plan for you*. There are five progressive steps:

1. *Silence* is the process of cutting the conversation line between your personality vehicles and their corresponding spheres of expression through an increasing rate of radiation.

2. *Listening* is the magnetic tension in which there is no conditioning thought.

3. *Registration* is the contact with a phase, or that part of the Plan related to you. It may be registered on the higher mental plane as pure impression, a great beauty, a challenge,

a sense of responsibility, or it may register as only a slight hint.

4. *Formulation* is the process of adaptation of the sensed plan. It is that point where real meditation starts. It is the stage of personal relationship with the plan of the Soul. The success of a man's life depends upon the right formulation and adaptation of the plan as he senses it.

5. *Expression* is the putting into action of the formulated plan, relating it to your daily activities and expressing it practically in your daily relationships.[35]

---

[35]*Cosmos in Man*, pp. 97-98.

17

Soul Approach through Jnana, Raja, and Agni Yoga

nana Yoga — Jnana means *wisdom;* Jnana Yoga means union through wisdom. Wisdom is defined as a state of awareness in which man:

a. sees that everything is changing and is illusion;

b. senses that in every living form dwells the *One Self;*

c. sees the difference between reality and unreality;

d. tries to stand detached in the changing world, as an unchangeable one.

Wisdom is a state of awareness in which the real need and the real answer are seen, the real cause and the real effect are seen, the real level and the way of approach are seen. To achieve these aims, the intellect and pure love are used under the light of the Plan.

In Jnana Yoga the aspirant starts to detach himself from his body, his emotions, his lower mind, and stands in the light of the Soul. Through the light of the Soul he sees the unreality of all forms, the unreality of all pleasures and attachments, and the illusions of knowledge....

In Jnana Yoga it is is the power of the intellect which is used to gather knowledge and to use it in love. It is the choice between light and darkness, love and hate, reality and unreality, goodness and evil. In Jnana Yoga the evolving *human soul* learns to live through the Light of the Angel of the Presence. He tries to see things through Its eyes, to sense the unchangeable one through Its intellect, to touch the stars through Its telescope, to reach the Source of Power through Its rays.

This is the yoga in which Soul infusion starts, and the growing soul uses the mental substance as his ladder, trying to enter into the light of the over-shadowing Beauty.[1]

...Higher awareness is direct knowledge. It is created when the radiation of the Inner Self comes in contact with the Intuitional and higher Planes. A great light is produced which penetrates into forms, qualities, purposes and causes, and *sees* things as they are — without the limitations of time, space and matter.

The Solar Angel (the Soul) has two poles: an awareness pole directed toward the Spirit, and a pole of intellect, directed toward the lower man. It is the bridging agent for man. In Jnana Yoga the technique is to make intellect active in the mental substance, through discrimination, concentration and comparison, so that the human intellect develops and fuses with the intellect of the Soul, and creates higher level expansion of consciousness.

Jnana Yoga may create crystallization on the mental plane and stop the progress of the pilgrim for ages, if it does not invoke the spiritual intelligence of the Soul as a guide....[2]

Raja Yoga is a technique of union with the Inner King. The Inner King is the Soul, the Guide, the source of inspira-

---

[1]*The Science of Meditation*, pp. 252,253.
[2]*Ibid.*, p. 255.

tion and light. Man has two ways to achieve unity with the Soul:

1. meditation,
2. service.

Raja Yoga meditation is a process in which the human soul tries to penetrate into the knowledge and wisdom of the Inner Guide and absorb it into himself. In Raja Yoga the human soul, working in the lower mind, climbs up through the more subtle levels of the mind and eventually penetrates into the aura of the Inner Guide. As he penetrates deeper, he absorbs more knowledge and more wisdom and tries to formulate it through the lower mental plane. As his meditation goes deeper, he eventually becomes one with the Inner Guide on higher mental planes, and the knowledge and wisdom of the Solar Angel become his own.

Here we must remember that the Inner Guide or the Solar Angel reveals Its knowledge and wisdom gradually. This revelation depends on the transformation of the life of the subject. The more you transform your life, the more you receive....

Through Raja Yoga the personality comes into being. Through Raja Yoga one achieves Soul infusion. In these two steps the human soul recollects himself, feels himself, and becomes a conscious soul. This is sometimes called "the second birth," when the human soul realizes his spiritual destiny, and becomes aware of the potentials hidden within his being.[3]

Raja means royal, highest or kingly. Raja Yoga is the technique of at-one-ment with the indwelling Lord, the

---

[3]*The Psyche and Psychism*, pp. 777-778.

Solar Angel. The best example of this technique is given by Patanjali in his *Sutras*, in which is the real, royal path of becoming a Soul-conscious man.

In this technique the human intellect meets the divine intelligence, or the light of the Soul, and eventually and safely is brought up toward Soul realization.

Through this technique the prodigal son becomes the returned Son, the Soul. This technique can be used only when the human intellect is advanced enough to attract the attention of the Inner Dweller.

In the *Yoga Sutras of Patanjali* the scientific technique is given to us to unfold our Soul consciousness and eventually act as Souls. ... In Raja Yoga, the unfolding human soul stands in the Light of the Solar Angel and tries to absorb that Light and be one with Its source. For this reason Patanjali suggests the technique of the *Four Viewpoints* which lead a man into causal consciousness, to the highest mental planes, and to the mystic marriage with the Angel. A liberated human being is one who is able to reach this state of consciousness, and act as the Lord of the personality.

True psychic powers begin with Raja Yoga, as the pilgrim faithfully follows the rules and lives a life of dedicated service. Raja Yoga has four *main* stages of unfoldment. In the first stage the pilgrim exercises occult meditation. In the second stage he enters into contemplation, which means that he starts to SEE in the light of the Soul the one Beauty. In the third stage he enters into unity with the Soul, and the powers of the Soul, higher psychism, unfold and are put under his command. In the fourth stage he becomes a radioactive soul, a fountain of light, love and power, a fountain of service.

The method of Raja Yoga is to stop mechanicalness of the mind, to stop its movements, to stop its modifications, and to make of it a clean mirror which reflects the great visions, ideas, and beauties seen through the eyes of the Soul. A Raja Yogi must be very watchful of his thoughts, words, and actions so as not to harm any living being, and always carry in his heart a fountain of compassion toward all sentient beings. He must use all his energies for the construction of the inner bridge, and for the service of humanity. He must be focused on his goal with all his heart and mind, and always stand in the light of the Soul. He must try to make all his life an extensive meditation, a process of sublimation, so that eventually he can achieve his goal which is Soul infusion and Soul realization. As his work proceeds and age-long traces of habits, mechanical actions, memories, and hidden illusions and urges are cleaned, the human soul gradually changes his focus of consciousness and focuses himself in the *Lotus*, in the mechanism of the Soul, and acquires the great wisdom of the Chalice accumulated throughout the ages. Man becomes a soul, and until the fourth major expansion of consciousness he acts as a shining soul in the light of his Guide, the Angel. At the right time the Angel leaves him, and man becomes his own Lord.

Raja Yoga in its essence is the true psychology. It is a practical, experimental approach to the Soul, and the technique to become one with the Soul.[4]

Raja Yoga teaches that man generates or accumulates energy as he stands in the Higher Self, concentrated and awake in the light of the Soul. That energy becomes a source of joy which radiates from a Raja Yogi.[5]

---

[4]*The Science of Meditation*, pp. 255-256.
[5]*Ibid.*, p. 260.

...True group consciousness starts on the path of Raja Yoga, as a man enters into Soul consciousness and responds as a Soul instead of a personality.[6]

Raja Yoga essentially has nine steps, and all of these steps must be used if the pilgrim wants to reach *Soul awareness*.

The first one is called *harmlessness*, non-injury on physical, emotional and mental levels....

The second one is called *spiritual observation*. This is a continuous watchfulness for beauty, truth and goodness....

The third one is *care for the body*. A Raja Yogi must regulate his sleep, his food, and he must economize his energy....

The fourth one is *breathing*. In the pure air there is a vitality which was called by the ancients *prana*, the life giving breath, the life force. A Raja Yogi must try to live in non-polluted air....

The fifth point is called *abstraction of the senses*. And the sixth point is called *concentration*. Actually these two go together. In abstraction the focus of consciousness, under the command of the will, withdraws itself from the physical, emotional and lower mental bodies, and from their respective objects and concentrates itself on the point of light in the higher mind which is called the *Soul*. This is a "let it go" process in which you turn your face and interest from sense objects, and slowly enter into the inner sanctuary where no outside impression reaches you. There you stand in light and are focused in peace....

The seventh step is *meditation*....

---

[6]*Ibid.*, p. 257.

The eighth step is *contemplation*, ... and the ninth step is called *samadhi*, trance or fixed attention in deep concentration.

Samadhi is actually a state of contemplation and identification in which the unfolding human soul enters into the light of the *Inner Dweller* and becomes one with that great Presence. In a short time his consciousness expands toward Soul consciousness, and the light and love and power of the Soul shine throughout his being....[7]

The following exercise is suggested to *all those who are sure that they are Raja Yogis*, and whose aim is to live as Souls, or as fountains of light, love and power.

Sit cross-legged on the floor and exhale all the air you have in your lungs. Then count to ten while holding your lungs empty. Start inhaling through your nostrils, filling first the abdominal area, then continue filling the chest and pull in the abdomen. This will be done in ten counts. Then you will hold the breath for ten counts, and exhale through your mouth for ten counts. This can be repeated five to eight times and done twice daily.

At the time of the breathing exercise your mind must be concentrated on a lofty thought — a verse from Patanjali, *The Bhagavad Gita*, the *Upanishads*, the *Dhammapada*, the *New Testament*, etc. — so that your mind does not become occupied with the mechanism of breathing.

This breathing exercise must be done in a really released way, inhaling and exhaling smoothly. This exercise should be done in the mountains, in gardens, at the seashore or at home, if the air is relatively pure and not polluted.[8]

---

[7]*Ibid.*, pp. 257,258,260-261.
[8]*Ibid.*, pp. 259-260.

AGNI YOGA

The Teaching that is given for this age and for the coming age is sometimes called the Teaching of fiery union, or in Sanskrit, it is called *Agni Yoga*. *Yoga* means union. *Agni* means fire in its triple manifestation. This is a union which must be achieved through the instrumentality of the three-fold fire. This fire will create integration, alignment, at-one-ment in man, in humanity, in the solar system and the Cosmos.

To bring about an integrated personality, man must use this threefold fire to create, to construct and to destroy. To bring about Soul infusion this threefold fire must be used. To bring about Self actualization, this threefold fire must be used. The separated parts of the human nature, through the action of the fire, will eventually function as a unit, enlightened and empowered by the electricity of the Self. This is called union through fire, or Agni Yoga.[9]

Agni means fire, and yoga means union. Agni Yoga means union through, by, or in fire. The fire we are referring to is the true Core of man. Man is essentially a Spark from a Cosmic Flame.

In occult literature, fire is divided into three parts:

    a.   fire by friction,

    b.   solar fire,

    c.   electrical fire.

Fire by friction is the electricity we use, or atmospheric electricity, which renders us great service as an agent of communication.

---

[9]*The Psyche and Psychism*, p. 170.

Solar fire is mental fire, or fire from the Sun, which causes enlightenment, expansion of consciousness and transmutation. It is like a bridge between the personality and the spiritual man. Our Solar Angels are sometimes called Fiery Meditators.

Electrical fire comes from the Central Spiritual Sun and is related to our Essence. This is Agni in its Solar manifestation.

We are told that fire by friction originates in the sphere of the Sun, which is the nourisher and sustainer of life in the solar system. Solar fire originates in the Heart of the Sun and is related to love and to the conscious realms of human beings. For the average person, solar fire is his consciousness. In the advanced disciple, it is love-wisdom. Electrical fire originates in the Central Spiritual Sun and is related to our Essence, the Self, the Spark within the form of man and to Infinity. It is the source of all creative urges.

From the point of view of Christian and other religious literature, the Central Spiritual Sun is the Father, the Source "from Whom all things proceed and to Whom all things return." The Heart of the Sun is "the word made flesh," the Christ. On human levels, it is the Solar Angel in man, Who is the bridge, a way by which achievement is possible. The visible Sun is the light of the Holy Spirit, the substance, or the personality. All of these are fire and in the Scriptures we are told that our God is a burning fire.

Agni Yoga refers to this fire. Through this fire a person must travel the path of transformation, the path of transmutation and the path of transfiguration. In other words, a person is going to be fiery. When he becomes purified, he will be a fiery being. And because no impurity exists in fire, the more fiery he becomes, the purer he will be.

How, then, does sickness come into being? Any place in your aura where the fire is extinguished is an entryway for fiery elementals which cause trouble. Microbes are fiery elementals of a low order.

Man, who is the Central Fire, the Monad, is going to become himself by passing through a fiery transformation. Then the physical body will be purified to the highest degree and man will be electrical. This is our goal. Then the body will not say any more, "I am weak; I am tired; I am getting old." All of these expressions do not refer to reality. When you are really your Self, you will be a Master, a fiery Angel, the fiery Self.[10]

Through Raja Yoga the human soul eventually masters the mental plane and becomes a Raja, a king of his own kingdom, of his own life.

Agni Yoga goes beyond this. A greater at-one-ment with higher level light and higher frequencies takes place when a man can free himself from the captivity of the mental plane and begin to function in the Spiritual triad or in the field of light formed by the mental, intuitional and atmic permanent atoms.

This is the real field of Agni-fire, where the human soul passes through transfiguration experiences. Here he deals not with knowledge or consciousness, but with *beingness* and awareness.

Through Raja Yoga the personality comes into being. Through Raja Yoga one achieves Soul infusion. In these two steps the human soul recollects himself, feels himself, and becomes a conscious soul. This is sometimes called "the second birth," when the human soul realizes his spiritual des-

---

[10]*Talks on Agni*, pp. 34-35.

tiny, and becomes aware of the potentials hidden within his being.

Through Agni Yoga, he enters into his "third birth" in which he realizes for the first time that he is a Spark of the Invisible Sun, free from personality and time limitations. It is in this stage that he can undo all that he did in the past. He literally finds wrong energy formations in his permanent atoms; distortions in his emotional body, which appear as glamors or emotional tumors, wounds and disturbances; destructive thoughtforms and seeds of future complications in his mental body, and gradually clears them out. He creates those patterns of energy which disperse, clear or melt away all unwanted and negative force formations within the aura of the personality.

The divine fire burns all impurities within the aura. It liberates the human soul to walk on the path of holiness and the path of initiation.

A Raja Yogi meditates and serves. An Agni Yogi lives a sacrificial life. To sacrifice means esoterically to make a higher principle take over and express itself through your mechanism. In this case both the "mechanism" and the higher principle are in an act of sacrifice.

On the Agni Yoga path the central fire of the Self radiates out of the periphery of the aura and attracts the fires of space. The fires of space are ideas, visions, energy waves or streams of currents coming from higher sources. All these are used by the Agni Yogi to expand his communication with Cosmos and become a creative co-worker with the Guides of evolution.

Agni Yoga is often called the Yoga of Synthesis and Yoga of Life. These terms reveal deep significances when meditated upon.

The path of spiritualization is the path of synthesis. On this path all separate things gradually become parts of greater and greater formations, and the Yogi develops the ability to correlate, synthesize and create holistic visions, which reflect the process of cosmic ideation in greater beauty and in greater accuracy.

An Agni Yogi is not only aware of this synthesis, but he transforms this abstract synthesis into a life of symphony. Thus even abstract visions and contacts become tangible in his daily life expressions.

An Agni Yogi is a fiery river who brings life from high mountains and stars, and glorifies the life of the planet with new cultures and with new visions.[11]

---

[11]*The Psyche and Psychism*, pp. 778-779.

18

Cycles

*T*he Presence within man observes various cycles to make Its guidance felt by man, who is active on physical, emotional and mental planes....

One of the cycles that affects the average man more closely than others is the lunar cycle. From the new moon to the full moon, the Inner Presence makes a special endeavor to reach the unfolding human soul and evoke a greater response to light, to love and to Divine Will....[1]

Our moon is a decaying organ in the solar system and, as such, it is a problem-producing factor for the earth specifically, and for the solar system in general. As a decaying organ within our body affects the body by hindering the circulatory flow of various electromagnetic energies, so the decaying moon disturbs, pollutes and hinders energies on their way to our Earth. There are cycles in which this condition is met and handled in a way that the decaying body is insulated and the hindrance is relatively absent for a period of fourteen days each month. This starts at the *new moon* when the solar radiation slowly overpowers the moon. At the time of each *full moon*, it is totally insulated, and energies coming from the different constellations or from various planets bypass the disturbing factors of the moon and reach our planet Earth.

---

[1] *Cosmos in Man*, p. 109.

Throughout ages, those who knew about the cycles, planned new moon and full moon meditation periods to help us reorient our whole being toward the Inner Light, the radiant Presence in each man, and to build a new channel of communication for light, love and power....

In Cosmos, in the solar system, and on the Earth we have the problem-producing factor of decaying bodies or organs. The same is true within our own spheres. A negative emotion, a criminal thought, a fear, a jealousy or an act of selfishness is nothing but a disintegrating and disturbing force-wave within our electromagnetic sphere. Starting with the new moon, because of inflowing solar and stellar energies, a man can insulate these factors, and build a communication line between his physical, emotional, mental natures and the Spiritual Presence within....

In some esoteric books we read that our Planetary Life enters into Its cyclic meditation at the time of the new moon. In the full moon period It reaches the highest point of Its tension, and at the exact moment of the full moon, It contacts the Solar Life, in the body of Whom our Planetary Life acts as one of Its centers. The ever-extending golden bridge of communication does not end here. The Solar Life in Its turn contacts those Lives (constellations) that form a special configuration in relation to our solar system. Thus a superb alignment is set up from man to the planet, to the Solar Life, and on to Cosmic Lives. When this alignment is achieved there comes a pouring down of energies from lofty Spiritual Beings and great Lives.

It is under such conditions that a window suddenly opens in our consciousness, and for a moment a flash of revelation strikes our Soul. We see, for a short moment, the reason for our being here and our responsibilities toward life as a whole. Relationships with greater spheres and energies expand our consciousness, expand our awareness and deepen our sense of responsibility, because these incoming energies are impressed by the Plan, the Purpose, and visions of Great Ones. The degree of our receptivity and assimilation depends on the degree of the alignment of our threefold personality with the Inner Presence, and on the mental focus at the time of full moon meditation.[2]

As the moon wanes during the period from the full moon to the new moon, the disturbing factors gain power, and their influence is felt by humanity and other kingdoms. This influence can be avoided if, during the waxing phase of the moon, a man charges himself with enough energy to reject all negative influences with his own radiation during the waning period. Energy is accumulated through meditation which is a process of contact with the Presence in man....

At each full moon our Solar Presence within us observes these cycles, and tries to reach man, to kindle the flame that will light his way toward freedom, compassion, peace and spiritual creativity. We must extend our hand to our Guide, especially at the full moon meditation period, and stand within Its Light, expressing it as the energy of blessings to all humanity. It is through such a closeness that Soul infusion can be achieved, and the path toward Mastery can be paved.[3]

Each full moon period is divided into seven days: three days prior to the full moon, the day of the full moon, and three days after the full moon.

---

[2]*Ibid.*, pp. 110-111.
[3]*Ibid.*, p. 112.

The first three days together are called the *days of preparation.* The first day of preparation is called the **day of confidence.** The second day is the **day of spiritual aspiration,** and the third day is the **day of dedication and decision.**

These three days must be observed in the spirit of renunciation and detachment. Renunciation and detachment are means to save and accumulate energy, clear our vision, and correct our alignment and relationships.

On the **first day** we must fill our heart with the **confidence** that Christ is, that the Hierarchy exists, and that in every man there is the spark of Life, the ever-blooming, ever-unfolding reality. All day our thoughts will center around these ideas without interfering with our daily duties and labor. Through such an endeavor we put our brain in the right condition for the future work.

On the **second day,** which is the **day of aspiration,** our astral vehicle is lifted to a very high level of sensitivity, beauty, adoration, worship and admiration. This day we lift our hearts to the grandeur of the achieved Sons of God and the spiritual life leading us toward Infinity.

On the **third day,** which is called the **day of dedication,** the mental body will be charged with will energy and extended toward transcendental values. A solemn decision must be made that all incoming energies will be used for the fulfillment of the Plan and for the upliftment of humanity as a whole.

This is the day of tension. We hold our whole chalice up as an open lotus toward the Rays of Infinity to be filled with the energies of the New Age.

The **fourth day**, the day of the full moon, is the **day of contact**. This extends over a period of twelve hours, but the highest point of contact is at the exact time of the full moon. Contact is made with the highest fire in you, with the fire of the Hierarchy, and with the center "where the Will of God is known." This is the time in which opportunity is given to disciples to expand their consciousness and enter into a new level of divine awareness. This is the day on which contacts are made with our Solar Angel, with our Master, and the day on which we may be impressed by even higher sources.

The full moon day is also called the **day of safeguarding**. Our Chalice is filled with the precious energies of the New Age and through them we are in contact with their sources, and thus stand in their light, love and power. This treasure must be protected and safeguarded.... This is the day of pure silence and contact, during which we are absorbed in our Inner Divinity.

The last three days are called the *days of distribution* and *sharing*....

The **fifth day** is called the **day of registration**. The contacted energies slowly descend into our mental equipment, into our personality, and are recognized there. It is at this time that new decisions are made and new plans are drawn up to carry out the work for the liberation and freedom of humanity.

The **sixth day** is called the **day of assimilation**, when the contacted fiery energies penetrate into our lower vehicles and cause transmutation, transformation and transfiguration.

The **seventh day** is the **day of radiation**. Through all our relationships, the higher energies that we have received are radiated toward our environment, toward our nation and toward humanity as a whole.

During each of these seven days, our meditation must be appropriated to the keynote of the full moon day, and a proper seed thought and invocation chosen for that special day.[4]

The full moon period is the right time to make a spiritual breakthrough for greater cooperation with the Hierarchy of the planet and with the light of the Inner Guide....[5]

It is the work of disciples to provide the ways and means for average people to resign the strength of their personality and enter into the enlightened power of the will of the Inner Guide..[6]

The keynotes for disciples are:

ARIES: **I come forth and from the plane of mind I rule....**

TAURUS: **I see, and when the eye is opened, all is illumined....**

GEMINI: **I recognize my other self and in the waning of that self I grow and glow....**

CANCER: **I build a lighted house and therein dwell.**

LEO: **I am That and That am I....**

VIRGO: **I am the Mother and the Child, I God. I matter am....**

LIBRA: **I choose the way that leads between the two great lines of force....**

SCORPIO: **Warrior I am, and from the battle I emerge triumphant....**

[4]*Symphony of the Zodiac*, pp. vii-ix.
[5]*Ibid.*, p. xvi.
[6]*Ibid.*, p. xix.

SAGITTARIUS: **I see the goal. I reach the goal and see another....**

CAPRICORN: **Lost am I in light supernal, yet on that light I turn my back....**

AQUARIUS: **Water of life am I, poured forth for thirsty men....**

PISCES: **I leave the Father's Home and turning back, I save.**[7]

The three most important signs are the sun sign, the rising sign and the sign the moon occupies.

The **sun sign** indicates the present problems of the person. It is mostly related to the personality, to the activity aspect of the person. It reveals the vices that must be overcome and the virtues to be developed.

The **rising sign** indicates the goal of this life or the immediate Soul purpose for this incarnation. It works for the future. It presents the force of the Soul and the goal for this life cycle, or for seven lives. It is the Soul opportunity.

The **moon sign** refers to the past, to limitation. It governs the body and shows where the prison of the Soul is to be found.[8]

The different ray personalities and Souls in a group contribute to each other and to the group as a whole when their consciousness is functioning upon Soul or Triadal levels. They complement and supplement each other to work out the Divine Plan....[9]

---

[7]*Ibid.*, pp. xviii-xxviii.

[8]See Bailey, A.A., *Esoteric Astrology*, pp. 18-19. (Excerpt from *Symphony of the Zodiac*, pp. 321-322.)

[9]*Ibid.*, p. 323.

At the time of the full moon, advanced disciples respond to the higher keynote and feel a great spiritual urge to serve, and they forget about their "Home," security, individual goals and blessings of reward. They forget these and turn toward humanity to help it proceed on its path of spiritual evolution. The main technique they use is to radiate their Soul virtues and release the corresponding energies through service.[10]

[A] great disciple, Hercules performed a great labor on the reversed wheel of the Zodiac during the month when the Sun was in Aries. The son of Mars, Diomedes, ruled a land in which he raised horses and mares of war. They were very wild and fierce, and all men trembled at their sound. They ravaged the land, killing people who crossed their way. Hercules was given the task of capturing these horses and stopping all of their evil deeds.

Hercules had a friend named Abderis, whom he called on to help him. Both of them cornered the horses and tethered them. Hercules felt so proud of his achievement that he wanted to show his victory to Diomedes. So he said to Abderis, "I am going toward the gate of Diomedes. You pull all these horses and bring them after me." And he turned his back and walked toward the gate. But Abderis was weak and when he pulled the horses out of the enclosure, they trampled him to death and escaped.

Again, Hercules pursued them, caught them one by one, tied them and drove them through the gate by himself. The people of the land proclaimed Hercules as their Savior.

We are told that Aries rules the head, or the mind. The horses symbolize thoughts and ideas. Thoughts are very dif-

---

[10]*Ibid.*, p. 325.

ficult to control, but unless we are successful in controlling them, there is no victory.

Hercules was advised first to control his thoughts, and with the help of Abderis, he succeeded in controlling them. Hercules symbolizes the Soul, the Self, and Abderis symbolizes the personality.

The Soul must always watch the thoughts and not depend on the personality because the personality misuses thought. The moment we depend on the personality, wild thoughts take over and the price is the destruction of the personality....[11]

...Aries is the transmitter of Cosmic Fire.[12] Actually, there are three transmitters of fire:

> Aries releases Cosmic Fire;
>
> Leo releases Solar Fire; and
>
> Sagittarius releases Planetary Fire.

Master Djwhal Khul says these three fires constitute the Yoga of Fire, which clears the way for resurrection. The Yoga of Fire is the progressive at-one-ment with the Inner Flame....

Resurrection is the process of uniting the fires of progressive magnitude. First comes the fire of the personality; second, we have the fire of the Soul; and third is the fire of the true Self, the Monad — three fires striving to be one flame....[13]

[During the sun in Taurus], a great hero, Hercules, was given the duty of rescuing a sacred bull captured by a king. This king intended to sacrifice the bull for himself. The bull

---

[11] *Ibid.*, pp. 44-45.

[12] See Bailey, A.A., *Esoteric Astrology*, p. 293.

[13] *Ibid.*, p. 59.

was taken to an island and Hercules, crossing the water, went to the island. After many difficulties, he liberated the bull. Sitting on the bull, he crossed the ocean and brought it back to its owners, who were three Cyclopes.

This is a very symbolic story; it seems to me that the bull is the human soul, the Divine Spark fallen into the matter of the physical, emotional and mental bodies, which form a unit.

On the path of evolution, the threefold personality (physical, emotional and lower mental natures) dominates the soul as a king and uses it as a slave....

Hercules is the symbol of the Solar Angel which crossed the sea of matter and reached the island and liberated the bull, the human soul, and brought it back to the cyclopes.

It is interesting to note that the names of the Cyclopes clearly indicate that they were the symbols of the three permanent atoms of the Spiritual Triad which is formed by the light of the higher mind, intuition and atmic will power.

The name of the first Cyclops is Arges, or *activity*, which is the function of the higher mental substance. The second one is Steropes, which means *lightning,* referring to the intuition. The third one is Brontes, which means *thunder*, power or will power. Thus, the human soul, the bull of desire, was changed into the bull of aspiration and direction.

In every human Spark, the will-to-be and the will-to-live are in existence. There is the desire to go out into matter and the desire to go out of matter into freedom. The Solar Angels met mankind the moment the lowest point of identification with matter was reached and the human Sparks were ready to turn their faces toward the Eye of the Bull, the Monad.[14]

---

[14]*Symphony of the Zodiac*, pp. 94-95.

Meditation prevents unwholesome abstraction into dreamland by keeping the Soul in right relation to the three-fold personality and by balancing the inner aspiration with the outer obligations and responsibilities.[15]

Taurus rules:

1. the Soul and personality rays of China;
2. the personality ray of Poland;
3. the Second Ray Soul of Great Britain;
4. the Second Ray Soul of Canada;
5. the Second Ray Soul of Rome;
6. the Second Ray Soul of Leningrad;
7. the Second Ray Soul of Moscow.

This means that these nations, countries or cities will absorb a great deal of Taurian energy and will go in "search for gold," or in "search for golden light divine."[16] This means that they will either obey their personality desires and personality demands, or they will follow their Soul desires and Soul demands....[17]

In this month [Cancer], a person is going to build Soul consciousness by lifting himself from his transient physical, emotional and mental natures, eventually becoming able to glimpse the existence and nature of his Soul and gradually creating a dialogue or communication with his Soul....

In the month of Cancer we are receptive to the energies of all zodiacal signs....

Cancer is related to the personality and also to the Soul. The average person is influenced by his personality; if he is

[15]*Ibid.*, p. 97.

[16]Bailey, A.A., *Esoteric Astrology*, p. 379.

[17]*Symphony of the Zodiac*, pp. 104-105.

a disciple, he is influenced by his Soul. Those who are on the personality level use the energy for their instinct of self-preservation. Those who are disciples use the energy to build great thoughtforms which will serve human upliftment and security.[18]

Leo energy, being fiery, produces the burning ground for a human being. It is through such a burning ground that the task of purification, transmutation, communication and mastery is carried on....

If the burning ground is on the personality level, there is mostly pain, suffering, renunciation and penance. When it is on the Soul level it produces great joy, because the Soul manifests Itself through the fire that purifies and expands the horizons....

Let us not forget that the ultimate goal of a Leo is to submit himself to the will of his Inner Guide and later to the will of the Divine Spark, the Self.[19]

When the Soul nature is active and a person stands in Soul-consciousness with pure white garments, he receives energy from the Heart of the Sun and radiates it as compassion, wisdom, or the Plan....[20]

The light that shines on the path of the subject is called "the Light of the Soul." This Light offers him great consciousness, fusion and synthesis. It shows him the existence of a plan within each Soul. It shows the existence of the jewel in each Soul....[21]

---

[18]*Ibid.*, pp. 194,195.

[19]*Ibid.*, p. 212.

[20]*Ibid.*, p. 206.

[21]*Ibid.*, p. 345.

One pan on the scale of Libra is the eye of the Soul; the other pan is the value of the person. It is proper that when our Sun enters Libra we weigh our values in the light of our Inner Guide and see if they are increasing or decreasing....

The unfolding human soul must increase its control over the personality, or increase its weight by beauty and spirituality, until it balances the Inner Guide to a certain degree....[22]

The Scorpio eagle fights mostly on the mental plane. His battle is waged with thoughts and ideas. Every fight is an expression of a never-ending inner battle for him. He fights against his physical, emotional and mental problems. He grows and unfolds only by fighting within himself. But it is very interesting that the fight is always introduced by his Higher Self and carried to victory by the Higher Self. The fight continues until he confronts the combined power of the whole lower army in his personality. This power is called the "Dweller on the Threshold."

The Dweller on the Threshold is the accumulated power of all blind urges and drives, all glamors and illusions with which a person has been identified throughout ages. When he is trying to free himself from limitations of the lower self, these limitations gather together as an entity and try to block the passage to the Soul and the Intuitional Plane.[23]

The light that shines on this path is called "the Light of day." The full power of the Inner Self, the full power of the Soul shines on his path; and in that Light he walks as a triumphant warrior.[24]

---

[22]*Ibid.*, pp. 240-241.

[23]*Ibid.*, pp. 257-258.

[24]*Ibid.*, p. 347.

The keynote for the Sagittarian disciples is, "I **see the goal. I reach the goal and see another.**"

A goal is part of the plan of the Soul, or the synthesis of all the best aspirations of a person....[25]

It is very interesting to realize that our life-goals do not conflict with each other. Actually, each goal that is projected from the Inner Guide to our mental apparatus is a piece of a big jigsaw puzzle in the universe. The whole image or picture is going to reach completion if we all find the pieces — goals — and put them in the right place in the puzzle, or play our true role in life....[26]

Christ said, "I am bringing you life more abundantly. Whoever drinks the water that I give shall never thirst."... Humanity is really thirsty. The proof of its thirst is its unquenchable greed, which can only be quenched if humanity assimilates "the Water"of Aquarius. Man will never be satisfied with what he has, or with what he will have, unless the energy of Aquarius pours into his heart, mind and Soul....

The more abundant life comes when one contacts his Soul, Christ and the Father's Home....[27]

...Outer growth is the result of those planetary and solar energies, which in cycles stimulate and push forward the mechanism of man. The inner growth also is cyclic and is the result of spiritual stimulations cyclically given by the Soul, by the Spiritual Triad, by the Hierarchy and by Shamballa.[28]

---

[25]*Ibid.*, p. 265.

[26]*Ibid.*, p. 269.

[27]*Ibid.*, p. 302.

[28]*The Science of Meditation*, p. 46.

19

The Rays

One of the richest and safest ways to come in contact with the Soul and use the treasures of the Chalice for our creative living and service, is to study and know the ray to which our Soul belongs. This knowledge is very important because it creates a closer rapport between Soul and personality and presents possibilities for greater infusion. To facilitate this infusion, and to secure greater guidance from the Indwelling Presence, we can meditate according to the Ray of our Soul.

Such meditation will give us tremendous advantage in creating a direct line of communication to the Soul, invoking Its help in all our activities upon the physical, emotional and mental planes, as well as in our individual and group situations....

There are seven types of energy which condition all activities and expressions of our nature and the kingdoms. Our Soul belongs to one of these energy streams. It may belong to one of the higher three rays, the Rays of Aspect, or to the lower four, the Rays of Attribute. Generally the Soul Ray is a Ray of Aspect, but the Soul chooses Rays of Attribute for certain cycles and for specific work in relation to Its obligations.

To know the Ray of our Soul is not easy when we are lost in the agitated sea of our physical, emotional and mental life. Once we step into greater dedication, service and sacrifice for our fellow man, we catch glimpses of the splendor of the Soul Ray, which inspires in us moments of great joy, sacrifice, danger, renunciation, life intention and heroic action. In these rare moments, we sense the nature of the Ray of our Soul, until that time when our personality fuses into the Soul light, and we eventually become a living Soul, harmonized with the Ray of the Soul....

Let us remember that the Soul on Its own level is in deep meditation and is trying to impress the man with the Divine Plan, and to impart to him the need for endless striving on the path. Our aim in these meditations will be to synchronize ourselves with the Soul's meditation.[1]

RAY MEDITATION TECHNIQUES

For each ray meditation we have selected words for seed thoughts. Meditating on these seed thoughts will be of great help in releasing latent energies within and opening new horizons. Also, as you ponder and meditate upon these seed thoughts, you cultivate corresponding virtues in your nature, and as these virtues are cultivated, organic and constitutional changes take place in your physical and subtle bodies; changes which will facilitate communication with your Soul.

We must also consider the personality ray and the way in which it can be brought into harmony with the Soul ray through meditation; first to create a balance and then a vehicle for the Soul to use to express Itself.

This can be accomplished as follows: After you know your Soul and Personality rays, use the Soul's ray meditation technique. Study, work and serve in your Personality ray

---

[1]*Cosmos in Man*, pp. 81-82.

field. For example, if your Soul is Second Ray and your personality is First Ray, choose Second Ray meditation, and carry on with your studies on the First Ray meditation....2

For the bridge-building process, the Tibetan Master gave us the Seven Words of Power for each ray in *The Rays and the Initiations:*

First Ray	I assert the fact.
Second Ray	I see the greatest light.
Third Ray	Purpose itself am I.
Fourth Ray	Two merge with One.
Fifth Ray	Three minds unite.
Sixth Ray	The highest light controls.
Seventh Ray	The highest and lowest meet....

The builder, as we know, is the Soul-infused personality; so while he is using the word of power, he must choose his Soul ray word which is dominating his personality ray.

These words of power will be sounded inaudibly by the disciple at the time of projection, while concentrating deeply on the meaning of the words to feel their essence. To do this, we must first of all study and find out our Soul and personality rays, and see whether the Soul ray is dominating, and then use the Soul ray words of power.3

2*Cosmos in Man*, p. 84.
Note: The meditations and seed thoughts for each ray can be found in *Cosmos in Man*, pages 84-95.
3*The Science of Becoming Oneself*, p. 147. (The best sources for the study of the Rays are the following books by A.A. Bailey: *A Treatise on the Seven Rays*, Volume I, pp. 202-212, 319-334, 401-403, 411-430; Volume II, pp. 259, 264-269, 282-285, 288, 291-303, 351-401, 442-443, 705-712; *A Treatise on White Magic*, pp. 109-121; *The Rays and Initiations*, pp. 575-589, 643-653; and *Esoteric Astrology*, pp. 596-601.)

As an example, if a man's Soul ray is *Will-power* or First Ray, and the Personality ray is *Love* or Second Ray, the Personality may be deeply colored or strongly influenced by the First Ray of the Soul. Love will be expressed by power and the power will function through the great inclusiveness quality of the Love Ray, on the personality levels.

This will continue to the Fourth Initiation. During this time of greater fusion between the Personality and Soul the two rays will gradually function as two sides of one reality, until the time comes when the Soul will depart from the Chalice, and the unfolding human soul will function as a *Soul*, changing its sub-ray to the parent ray. Here is the subtle point. This ray which was the ray of the Solar Angel, is in its turn a sub-ray of the Monadic Ray, which was the ray of the unfolding human soul. For example, let us say that a man has:

— A First Ray Monad
— A Second Ray Soul
— A Fifth, Third or Seventh Ray personality

During his evolution and on the path of discipleship and Initiation, this Fifth, Third or Seventh Ray of the unfolding human soul will change into the *Second Ray*, the ray of the Solar Angel, the Soul. Then on the path of advanced Initiation this Second Ray will become the servant of the First Ray, and eventually will change into its true parent ray, the First Ray (through the Third Ray).

To learn what the Personality ray is we must clearly understand that the Real Man, the Spark, the Monad, is as a diffused light in the three lower bodies. As the three bodies begin to become organized, individually and collectively, the diffused light condenses and slowly becomes a center by itself. This center is the lower self. So we may say that the lower self is spread throughout the three bodies. In most individuals the lower self is under the control of one of its three bodies, serving its ends and purposes. Gradually, as the bodies develop and as the stream of light from the Solar Angel penetrates into them, the diffused light of the Monad begins to recollect itself and form a center. This center is the character of man. By character we mean special or exceptional character, for it highly influences the three bodies....[4]

---

[4]*Cosmos in Man*, p. 76.

20

The Soul Note

*I*n man, the Spark sounds a triple note and draws seven layers of matter around Himself, creating a seven-fold vibration. Eventually He becomes imprisoned on the lowest plane of manifestation. The Solar Angel performs similar work, and in sounding certain words, brings the lower man, the physical, emotional and mental man, into existence....[1]

A man is like a musical instrument with seven strings....

The seven strings represent our vehicles of expression, each of which has its own note. In the beginning the notes are not clear, but are fluctuating and changing constantly, depending upon the outer conditions and inner states of our being; until one day when, one by one, the notes have been purified and brought in tune with the other strings by the touch of the Inner Musician.

These seven bodies are divided into three parts which are often designated by various symbols. They may be called Spirit, Soul and personality. The Soul is the Inner Conductor who holds the tuning fork, the *Word*, the *note* with which the personality must be in tune if it is to create a channel for the spiritual energies of higher planes, the higher strings....

---

[1] *Cosmos in Man*, p. 238.

The average man cannot find the true note of his Angel, and even though he may find it by chance, it will cause him more difficulty than it will be of help to him....[2]

Sometimes there is confusion in distinguishing between the Soul note and the sub-tones of the physical, astral and lower mental planes. These planes being separate units and an aggregate of lives, have their own sub-tones. It is possible that people may pick up these sub-tones at times, creating a constant buzzing in their heads, which often leads to a state of bewilderment. A ringing in the ears bears some relation to this fact, but more often the cause is biological. This note heard in the head is probably one of the sub-tones of the personality vehicles which is being confused with the real note of the Solar Angel or the real note of the unfolding human soul....

Man loses the note when he is in the process of transferring his focus of consciousness from the physical to the emotional plane. When, however, his consciousness is settled in the emotional body, he starts to hear the note in a clear tone. He continues to hear the note until he begins to shift his consciousness from the emotional to the lower mental and from the lower mental to the higher mental. Here on the higher mental plane he discovers that both his and his Solar Angel's notes are fused into one.

...It is the note of the unfolding human soul, which must eventually tune in with the note of the Solar Angel and fuse with the Monadic note of his essence, finally settling the agelong battle between the higher and lower selves. In this process there is a period when the unfolding human soul, identified with the personality conflicts with the

---

[2]*Ibid.*, p. 239.

note of the Solar Angel. This conflict endures for a time because man thinks that fusion with the note of the Solar Angel will cause him to lose whatever he is or has. This is the rich man confronting the Christ....

The true *Soul Note* has a powerful transfiguring effect upon your personality and bestows upon it the power of the true Will....

In sounding the OM at the aspirant stage, we let loose a new vibration throughout the personality to reach the cores of the cells and atoms of the three bodies, making them radioactive and in tune with each other, and opening a channel for the circulation of Soul energy.[3]

Before you can profit from sounding the OM, you must have reached the level of the OM, which brings you into the light of the Soul on the mental plane. This means that your mind, emotions and physical activities must be carried on with a sense of responsibility and loyalty to the law of evolution under the guidance of the Inner Light....

We must unite with the OM and imagine that we are liberating ourselves from our physical, emotional and mental bodies, but at the same time, create harmony in them so that the Soul-life can pour through them and create beauties in our environment....[4]

After a period of time, when you are sounding your own soul's note, you will hear the major note of your Angel, and the two will form a chord, or vibrate in unison, uplifting the focus of your consciousness to the higher mental planes.

---

[3]*Ibid.*, pp. 240,241.
[4]*Ibid.*, p. 242.

If your ear is not clear of the noise of physical urges and drives, from the noise of physical complications and material values; if your ear is clogged with the noise of negative emotions, conflicting thoughtforms, habits, selfishness, pride and many kinds of vanities, you cannot expect to hear the Voice of Silence, the OM. The OM is the magnetic pull of your Angel calling you back to your Source through detachment, release and freedom.

When your ear is cleared of the noises, you are ready to hear your Soul note, the note of liberating energy. The question may be asked, "Should we sound the OM before we reach such a state?" The answer is, "Yes," because it is through striving toward the core of your being, and through the effort to reach your Source by cleaning poisons from the outside by sounding the OM, that eventually the inner OM and the outer OM meet and synchronize.

Knowing your need, you can sound your note on the plane of that need. It can be sounded on the physical, emotional or mental planes, but real help comes when you find and use your Soul note; the note which gradually unveils the plan of your Soul for this life.[5]

...When [a person] finds his higher mental note, he has found the note of his Solar Angel and the note of the group in which he is working. Here, he can use that note to increase his light, to synchronize himself with the Inner Presence, and to be of tremendous service to his group....[6]

The OM is sounded in different keys, because every man has a different note, according to his constitution. Your physical body has one note, your emotional body another,

[5]*Ibid.*, p. 243.
[6]*Ibid.*, p. 244.

your mental body has its note, and your Solar Angel still another. If you are an integrated personality, the physical, emotional and mental notes are harmonized or united into one chord. There then remains the task of playing this chord in harmony with the Soul note.

How does one find his *own note*? Finding one's own note is one of the secrets of initiation which has not yet been given. Instinctively you may sound it correctly, or when you take the Third Initiation, your Master will tell you how to sound your OM. You will hear it and recognize it. Sometimes, while you are meditating, your Soul will give the note. When this happens, from then on, you must use it. It will be a very subtle tone, but once you experience it, you will recognize it by its soft, bell-like tone resembling that of a tuning fork.

Our Solar Angel is in continuous, deep meditation from our birth to our death. Meditation for the Solar Angel means absorbing the Divine Plan, digesting it and radiating it out to the world. Thus, we can see the importance of regular and rhythmic meditation. Through meditation we slowly enter into the sphere of vibration or radiation of the Soul, where we are gradually purified, sublimated and transfigured, until one great day when we become *one with our Soul;* this union is called the mystical marriage. The Spark slowly blooms and moves closer to the Source. When It reaches the Solar Angel, Its vibration and the vibration of the Solar Angel become as one, completely unified. It is like two violins being tuned together. A quarter of a degree difference in tone can be detected by a sensitive ear, but if the two instruments are perfectly in tune with each other, no difference can be heard by the most sensitive ear. The two violins have become as one. In like manner, the Soul and the one becoming a soul, unite and become as One. This can be accomplished only through meditation.[7]

We must sound the OM three times before meditation. The following steps are suggested for the sounding of the OM:

— The first OM is very soft, almost a whisper.
— The second one is a little louder.
— The third is still louder.[8]

1. For the first OM the mind must be concentrated, but relaxed. The lips must form an "O" and the full, round "O" sound must be sent forth. This "O" must rise as if you were pushing the sound to the roof of your mouth, on up to the middle of the top of your head, and out. As you are doing this, you must visualize your mental vehicle as becoming purer and more subtle.

2. The same visualization will be used for the second OM, but this time for the emotional body. Try to see the emotional body as a fine mist around you.

3. When sounding the third OM, relax the physical body completely, and imagine that your aura is becoming a golden color.

The duration of the OM is divided into two parts, the "O" and the "M." The sounding of the OM must be preceded by taking a deep breath. Its true effect starts after it has been sounded. We must allow an interval of silence as we

---

[7]*Ibid.*, p. 246.
[8]*Ibid.*, p. 244.

end it, and in that short period of silence the effect of the OM enters deeper and deeper into the bodies....[9]

The OM is sounded on various levels, according to the level and awareness of a person. If a man's consciousness is not beyond the physical level, his OM will have very little effect. If his consciousness is advanced and the OM is sounded on the mental plane, the effect will be stronger. If it is sounded on the Soul level, as a Soul, the effect will be very potent. It is here that the OM can be used for magical purposes; for the creation of subtle forms to further the expression of the Plan and Purpose of God; for cooperation with the law of evolution through transformation, transfiguration, and alignment with greater sources of energy and awareness.[10]

...We will divide people into three groups, according to the three stages of development:

— Those people who speak from the level of Soul consciousness.
— Those who speak from the level of their aspirations, visions and dreams.
— People who speak from the level of their physical urges and emotional drives.

Whenever a person sounds the OM, or speaks on any subject, he charges his voice with the force of the level upon which he is functioning. It is important, therefore, that before a person sounds the OM or gives a speech, he must deliberately raise his level of consciousness to the higher

[9]*Ibid.*, p. 245.
[10]*Ibid.*, p. 247.

mental plane through alignment and visualization. It is possible to climb a mountain and for a short time enjoy the beauty of the heights, but when in that short time, you become able to touch your Soul and sound the OM, or speak the words of your Soul, you raise your own level of being tremendously and you release greater energies into your system.

Through such alignment, upliftment and effort the day will come when you will hear an echo from within, and eventually this echo will become a clear note, the note of your soul. You will have found the lost Word which was You....[11]

After ... three OMs are sounded solemnly, you will have a short period of deep silence, in which you will feel that the Solar Fire of the Angel starts to circulate throughout your three bodies, creating a magnetic expansion toward Infinity.[12]

It is not easy to find your Solar Angel's note; we are told that this is one of the secrets of the initiations. When the time is ripe and when your three bodies are aligned and have entered into a high level of purification, then your Solar Angel gives you the key. This may happen in one of your meditations, or in one of your higher contacts on subtle levels.[13]

In sounding the OM actually we are releasing the true notes of each atom on the three planes, and synchronizing them with the note of the Soul.[14]

---

[11] *Ibid.*, pp. 247-248.

[12] *The Science of Meditation*, p. 115.

[13] *Ibid.*, pp. 115-116.

[14] *Ibid.*, p. 118.

...[T]hrough sounding the OM, the soul in the three worlds of personality is focused on the higher mental plane, and released from the enchantment of the three lower worlds. Through the Sound, the soul is freed from the mental plane and focused in the intuitional level and, eventually, the "Temple of Solomon," the Causal Body, is destroyed and the Solar Angel is set free.[15]

The first OM hits the mental unit, and then extends to the mental permanent atom. First the lower mind calms down, and as the sound reaches the mental permanent atom, it creates a radiation from both the mental permanent atom and the mental unit; then the lights of the two points extend in circles, interpenetrating each other and forming a web of light. This light, or energy, cleans the undesirable thoughtforms, melting or burning them, and builds a sphere of communication between the lower and the higher mind. The sphere of light then becomes charged with the light of the Solar Angel, or Ego. This stimulates the etheric head center and drives away elements of inertia from the mental body.[16]

It will be possible in the future to form healing groups which are on the Soul level. Such groups will be able to discern the true notes of other people's bodies and, by sounding the OM, cure them of many complications in the physical or subtle bodies....[17]

---

[15]*Ibid.*, p. 111.

[16]*Ibid.*, pp. 112-113.

[17]*Cosmos in Man*, p. 242.

21

Soul-Infused Personality

T *he need of every disciple is ever to develop a closer and more direct alignment between soul and personality....[1]*

—The Tibetan—

The Solar Angel lives on the higher mental levels, radiating light, love and power. Its light-aspect gradually penetrates the physical, etheric, astral and mental atmospheres, as the aspiration of the human soul grows and deepens. At first, most of the atoms of the three bodies do not respond to the light-aspect of the Soul. Gradually the sensitivity of these atoms increases, and the bodies attract more light of intelligence from the Soul. The increase of this light-energy causes the human soul to integrate the three bodies, forming them into a unit, called the personality....

The personality passes through three separate stages of development. In the first stage it is a selfish unit working only for its own individual nature. In the second stage, a conflict begins between the Soul expression and the personality reaction. Most of the time the personality rebels against the silent suggestions of the Soul. In the third stage, the personality yields and gradually fuses with the will of the Soul. Here starts the path of discipleship; the unfolding human

---

[1]Bailey, A.A., *Discipleship in the New Age*, Vol. I, p. 126.

soul realizes the part he should play in the great Plan. Eventually the second energy, the love energy, starts to pour into the personality. A faint bridge appears between the man and the Soul. The man starts to feel the touch of the Soul; his aspiration increases; and then the power of the Soul begins to flood the personality. These three energies of the Soul gradually penetrate the whole substance of the three vehicles, and man becomes a Soul-infused personality. The unfolding human soul and the Solar Angel become fused. The personality now ceases to be a concealing veil or misleading mask. It becomes a truer picture of the inner man, who shines through the physical body as acts of service, through the emotional body as love and compassion, and through the mental body as knowledge and right human relations.

The Solar Angel affects man in seven-year cycles. First, It energizes the physical-etheric man through the life thread anchored in the heart center. Then It starts to affect the emotional life from ages seven to fourteen and the mental life from ages fourteen to twenty-one. During these twenty-one years the Solar Angel charges the bodies or the three vehicles. It lightly touches them, which has an organizing effect upon the bodies; they become integrated and prepare for more advanced work in the future.

At age twenty-one, the second touch of appropriation of the etheric body commences; it passes to the emotional body and then to the mental body. This time the touch is stronger and can be very rewarding for the man if, in previous cycles, his vehicles have been developed and used in higher activities. Theoretically, at age forty-nine man is mature, and if he has been wise enough to unfold and develop himself, he will see the true path and have enough energy and light to enter it in full consciousness. The contact of the Solar Angel with the sleeping human soul liberates him from glamors and illusions, expands his consciousness, and develops his sense of reality.

Most of the actions of the personality are automatic and mechanical. The personality is a stimulus-response apparatus; many of our actions are mechanical responses to physical, emotional and mental stimuli. We have a choice of two ways of responding — the personality way and the Soul way. A great part of our life is controlled by the first, which makes man the victim of his surrounding conditions, events and blind urges of the physical, emotional and mental vehicles. But as the Soul light penetrates into the mental layers and awakens the human soul, a transmutation process starts. Gradually the mechanical actions of man decrease, and conscious actions increase until the whole mechanism comes under the control of the Soul consciousness. This process is called Soul infusion.

Soul infusion is not easily achieved. It requires continuous hardship and struggle, pain and crisis, service and sacrifice. Agelong habits of the personality do not yield easily, and man passes through great depressions, conflicts and "dark nights." These things come about because the inpouring Soul light creates friction in the substance of the three worlds. Man passes from one crisis to another until, gradually, rhythmic vibration permeates the three bodies simultaneously. Man has become a Soul-infused entity.

Soul infusion causes diverse effects upon different bodies. In the etheric-physical body it creates a radioactive energy; the physical man is full of energy, which he can control and use beneficially; his senses are very keen; he projects peace, poise and serenity. In the emotional body, Soul infusion brings peace and calmness; it generates extreme sensitivity to higher impulses; man's emotions become strong and positive; his imagination becomes extensive and creative; he devotes himself to higher causes and acts enthusiastically. In the mental body, Soul infusion produces clear thinking, pure logic and a living goal. The Soul-infused personality sees things as they really are. The mind becomes illumined and the Divine Plan can be visualized. This creates group-consciousness, a sense of unity, synthesis and tolerance. A limitless horizon appears and deep aspiration toward the Divine realities is created. The form cannot veil his vision. Man sees the motives and causes. The hidden storage of his Soul's knowledge becomes evident. He becomes aware of all past experiences of the Soul. When man learns to control his mind, he can use it as a searchlight for deeper truths and as a creative agent for life in general. He starts to look beyond the mental field and experiences great expansions of consciousness, leading from the unreal to the Real.[2]

The Masters of Wisdom say that the three disciples at the time of transfiguration symbolize the three worlds of human endeavor, the personality or the lower self. Christ symbolized the *way* or the Soul-infused personality, the transfigured personality, at which time "the voice of the Father," the voice of the real Self, was heard....[3]

The process of Soul infusion in the literature of mystics is called spiritual marriage. The bride is the purified, ornamented virgin in a white robe who awaits the bridegroom. She is pure, holy and endowed with various graces. The

[2]*The Hidden Glory of the Inner Man*, pp. 124-127.
[3]*Ibid.*, p. 35.

bridegroom is the vision, the crown of her head, who will give him a new meaning, a new life and who says to her in a sweet voice:

> *Behold, thou art fair, my love;*
> *Behold, thou art fair....*
> *There is no spot in thee,*
> *Thou has taken away my heart....*
> *How fair is thy love, my sister, my spouse.*
> *Thy lips, O my spouse, drop as the honeycomb....*
>
> *I sleep, but my heart waketh;*
> *It is the voice of my beloved that knocketh, saying,*
> *Open to me, my sister, my love, my dove, my undefiled.*[4]

In ancient mysteries, the performance of the ceremony of opening the door was very beautiful, and the description of it can be found in the literature of many nations. It was the ceremony of initiation, the ceremony of touching the Inner Reality, which is represented by the bridegroom.

In an Oriental church this ceremony has a deep significance and is performed in a very mysterious way. A priest stands in front of a huge curtain, singing and asking to be taken in. From the inner side another priest, representing the Soul, asks him some questions. After giving the correct answers, the priest on the outside enters while the choir sings joyous hymns. This was referred to in the *New Testament*, where we are told that the veil of the temple was "rent in twain" from top to bottom.

---

[4]*Song of Solomon,* IV and V.

According to the Bible, there was a tabernacle closed by the first veil, which held a candlestick, a table and show-bread. Then there was a second veil, behind which was another tabernacle, called the Holy of Holies, containing the golden pot that held manna and Aaron's rod that had budded....Thus there was an innermost tabernacle called the Holy of Holies, another in front of it called the Sanctuary, and an outer court. We must consider also that only the high priest, symbolically the Soul, could enter into the Holy of Holies.

In this wonderful symbolism we have described for us:

    a. The outer court — the personality and a veil.

    b. The Sanctuary — the Soul, the Son and a veil.

    c. The Holy of Holies — the Divine Spark or the real spiritual man — where we can have direct contact with the Great Presence.

To realize his own essence, man must throughout the ages rend these "veils" which separate the personality from the Soul and his soul from the spiritual fire, his true essence.

Let us repeat the words of Solomon: "My sister, my love, my dove, my undefiled, open to me..." and, at the same time, let us imagine the *Master* Who knocks at the door. In the Bible, this picture is given to us in three wonderful events. The first has already been mentioned. The second is found in the *New Testament* where the Master of the Bridegroom is returning from the wedding and knocking at the door. The third description is more mysterious and beautiful, and is found in *Revelations*, where it is written:

> *Behold I stand at the door, and knock.*
> *If any man hear my voice and open the door,*
> *I will come in to him and will sup with him, and*
> *he with me.*

All these symbols refer to the process of Soul infusion whereby the personality becomes the embodiment of the beauty, inspiration and energy of the Soul, which expresses Itself as knowledge, love and sacrifice. It is interesting to note that the door or the veil is made not of wood, but of cloth, and may be opened from within or without.

In the Ageless Wisdom, we are told that parts of the above-mentioned triplicity (personality, Soul and Divine Spark, or Pure Spirit) are separated by very subtle veils, which both link and separate them from one another. For the personality (the outer court), the existence of the first veil is a safety valve. Without the protection of the veil, the energies and inspirations coming from the Soul would burn and destroy the personality. The veils also transmute the incoming or outgoing energies and forces according to the capacity of the personality and transmit them to the vehicles.

The ceremony of knocking at the door means communion which the Soul wants to establish with the personality when It finds that the latter is "undefiled" and can open the door, or is ready to receive spiritual energies. When the man hears the "knock" he is first an aspirant, then a disciple at the portal of initiation. Every knock on the door is a vision, an inspiration, an invitation to the personality.

In esoteric literature, these veils are called "the dweller of the threshold" which close the entry into higher planes. The personality in itself is a veil. In the Ageless Wisdom, esoteric instructions are given which are called "bridge-building processes." The bridges are those lines of communication which are established when the gaps between the veils are bridged, or the curtains are destroyed. One span connects the integrated personality to Soul-consciousness, another connects the Soul-infused personality to the spiritual Essence, and the last span ascends to the Spark. Although the spans have separate links, they are parts of the same bridge.[5]

In esoteric literature the completed bridge is called the Rainbow Bridge, through which man achieves continuity of consciousness; he can be aware of his Soul's activity, he can raise his consciousness to the astral and mental planes, he can achieve Monadic communication, and he can register these in his brain all at the same time. Also, he can, at will, enter sleep and, emerging from his body, consciously communicate with his fellow disciples and Souls and remember these events in detail in his waking consciousness.

In the ancient *Upanishads*, we find the following significant words: "Whoever knows the Thread (the bridge) and the inner Ruler, knows God, knows the worlds, knows the souls, knows all."[6]

...After the Spark achieves the stage of Personality He should move forward until He experiences at-one-ment, a mystic marriage with the Solar Angel. This is the stage in which the light of the Solar Angel embraces the unfolding Monad, dispersing accumulated hindrances around Him and stimulating radiation of the Spark, the core of the Monad. This mystic marriage is called the process of Soul infusion. After Soul infusion man is on his way to another stage.

For the first time man feels that he is not the body, not the emotions, not the mind, but a still higher entity; an entity not limited by his three vehicles or by time and space.

---

[5]See *Christ, The Avatar of Sacrificial Love*, Chapter 19, about veils.
[6]*The Hidden Glory of the Inner Man*, pp. 36-39.

This realization slowly deepens and he learns that to be a Soul means to be free from the limitations of all his vehicles and to be aware of a plan in the universe, a plan with a great purpose behind it.

The Solar Angel is still present until the Fourth Initiation which is a stage of great expansion of awareness. When the unfolding human soul enters into the Fourth Initiation he has built the Rainbow Bridge between the mental unit and the mental permanent atom. With the help of the Solar Angel he has built the higher bridge between the mental unit and the Spiritual Triad which is actually the domain or vehicle of the Solar Angel. At the Fourth Initiation when the Chalice or the Causal Body is destroyed, the Solar Angel departs. It often leaves Its own buddhic-atmic vestures to man who uses them until his vestures become ready at the Fifth Initiation. Man is now a Soul. The physical, emotional and mental bodies or the "personality vehicle" now presents a mechanism through which the Human Soul, functioning in the Spiritual Triad, expresses Himself in these three lower worlds and uses them as fields of service. Here man is a duality. He will be a unity when he enters his monadic consciousness.[7]

Until man achieves continuity of consciousness, he is under the direct supervision of his Solar Angel who watches over the developing human soul while he is in incarnation and while he is out of incarnation. After the man passes away, he is still in the hands of the Angel, but he is not conscious of this fact. When he enters into the process of birth, the Angel hovers above the embryo until he is born. Thus, age after age, the Solar Angel watches, inspires and tries to

---

[7] *Cosmos in Man*, pp. 40-41.

establish communication with the human soul as It leads him to his destiny.

There is a mysterious announcement in the *New Testament*, which became the stumbling stone for many an honest person; it says, "No man can go to the Father except through me." This is a very occult statement; "through me" means through the Christ, or Christos, the "hope of glory" within man, the "Path." Actually, Christos means the Savior, the Liberator; it also means a state of Consciousness, Soul Consciousness. No man can pass to the Father Consciousness, except through Soul Consciousness, or Son Consciousness. This Son, this Soul, or State of Consciousness, is called in the Ageless Wisdom, the *Solar Angel*, the Guardian Light within the man.

No man can enter into conscious immortality except by raising himself to the consciousness of that Inner Guide and becoming fused with It. It is this state of consciousness that is symbolically represented as the marriage between bride and groom. You will find this symbology in all Sufi literature, and in Christian literature. The Song of Solomon is a great epic about this fusion between the unfolding human soul and the Beloved, the Inner Guide, Whom we call the Solar Angel.[8]

It is beautiful to listen to the Inner Guide's voice. By paying attention to it, we become identified with our divinity. By not listening to it, we become an effect. Soul infusion comes when we listen and become one with It.[9]

Soul infusion means a gradual awakening to the purpose of Creation and ever-increasing awareness of the part the

---

[8]*Ibid.*, p. 194.

[9]*The Psyche and Psychism*, p. 276.

individual plays in the fulfillment of the Divine Purpose. Soul infusion not only gives this prospect; it generates in man an inner urge to participate in the Cosmic Purpose by doing his share according to the level of his achievement. Soul infusion provides man with endurance and enthusiasm to continue his high-level activities of light, despite difficulties, obstacles and trials. Nothing can stop his unfoldment and service. He feels a fountain of inspiration and courage within him which changes all his obstacles and problems into creative urges. From this moment on, man starts to walk as a disciple of the great principles. He is aware that he has a Guide, the Solar Angel; he is also aware that he is living, feeling and thinking in the light of that Presence according to the Plan. This he sees in the eyes of the agelong Presence. He has become a liberated person.[10]

> *When, therefore, your life is fundamentally invocative, then there will come the evocation of the will. It is only truly invocative when personality and soul are fused and functioning as a consciously blended and focussed unit.*[11]

SOUL INFUSION

The human soul and the Solar Angel are fused. This is "the marriage in heaven," when the mental field is irradiated with the light of consciousness of both the Solar Angel and the human soul. This is achieved during the first, second and third initiations.[12]

---

[10]*The Hidden Glory of the Inner Man*, p. 127.

[11]Bailey, A.A., *The Rays and the Initiations*, p. 35. (Excerpt from *The Science of Becoming Oneself*, p. 92.)

[12]*The Psyche and Psychism*, p. 915.

As the process of disidentification of the human soul goes on, the influence of the Solar Angel increases upon the personality, or, better to say, upon the three lower vehicles. The time comes when the three vehicles radiate the light of the Solar Angel in Its full power and beauty. This stage is called Soul infusion, and we have now a soul-infused personality.

But there is a deeper story. In Egyptian mythology we have a very significant legend in which we are told that Osiris, the king, was mutilated. His head was cut, his body was broken into pieces, his internal organs were removed, and all the parts of his body were scattered over land, sea and air. But Horus, the son of Osiris, with his four children collected the parts of the body of Osiris, reconstructed his body and restored life in it; then Osiris began to talk. Later, when Osiris decided to go to heaven, Horus and another king presented him with a ladder on which he stepped into heaven and entered into the company of the shining and living gods.

This legend has the whole story of the descent of the spirit into matter, into the threefold personality, where the Spark was mutilated, diffused, and scattered in the physical, emotional and mental worlds — earth, sea and air — and was lost as the *Lost Word*.

Horus is the Solar Angel who is the real magnet in man. He is gathering this diffused and scattered spirit into a human soul who, through the process of initiations, is becoming whole and entering within the compass of the kingdom of God. He is becoming a liberated soul, and then, through building the Antahkarana with the help of the Solar Angel, he is rising to himself, to his kingship.

Actually, the great disciple, Paul, knew about this mystery when he was writing to the Galatians: "My little children, of whom I travail in birth again until Christ be formed in you."[13]

The process of alignment resembles the process of tuning an orchestra with its many kinds of instruments.

Let us assume that our orchestra has seven mandolins, seven guitars, seven violins and one piano.[14] The mandolins cannot play any real music if they are not in tune individually and with each other. Let us say that the mandolins represent the physical-etheric body with all its systems. Now these mandolins cannot respond accurately to the touch of the artist to produce beautiful music if they are not in tune, individually and as a group. In like manner the physical body cannot be used as a creative instrument if it has no harmony, if it is not in tune with itself and its many parts. This applies also to the guitars, which, let us say, symbolize the emotional body or the emotional nature of man. This applies also to the violins, which, let us assume, symbolize the mental body or the mental nature of man.

Now assume these three kinds of instruments wish to play together. The mandolins are tuned up among themselves. The guitars and the violins are also tuned up individually and by themselves. But suppose the tone of the first kind of instrument is flatter than the second, and the third is two tones sharper. Can they play music together? Of course not. They can produce noise, but not music. Now what can they do?

---

[13]Galatians 4:19, *Holy Bible*, New Analytical Version. (Excerpt from *The Science of Meditation*, pp. 116-117.)

[14]See the "Seven and Sevens," Ch. 14, *The Science of Becoming Oneself.*

These three kinds of instruments must get together and tune up their strings with one another. Then if the first instrument plays the note G, all the other instruments will respond with the same note. Now they are in tune. Now they can make music. This means that the physical body, the emotional body and the mental body are aligned, and they can act as a unit to perform advanced works because now there is closer communication and closer responsiveness between these three bodies than before the tuning. If any "note" is played on any of these bodies it passes to the others without obstruction and friction, and to each stimulus all these three respond harmoniously but in different tonalities. When this is achieved, we say that the man is an integrated personality.

Now suppose these three instruments will play with a piano. These three groups of instruments can change their tones, but not the piano. So these three groups of instruments are forced to tune themselves with the piano.

The piano does not vary its tone. It is set. The piano symbolizes the Soul, and the instruments will take their key from the piano and tune themselves to its note. Now all mandolins, all guitars and all violins begin a process of tuning. This takes quite a long time, until the exact note of the piano resounds through the notes of the other three groups of instruments. When this is achieved we say that man is a Soul-infused personality. Soul infusion is a process in which man creates an unimpeded line of communication between all vehicles and the Soul; the fiery note of the Soul is finding response in its three instruments, producing a shining beauty.

Once this perfect alignment and communication is reached within and between the bodies, the disciple is able to withdraw himself into the higher planes of the mind in order to absorb the light, the love and the power of the Soul and transfer it down to all the lives of the lower vehicles. This is the moment in which the piano is the soloist and all the rest of the instruments are absolutely quiet. Man is in Soul contact and the symphony of the Soul radiates out to space. This is achieved in a moment of deep meditation.

Then comes the descent, and all instruments of all three bodies are ready to begin again their part of the work and translate into their own levels the idea, the vision, the beauty seen and experienced in the light of the Soul.

Inspiration and creativity are not possible until the disciple learns how to align his bodies with the Soul.

The three bodies must be refined and tuned; they must have a high degree of sensitivity and the power to respond accurately. Then they will be able to register the "music," the ideas, touched on the Soul levels and translate them mentally, emotionally and physically, without distorting their original beauty.

The works of great artists touch you on all your levels. You enjoy them physically, emotionally, mentally and spiritually. But to understand them completely you must develop a high degree of alignment between the personality and the Soul, so that you may respond to them with all your refined and aligned levels.

We should not think that alignment is an easy process. Those who were able to align their bodies with the Soul worked very hard. They have passed through physical, emotional and mental discipline until they could work consciously with their bodies and eventually learn the art of perfect alignment. Many, many lives are dedicated to tuning one's individual instruments; many more lives in tuning them together. These lives are called the Path of Probation, or the path of inspiration, on which the bodies are refined and gradually aligned.

After this cycle is over, man enters the Path of Discipleship, where he learns to align his personality vehicles with the Soul.[15]

...The first source of right inspiration is your **Inner Guide** or your Solar Angel. If you live physically, emotionally and mentally along the lines of beauty, goodness, righteousness, joy, and freedom, the contact between you and your Inner Guide becomes stronger and stronger, and your Guide inspires you in every action, feeling and thought. Eventually you and the Inner Guide become one. This is the experience of *Soul infusion*.[16]

A person who has Soul infusion will have the ability to transform his vices into virtues, utilizing his vices as fertilizing elements for his virtues.[17]

Transmutation is the result of the action of *fire*. We transmute our physical body, for example, through the fire of mind used through *concentration*. Actually, concentration is the response of the man to the evolutionary process and to the magnetic pull of the Solar Angel.

Transmutation leads us to the first major expansion of consciousness, in which the physical body and the life force are under the control of the human soul.

On higher levels this means that personality force is superseded by the energy of the Solar Angel, in transmuting

---

[15]*The Science of Meditation*, pp. 99-101.

[16]*Challenge for Discipleship*, pp. 358-359.

[17]*Ibid.*, p. 375

desire into aspiration and aspiration into determination. This leads into the process of *transformation*.

Transformation is mostly concerned with the astral body. When the "motion" of the astral body changes into the quality of rhythm, we say that the astral body is transformed, and the intuitional substance has taken the place of the astral substance. It is here that desire changes into aspiration, or the desire of *havingness* becomes aspiration toward *beingness*. Man ceases to have the desire of accumulation and develops the aspiration to be. This is the quality of a disciple, and as he progresses on the Path the energy of buddhi becomes his light and the source of his inspiration.

We are told that the transforming agent is the Soul, and the nature of the Soul is *solar fire*. The transformation occurs when the man opens a channel through occult meditation for this fire to flow down. Transformation leads us to the second major expansion of consciousness, which is called the second initiation of the threshold. Transformation of the astral body and of desire into aspiration leads the disciple into Transfiguration. And on the path of Transfiguration he becomes a true *Initiate*.

The agent of Transfiguration is the *electric fire* of the Spiritual Triad, which gradually pours down to the personality vehicles through the process of advanced meditation or contemplation. This light of the Spiritual Triad, which works through the higher mind, releases the lights of the atoms of the three bodies of the personality and produces that great experience which is called Enlightenment or Transfiguration. It is with this achievement that the astral body disappears with all its glamors, the illusions of the mental body are washed away, and the man stands in the light of the Spiritual Triad....

In Transmutation the fire of mind is invoked. "Let light descend on Earth" (physical-etheric earth).

In Transformation the Love of the Great Soul is invoked. "May Christ return to Earth."...

In Transfiguration the fire of the Triad is released. ... "Let purpose guide the little wills of men."...[18]

As we stand in the glory of our Soul, of our Master, of our Great Lord, we pass through the fire of transformation. In this transformation, we pass through purification; the Plan is seen more clearly; our willpower to serve and sacrifice increases, and the star of the purpose of life shines within our Souls.[19]

---

[18]*The Science of Meditation,* pp. 159-160.
[19]*The Psyche and Psychism,* p. 1159.

22

Contemplation

A mind free of thought can be achieved through the practice of contemplation, which is fusion with the Inner Light, the Inner Being, but this can be accomplished only after the mind is totally purified by the fire of true thinking — *true meditation.*

Contemplation is a state in which man is no longer identified with his own mental plane or mental substance, but is free to communicate with the Inner Being and to reflect the beauty of this contact in the mirror of his mind.[1]

In contemplation your mind is not blank, but reflects the things your Soul sees in the higher mental and Intuitional planes.[2]

The mechanism of contemplation is as follows:

    a. The evolving human soul gradually controls the lower mind, and stops its mechanical modifications or responses. This is learned through concentration and meditation.

    b. Gradually the real man, or the evolving, unfolding human soul, or the fallen spark, builds a bridge between the Solar Angel

---

[1] *The Psyche and Psychism,* p. 713.
[2] *Ibid.,* p. 781

and the four levels of the lower mind, and slowly penetrates into the realms of the Thinker, the Inner Reality.

He experiences the intense love, the ageless light, and the irresistible will of the Inner Thinker, Who stands there as the representative of the Planetary Logos, for the Plan, and as a path to the Purpose of that glorious Being. This is just the prelude to contemplation, through which great masterpieces come into the world, masterpieces in all branches of human endeavor.

c. In the next stage the mental substance, as a bright and scintillating sphere of light, polarizes toward the Inner Thinker. All modifications are stopped and the brain, as a magnetic plate, is polarized toward the mind.

The unfolding human soul, using his powerful intention, starts to climb through the Rainbow Bridge with the will power latent in him and slowly enters into the sphere of the Solar Angel. For a short moment his "eyes" meet the Eyes of the Soul, and he sees, through the Eyes of the Soul, the wonders of creation and the ever-growing Plan. This is the moment of blissful joy, ecstasy, illumination and inspiration. The unfolding human soul looks at the wonder of the higher worlds but does not pass any message to the lower mind, which waits in great expectancy. When this blessed moment of contemplation is over a great stream of joy descends toward the lower vehicles; then the real man sends down those messages which are needed for the working out of the Plan, and those energies which are needed to push and reveal the Plan all over the world. Contemplation is "seeing" through the Eye of the Solar Angel with the eye of the unfolding human soul. Two eyes are united.[3]

Real contemplation leads us toward work and service with clear understanding of the Plan and the need of the time. Thus contemplation is a real contact or an act of fusion, a marriage between the Thinker and the human soul. This contact is an open window toward Infinity, where the soul goes often to renew his vision and to bring down new beauties for the service of humanity.

Contemplation is a great experience of your reality as a soul. Only in true contemplation can you detach yourself from your brain and mind, observe them as your tools, and feel your identity in the light of the Soul. Only in contemplation can you truly experience the existence of the Thinker within you as an ageless Silent Watcher, Who watched your steps since the Lemurian times throughout your incarnations.[4]

In contemplation the human soul is in his greatest tension as he tries to synchronize his own vibration with the radiation of the Thinker. While in great tension his recognition grows as he merges and fuses with the Solar Angel, the Nirvani, or the Inner Lord, as It is called in various places.

The predominating energy, which is released at the time of contemplation, is will energy or the life aspect of the Existence. The energy of abundant life floods all the vehicles of man, and he becomes magnetic and radioactive....[5]

---

[3]*The Science of Meditation*, pp. 163-164.

[4]*Ibid.*, p. 164.

[5]*Ibid.*, pp. 164-165.

Contemplation for the disciple is face-to-face communication with the vision of the Thinker, and is a source of inspiration and illumination....[6]

...Contemplation is an act of Soul infusion in which the fountain of joy and the blueprints of the Plan are touched....[7]

---

[6]*Ibid.*, p. 166.

[7]*Christ, The Avatar of Sacrificial Love*, p. 35.

23

Positive Effects
of
Soul Contact

SOUL CONSCIOUSNESS AND ITS SOCIAL EFFECTS

My warriors, guard thyselves with the Shield of God's Will, and the Divine Song will ever find echo within thee. Before the Deluge, when men were wedding and feasting and bargaining, Noah was already selecting the most stalwart oaks for his Ark.[1]

—M.M.—

Once a person recognizes himself as a soul, and affirms that he is a soul, an immense change takes place in his life. A great flood of light pours into his mind and clears away the agelong obstacles, illusions and thoughtforms that have kept him a slave of his past.

The first effect of this change is that energy accumulates in him. Because he does not misuse it, he no longer has any leakage due to wrong thinking and negative emotions. Therefore he continuously receives precipitation of energy. Such a person has become a fountain of power which heals, uplifts and leads.

The second effect of the change is that the person becomes an agent of liberation in his social and national

---

[1] Agni Yoga Society, *Leaves of Morya's Garden*, Vol. I, para. 120.

environment. He works to liberate the human soul from all inertia, glamors and illusions which are making our planet a place of sorrow, slavery, racial discrimination, fear, prejudice and selfishness. This task will put tremendous pressure on his vehicles and cause him much suffering ... and joy.

The third effect of Soul consciousness is the creation of simplicity in living and sincerity of expression.

The fourth effect is a dynamic sense of communication and right human relations. We cannot create right human relations until a large percentage of humanity becomes Soul conscious and realizes the supreme meaning of the words:

"The sons of men are one
and I am one with them."

The fifth effect will be transmutation of a person into a magnetic and radioactive personality, who will automatically group people around him to serve the cause of human liberation. The universal or global revolution has not started yet. Greater revolutionists will gradually appear in all the fields of human endeavor, and this time they will inflame the hearts and souls of all true humanitarians throughout the world who will be charged with the spirit of greater dedication, aspiration and sacrifice. These leaders, having achieved Soul consciousness, will not stop at any obstacle, and through stupendous self-sacrifice, they will lead humanity as a whole toward a higher dimension of living. The introduction of this is set forth in part in the Universal Declaration of Human Rights and in the United Nations' Charter.

Throughout the ages, opponents of progress for humanity and its unfoldment have opposed the universal liberation of mankind, the concepts of soul and immortality, and man's transformation into Divinity. Soul consciousness will end all religious, political and financial exploitation, thus leading humanity progressively forward. The coming revolution can be kept on the mental level, without tears or bloodshed, if the greater percentage of humanity responds to the rays of the new age and synchronizes all its life expressions with them. If the greater part of humanity does not respond to the keynote of the new age, however, and if the political, economic and social conditions continue as they are at present, then the leaders of the new age, the Soul conscious people, and all people who are dedicated to the liberation of humanity will arise and the revolution of the planet will commence. This will be a revolution for the liberation of all humanity and will be the most crucial revolution in the history of the planet.

To the degree that a person approaches his Soul and becomes a Soul does he become an independent human being and a being of greater cooperation. Many people think that independence is conditioned by outer events, but in reality it starts from within. Man cannot be independent unless he breaks all the inner chains, the inner slavery, and the inner imprisonment. Once freed from inertia, glamors and illusions, he enters the freedom of his Soul consciousness and becomes an independent, self-activated, and self-determined person. Before this inner freedom has been achieved, his outer freedom contributes only to his own destruction and suffering.

Education and knowledge often lead man to group or national independence, to attacks and wars. Soul consciousness does not work for personal, group or national freedom alone; it works for the planetary and global independence and leads to an everlasting sense of unity, because the Soul is group conscious and stands for all humanity and its highest good.

When people who stand above racial discrimination, religious separation, dogmas, and doctrines increase on the planet, they will recognize one another and will hold each other's hands from east to west and from north to south. Then a new dawn will break upon humanity and "the orphan of the planet," mankind itself, will experience a great release of joy which has been imprisoned within man for ages and ages due to human slavery and ignorance. This will be the age of health, trust, joy, understanding and cooperation.

The sixth effect of Soul consciousness will be the elimination of the fear of death and the acquisition of a continuous radiation of sacrifice for one's fellow man.

The seventh effect is a universal sense of harmlessness and a deep, fiery devotion to the flame of life in every form, from the flowers on the earth to stars in the firmament.

Then the vision of St. John will come true:

> *And I saw a new heaven and a new earth; for the first heaven and the first earth had passed away and the sea was no more ... and He shall wipe away all tears from their eyes; and there shall be no more death, neither sorrow nor wailing, neither shall there be any more pain....*[2]

---

[2]*The Hidden Glory of the Inner Man*, pp. 135-138.

"Let the soul control the outer form, and life, and all events."

The soul in us is the sense of unity. As we have a sense of smell, a sense of taste, a sense of touch, etc., so also do we have a sense which can be called **the Soul.** This sense is the sense of unity, it operates for unity, and it is expressed only by acts of unity because it stands for unity.

A man's soul is the eye of his true Self, and this eye when opened sufficiently can see only unity in the diversity of forms. It sees the essence which expresses itself in manifold ways, means, colors and forms.

Let this sense control our outer form, and life, and all events.

Let all these be expression of Soul, of harmony, with the interests of all at heart. Let our mouths speak the language of the Soul. Let our feet walk the path of the Soul. Let our minds operate in the light of the Soul, and let all events be expressions of that inner sense of beauty and unity.

"And bring to light the love that
underlies the happenings of the time."

Underlying the happenings of the time are the law of justice, the law of cause and effect, and love. Love is not a sentiment but rather a universal law which underlies the waves of the ocean of life. It is not the direct cause of waves (happenings) but it underlies all waves and motion. The waves and agitation are caused by various agents, but the ocean remains as one whole — unmoved. Let our Soul, one of our higher senses, bring us to the understanding that no matter how threatening the waves of the events are, eventually they will subside because divine love is the ocean and that love eventually will enlighten us and enable us to understand the purpose for which we have been placed on this planet in this little solar system.[3]

How can you, the human soul, be the friend of your physical body, your emotional body and your mental body, as well as your own friend? Many people complain, "I am very lonely; nobody loves me...." But if for one minute you realize that you have the greatest friend within yourself, you will never feel this way.

Every human being has a great friend within himself, and that is the Guardian Angel or the Inner Presence, the source of inspiration, the source of Beauty, Goodness and Truth within you. Even if you have never heard about this "fellow," he is your best friend. Even if you have never heard of him, you often talk with him.

I have seen many people who, when they are alone, say, "What am I going to do now?" To whom are they talking? They know instinctively that there is someone within them, and they ask that unseen Presence, "What am I going to do now?"

This kind of expression immediately reveals that instinctively you are feeling a Presence within you and you are talking with that Presence. **When this Inner Guardian is contacted and if you make It your friend, you will see that It will inspire ten things in you:**

1.   When you start contacting this Great Presence within you, you will be filled with love. Because It inspires you to love, you will want to love the physical, emotional and mental bodies more and not do anything wrong to these bodies. For example, if you love your body, you give it rest

---

[3]*Five Great Mantrams of the New Age,* pp. 27-28.

so that it sleeps. If you love your body, you always try to make it healthy. If you love your body, you do not pour a bottle of whiskey down its throat. If you love your body, you clean it and feed it the right food. You take the love from the Inner Presence and give it to the physical body.

2. When you come a little closer to your Inner Presence, It gives you harmony because Its nature is harmony. You think harmoniously; you feel harmoniously; you live harmoniously within your family, within your group, within your nation, within humanity. You bring harmony between the three bodies and you and the Inner Guardian. Your whole instrument is now healthy because it is harmonized, and so the Inner Guardian can play Its music on this harmonized instrument.

If this instrument is not in tune, how and what is the Inner Guardian going to play? It hits the note A, but the body sounds a different note. Only if the mental, emotional and physical bodies and the human soul are harmonized with the Inner Guardian can the beauty, goodness and power of the Inner Guardian radiate out.

When this beauty radiates out, the first results are health, joy and intelligence. The mechanism is now functioning in the right way. It is not distorted. We call this personality health, personality joy, personality intelligence.

3. If you increase your contact with the Inner Guardian, some kind of striving starts within your personality. The physical body says, "I am going to exercise, jump and do things so that I am beautiful," because the soul says, "Friend, be healthy. I want you to be beautiful so that I can do lots of things. I do not want you to be sick because I can do nothing if you are sick."

The soul inspires striving in the physical body, in the emotions and in the mind. Emotional striving is aspiration toward higher beauties. Mental striving is aspiration toward more knowledge, research, penetration and depth....

4. Then solemnity starts. The Solar Angel inspires the human soul to be solemn. Solemnity means that mentally, emotionally and physically, with your thoughts, with your words and with your actions, you always try to live in the presence of God.

5. After solemnity is proven in your life, the Solar Angel transmits another light in your personality, called enthusiasm. The ancient Greeks called enthusiasm the "Fire of the Gods." Gradually your physical, emotional and mental atoms start burning in the fourth, fifth, sixth and seventh dimensions, and the burning increases. Because it increases, everything you do, say and think becomes totally charged with fire. This is why one enthusiastic person can change a group and three enthusiastic people can change a nation — because they are fiery.

6. If this continues, all your thoughts, your emotional reactions, actions and responses, and your physical actions become righteous. Righteousness is not easy. The five above qualities must be achieved before you become righteous....

As you do not deceive your bodies, you do not deceive yourself and you do not deceive others. You must be really pure in your consciousness in order to be pure to others. But people often start the other way. They say, "Speak truth to them. Express love toward them." How can someone express love if he does not have love within himself? How can someone be righteous if he does not have righteousness within himself?

The foundation of cultures and civilizations is man. You yourself must be beautiful in order to be a beautiful stone in the temple of God. If you are not beautiful, you cannot make others beautiful. You can talk beautifully; you can dress beautifully; you can write beautifully; but you cannot change people and make them beautiful if in your essence you are not beautiful. This is because when you talk, invisible frequencies, rays, and energies flow through your words and reach people's brains subliminally and say, "He is talking very beautifully, but don't believe him. Inside, he is not righteous."

7. **If you become righteous, the Solar Angel gives you a greater responsibility: It says that you are going to be noble.** Nobility is graduation into kingship. When you feel you are integrated with the Solar Angel, you act nobly, you think nobly, you speak nobly, you feel nobly, and all your relations are noble.

8. **After you are noble, the Inner Guide inspires you — to paint, to compose, to write, to speak, to heal, to discover, to build.** You receive inspiration to serve and fly. Inspiration is like the wind in your sails. You are on the ocean with floppy sails, and suddenly the wind comes and fills your sails and your boat starts to fly across the water.

9. **Then the Inner Guides gives you guidance.** Guidance means that you now have full knowledge to lead people, to guide people, to see them exactly as they are, and not to be deceived by phenomena, bribery and flattery. You know exactly what is in the hearts of other people, because you have the guiding light within you. And because you have that guiding light within you, you become a light for others. This is how you build friendship. You become your own friend, and you become the friend of your Solar Angel.

When this friendship is formed, you become the friend of humanity and the friend of God. God trusts you because you are a friend.

There is a very beautiful Sufi writing which says that advanced Initiates are the friends of God. A friend of God is someone to whom every secret is entrusted....

10. The Inner Guide inspires in you self-respect. Not so many people know what they essentially are. They think they are equal to their body, possessions, certificates, positions, knowledge or deeds. And because all these are not solid measures, during life and its many problems they become confused about themselves and lose their respect for their own Self....

Once a person begins to realize what he is in his essence, he begins to live a respectful life. He never thinks, speaks, or acts in ugly ways to lose his own respect for his Self.

A self-respectful person not only respects himself, but he also respects others. He tries not to be disrespectful to others, and he evokes from them a mutual respect. Such a person has no jealousy. Whenever someone else is respected, he feels he is respected too. Whoever respects him, he feels that person respects himself. He always tries to live in a way that evokes respect from others.

He educates himself to serve, and through service he earns money. He lives in a nice house. He drives a good car. He dresses well. He takes care of the Divinity in him. Whatever he has, he believes belongs to the Self Who is one with the All-Self....

How can you come closer to the Solar Angel? As you exercise love, you come a little closer. As you exercise harmony, you come closer. As you exercise striving, solemnity, enthusiasm, righteousness and nobility; as you receive more inspiration from higher sources; as you guide yourself with higher principles, you fuse yourself and your bodies with the Inner Light and become a Soul-infused personality.

A Soul-infused personality means that you are now absorbed in the light of the Inner Presence, and It is radiating Its light through you. The transformation took place. You are now in the stage which we call the *transfiguration experience*. Transfiguration is the moment when you suddenly realize that you are not the same person. You totally change; your measures change; your relationships change....

When you become the friend of your bodies and the friend of your Inner Guardian, you become healthier, happier and more energetic. But if you become the enemy of your bodies and do not have good relations with your Inner Presence, you develop various tensions, sicknesses and insanity. When you are in harmony with your Inner Guardian, you live in light, in love, and in power, and you handle your bodies in the best way possible, just as you handle your car and keep it up-to-date to meet the requirements of the highways of life....

Once you become the friend of your vehicles and the friend of your Inner Presence, people will look at you as their friend because you will become a source of blessing for them.

> *Let a man lift himself by his own Self. Let him not degrade himself. For the Self alone is the friend of the self, and the self alone is his own enemy.*[4]

---

[4]*The Bhagavad Gita*, translated by H. (Torkom) Saraydarian, Chapter 6, Verse 5. (Excerpt from *Challenge for Discipleship*, pp. 211-214,216,217.)

Soul impression is very different from channeling. **The following are signs of Soul impression:**

1. It is in the nature of inspiration and is always related to the hierarchical Plan, and to the service of the Plan.

2. It charges the subject and increases his creativity, vitality and joy.

3. The man becomes more magnetic.

4. He understands all that he receives and intuitively agrees with it. Soul impressions are not formulated phrases or orders, as is the case in channeling, but waves of Beauty, Goodness, Truth which the subject himself formulates and uses according to the need.

5. In Soul impression there is always a new Teaching. It is just like the continuation of the building of wisdom. There is always a new angle, a new approach, a greater depth, a greater synthesis. The Soul never wants to repeat what is given already. If the subject is not aware of an instruction given years ago, he directs the man to the right book or to the right teacher to learn it. The Soul always respects the law of economy.

6. Soul impression deals with wholes and in the interest of all humanity.

7. Impressions coming from the Soul first express themselves as virtues, such as humility, harmlessness, sense of unity, sincerity, simplicity and so on. Then they deal with the expansion of consciousness and service. Thus, a man who formulates spiritual impressions is a man who lives up to the standard shown in his speech and written words.

8. Soul impressions evoke higher mental and intuitional responses, being highly organized and charged with universal ideas and visions.

9. Those who receive impressions are highly organized, Soul-infused personalities. They have highly developed minds, hearts and intuitive faculties. They are intensely creative in many fields, and have long years of service behind them.

10. Those receptive to Soul impressions turn into powerhouses of psychic energy, which encourage, heal, lead and protect others.

11. Those who receive Soul impressions have increasing control on their urges and drives and the power to transmute them into their higher correspondences.

12. Those receiving Soul impressions never make self-claims, but labor hard and sacrifice. They do not make demands, but let the Law of Karma work for them.

13. When a man is in contact with his Soul, his field of service expands gradually.

14. Soul impression, when registered and worked out over a period of time, leads man into ashramic contacts. This contact reveals to him his further responsibilities and duties.

To protect ourselves against distortion we need to learn the science of meditation, which is the science of contact with the Transpersonal Self or the Soul. Only through such a contact can we enlighten our minds, and draw psychic energy into our aura, which eventually turns into a shield.

The nature of evolution is that we ourselves, through our own hands and feet, must solve our problems and protect ourselves. Outside protection and guidance gradually are taken away so that man learns to stand on his own feet. So-called "spirits" often promise to protect us, but they disappear in our darkest hours. The help that we receive from our Innermost Core never diminishes, but year after year, it increases and turns into a powerhouse of courage, striving and daring.

Those who come in contact with their Souls are naturally protected by the Hierarchy. Those who are in conscious contact with the Hierarchy are invincible.[5]

...[An] individual's past memories, the failures of the present, and uncertainty of the future can have no effect on a disciple whose consciousness is focused on Soul levels. He is not occupied with his little self and its affairs, but he is highly oriented toward the Plan and is extremely busy serving the Plan.[6]

Immortality is sensed immediately when your Soul eliminates the prisons of your physical, emotional and mental limitations....[7]

...It is in Shamballa that the message of the Solar Lord is analyzed and proper steps are taken to transmit it to the Hierarchy.

The transmitted message from Shamballa is worked out by the seven main Ashrams as the seven main Teachings within the seven human endeavors. Thus the message turns into a Teaching related to politics, education, communication or philosophy, arts, sciences, religions and economics.

The central note in all of them is clear within the Ashrams, but as the Teaching merges with the lower strata of the human mind, the keynote fades away, and each department of human endeavor carries out its work separately. As the human mind develops, holistic movements

---

[5]*The Psyche and Psychism*, pp. 98-100.
[6]*The Science of Meditation*, p. 213.
[7]*The Flame of Beauty, Culture, Love, Joy*, p. 34.

appear, which are nothing else but efforts to find the keynote of the seven human endeavors.

The Solar Angel in each human being is a member of the Hierarchy, and It directly receives Its instructions from the Christ. The human soul, being identified with the physical, emotional and mental vehicles and entrapped by maya, glamors and illusions, often receives very little light from the Solar Angel, Who tries through deep meditation to reach the developing human soul. As the human soul advances and gets closer to the Solar Angel, he receives more light, more love and more life, and transforms his vehicles and his environment.

On the human level, the Teaching passes to the seven types of thinkers. Those who are on the *political* line use the light to create political ideologies and try to impose the will of the Sun — as far as their level permits them to grasp it — upon the minds of men.

Those who are on the *love-wisdom* line try to create a plan. They try to use the light to unify and synthesize. Ideas formed on this line are intended to harmonize, to teach, to heal. Out of this line come psychiatry, psychology, religious ministries and great philanthropic movements.

Those who are on the line of *philosophy and communication* create ideas related to the deeper meanings of life, to objective and subjective communication. This third type of thinker makes practical use of the Beam of Light given to them by higher sources.

Those who are on the line of *creative arts* use the light for their creative ideas in music, painting, dancing, carving, building, etc. The whole Teaching about all forms of art comes from the Fourth Ray Ashram and is adapted to the level of those who come in contact with this Teaching.

Those who are on the line of *science* use the Beam of Light in their research and discoveries. All knowledge generated in the field of science is a response of the human mind to the Beam of Light coming from above, from the one Teacher, via the man's Solar Angel.

In those who are on the line of *devotion,* the Beam of Light produces religious ideas and aspirational and devotional techniques.

In those who are on the line of *economics and finance,* the Beam of Light reveals all that they need to discover in their field. Thinkers on this line create law and order, ceremonies and rituals.

The Beam of Light brings seven kinds of gifts to the seven types of people who receive their Teaching via their own Teacher, their Solar Angel.

If they are Soul-infused personalities, or in other words, if the human soul is in the radiance of the Solar Angel and has direct communication with It, the ideas coming to him are pure, interrelated, and directed to the same overall purpose. If the human soul is focused in the lower levels of the personality, he receives distorted ideas; he builds illusions and misuses the light for his personal and separative interests.

The Teacher for the Hierarchy and for the seven lines of human endeavors is the Christ. The transmitters are the Master and Solar Angels.[8]

...Purity of mind is achieved when the mind thinks in the light of the Inner Guide and for the greatest good of the greatest number of people....[9]

---

[8]*The Psyche and Psychism,* pp. 492-493.
[9]*Ibid.,* p. 209.

The personality searches for pleasure and comfort, but the developing human soul, once contacting the Inner Guide, no longer is trapped by pleasure and comfort....[10]

When impressions hit our consciousness, the human soul becomes aware or conscious of them. He is not the receiver but the observer. In the early stages, he uses impressions for the interests of his lower bodies. When he advances, he translates the impressions in different dimensions and uses them as stepping stones for his progress. Sometimes his interpretation and the interpretation of the Soul do not agree, and then he has inner conflict. The human soul says, "I want to repeat this sensation. It feels good." The Solar Angel says, "These sensations can trap you and hinder your path."

Most of the time the human soul insists on his own interpretation and continues the way he wants to act. If it happens again and again, the Solar Angel keeps silent so that the human soul learns his lessons through karmic complications.

In the early stages, the field of consciousness, formed by the beam of intelligence, propelled by the Soul, is not accessible to the human soul. That is why he is almost an unconscious being. Later he begins to enter into that light occasionally.[11]

... To awaken means to fuse one's own consciousness with the field of consciousness formed by the beam of intelligence projected from the Inner Guide. Every time you do an unconscious act, you are out of that lighted field. Your

[10]*Ibid.*, p. 228.
[11]*Ibid.*, p. 918.

progress is guaranteed only if you stay in that lighted area and progress upward. That is what cosmic living is.

When we are focused in the lighted area, we have a chance to see the interpretation of the Inner Guide and make a choice. Often we reject Its interpretation, which comes to us as the voice of our Conscience, but we push it away if the pull of lower pleasures is great.

There is another point. The human soul translates the impressions reaching the center through his own level of achievement. We must remember that the consciousness does not receive impressions but reflects them. Sometimes we watch the reflector, sometimes not. Sometimes we do not want to be bothered by the images or impressions reflected on the sensitive field of our consciousness; thus we lose many opportunities to learn and to become aware.

Thinking for the human soul is:

1. seeing the interpretation of the Soul, and

2. reconditioning the field of consciousness by using the lighted substance to build new thoughtforms to explain the interpretation of the Soul.[12]

Through these three methods, observation, concentration, and dedication, the focus of your consciousness is shifted from the lower planes to the mental plane. At this stage you demonstrate increasing creativity. Then gradually you, as a Soul, function on the mental plane as consciously as you worked on the physical plane....

---

[12]*Ibid.*, p. 919.

As the bridge crosses the mental plane, the human soul contacts the Inner Guide consciously, and even sees It face to face. From that moment on the wisdom of the Solar Angel becomes available to him, as he serves humanity in accord with the Plan of the Hierarchy. Then it is very possible that he can have a contact with the Great One Who is watching his evolution age after age.[13]

In the modern understanding, one is a true Disciple of Christ if he is in contact with his own Soul and, through his Soul, with the Christ. Neither titles, position, nor grades confer on anyone the state of being a disciple or a minister of Christ. Priesthood or ministry is not based upon knowledge, diplomas, studies or "authority," but is based upon inner conscious communication with our Soul, with Christ, and upon the resultant life of sacrificial service....[14]

Talent is the result of contact with the Soul. You do not have talent if you are not in contact with the Soul. Your talent increases as you reach greater fusion with your Soul and try to express that fusion creatively.[15]

...Worship increases aspiration and leads often to spiritual ecstasy, which is the result of inspiration coming from the Soul through the process of worship.[16]

During man's lifetime, force is largely used; the force of his lower vehicles with which he is identified. As he begins to focus his consciousness on the higher mental planes and is in touch with his Solar Angel or Spiritual Triad, he begins

---

[13]*Ibid.*, p. 505.

[14]*Christ, The Avatar of Sacrificial Love*, p. 127.

[15]*The Flame of Beauty, Culture, Love, Joy*, p. 57.

[16]*The Psyche and Psychism*, p. 129.

to express energy instead of force....[17]

Consciousness is the result of action of the Solar Angel on the mental plane, the purpose of which is to align all the atoms of the vehicles, thus building a path of light for the returning pilgrim as he endeavors to work out the *Divine Plan*. This energy is called *solar fire*.[18]

The strongest force in the world is an idea, an idea that originates from your Inner Being, who is in contact with the Divine Plan.[19]

...[R]emember that a white magician is a man who stands in the light of his Soul, and operates from there with the soul aspect of all forms.[20]

Creative imagination is a technique of the unfolding human soul, who pushes himself up through his desires and aspirations, and tries to translate all the impressions coming from the Soul, or intuitional levels, as images or symbols upon the higher astral planes....[21]

Energy is produced when the lower atmospheres of the Soul have been cleared of crystallized forms, allowing the light of the Soul to shine forth.[22]

Man steps out of his mental consciousness through the help of the Inner Guide, and for the first time, he senses tremendous synthesis, a tremendous sense of unity, a tremendous clarity

---

[17]*Cosmos in Man,* p. 252.

[18]*Cosmos in Man,* p. 251.

[19]*The Science of Meditation,* p. 144.

[20]*Ibid.,* p. 147.

[21]*Ibid.,* p. 170.

[22]*Cosmos in Man,* p. 254.

of vision. This is a sign that he is entering into the awareness of the Intuitional Plane....[23]

...It is the Soul that can project Its light to the Intuitional Plane and to the world of the personality, revealing them to each other. Once the personality is integrated and fused with the Soul, the light of the intuition creates wonderful responses, as is the case with great artists, scientists or leaders.[24]

Under certain conditions, when the Inner Guide sees that great progress upon the path can be achieved by a disciple, It reflects a part of his past life which has immediate connection with the problem he is facing or with the planes upon which he is contemplating....[25]

In esoteric literature the state in which the consciousness of man functions in the light of his Soul is called the awakened state of consciousness. The state in which man is the victim of his lower self, his glamors, and his illusions is called sleep, or the state of ignorance and darkness. In olden days a person was called ignorant if he had no experience of communication with his Soul and existed within the limits of his five senses. Knowledge comes from within, and a person becomes a true knower when his mind is infused with the light of his Soul. Only then does he begin to realize the depth of his former ignorance and start to use all his new knowledge to work out the Great Plan behind the manifested life.

Only Soul-knowledge can lead us toward happiness, joy and bliss, the state of being our true Selves. The great Sankaracharya says:

---

[23] *Ibid.*, p.116.
[24] *The Science of Becoming Oneself*, p. 141.
[25] *Cosmos in Man*, p. 192-193.

> *There is no higher cause of joy than silence*
> *where no mind pictures dwell; it belongs to him*
> *who has understood the Self's own being, who is*
> *full of the essence of the bliss of the Self.*[26]

...We are told that every cell, every atom in the human mechanism has a nucleus of light. This light increases and becomes more radioactive as man goes deeper into the intuitional world. This is the basic cause of the phenomenon we call Transfiguration. For a longer or shorter period of time the nuclei of light of the three bodies radiate under the impact of the Soul and intuitional light....[27]

...As a man approaches Soul infusion he absorbs greater amounts of Soul energy, or psychic energy and expresses it as goodwill....[28]

People who work for the Masters cannot be called mediums; they are initiates who have succeeded in contacting their own Souls and then their Master, and because they have built the Antahkarana they are able to see things in the light of their Master, and on occasion can express the Teaching or message given to them by their respective Masters either in waking consciousness or in subjective ashrams.[29]

The unfoldment of the petals and flames is also related to the initiations. The first initiation is taken when the first four

---

[26]Sankaracharya, *The Crest Jewel of Wisdom,* Verse 527. (Excerpt from *The Hidden Glory of the Inner Man,* pp. 21-22.)

[27]*The Science of Becoming Oneself,* p. 84.

[28]*Triangles of Fire,* (First Edition) p. 21.

[29]*The Science of Meditation,* p. 218.

flames of the Egoic Lotus are unfolded. We are told that at this time the light of the Solar Angel penetrates into the area of the pineal gland. As a result of this the vital airs in the head scintillate and irradiate light. This affects the atoms of the brain and releases their light. Then three lights are fused into a focused point which appears as a radiant sun.[30]

The emotional body is the battleground of man and of the race. It is here that the first great battle is bitterly fought. On this battleground are both negative and positive forces. Negative forces come from the lower nature and from accumulated past experiences; positive forces come from the higher sources of the Soul or the Intuitional Plane....[31]

It is impossible to win the battle on the emotional plane if we do not stand apart from it on a higher level, the level of the mind. We can fight against the evil army only if we hand the command to the Inner Lord. The Inner Lord can fight upon the emotional battlefield only through the forces and energies of the mind.[32]

...The source of all progressive discoveries, arts and unfoldments is the storehouse of knowledge and wisdom of Soul, into which we try to penetrate through our meditation and radiate the contents through our service for humanity.

The fact that man through meditation or pure thinking finds the answer to his many questions demonstrates the existence of One who knows, One who is willing to help, the One who is within our reach.[33]

---

[30]*The Science of Meditation*, p. 191.
[31]*The Science of Becoming Oneself*, p. 28.
[32]*Ibid.*, p. 29.
[33]*Christ, The Avatar of Sacrificial Love*, p. 120.

It is with ... power of a quick response to the need that real service is rendered and a fellow man is led toward the inner light. The word "quick" has a deep significance here; it is almost an immediate, straight recognition and response that is urged from the Soul level without creating any reaction or friction in the personality. Once the personality reaction is overcome, the true psychic powers start to function.

[Another] ... power is called, *"the correct manipulation of force."* You have your physical force, your emotional and mental forces, your money, your position, your talents and so on. These are all forces. How do you use them? On what level? Toward which goal? Correct manipulation is the key-word. All these forces should be used for the ends of the Divine Plan, for the given cycle and age. And to do this you need the great light of the Soul, and you need to be a Soul before you can be really able to manipulate force correctly.[34]

...Group vibration is the keynote by which groups are recognized and evaluated. Group vibration refers also to the Soul Ray of the group as a whole. Through such a response the individuals, and individual and partial interests are overlooked, and only the group need is responded to. The person no longer serves separative interests, but interests that are dedicated to the group idea, to humanity and to the planet as a whole.

Such a man is sensitive to the Soul aspect of the group, and rejects response to any vibration coming from separative sub-planes. Actually a real group, in its esoteric sense, cannot be a group unless all, or the majority of its members are at least Soul-infused personalities. No group can radiate a uniform vibration unless it is on Soul infusion level....[35]

---

[34]*The Science of Meditation*, p. 222.
[35]*The Psyche and Psychism*, p. 165.

Energy is produced when the lower atmospheres of the Soul have been cleared of crystallized forms, allowing the Light of the Soul to shine forth.

The Soul, one of the main inner energy sources, is like a sun within us. In most people, however, there is a thick layer of clouds between phenomenal man and the Soul. The first step in gaining contact with this inner source of energy is to exercise observation and discrimination between "you" and your vehicles on the three lower planes. Observe the world around you. For a long period of time do not think about what you are seeing; just observe things as they are. Then start to use your power of discrimination and see both the illusion and reality; the constructive and the destructive; the time killer and the builder. After exercising your discriminative ability, you will choose those ways which are constructive, saving yourself much time, energy and money. The saving of time, energy and money will help you more and more to go deeper in the right direction in the accumulating and the using of energy. Every right step upon any level of your being evokes the light of your Soul.

The next step is clearing yourself of illusions, glamors and the many attractions of the material plane. Let us understand that the Soul is a nucleus of fire within us. As we succeed in clearing the atmosphere of the Soul, Its radiation increases proportionately. Every word, thought, action or emotion that obscures the radiation of the Soul, or is out of harmony with the Soul vibrations, decreases the vitality of our body in the long range and gradually dims the light of our mind, causing illness and disease.[36]

---

[36]*Cosmos in Man*, pp. 258-259.

...Soul powers, Soul beauty, Soul energies cannot be given to us, unless we prepare and raise ourselves up to the Soul level. All psychic powers are inherent within us, and they are unfolded as we proceed on the Path of Evolution.[37]

Spiritual tension is not strain. It is a tremendous radioactivity that flows out of you; and because of this radioactivity, you are a center of peace since no disturbances can penetrate through your field of radioactivity and bother you. Thus, you have a shield or an intense atmosphere around you through which the mechanical thinking and solar plexus emotions of other people cannot penetrate. You are a living fortress and you know within your own heart that you are safe and beautiful and nothing will hurt you. That radioactivity starts within us when we touch our Soul consciousness and release it into all our activities and expressions.[38]

The ability of discernment comes into activity on the Soul levels. The Soul levels are the third, second and first mental sub-planes, and whatever activity is done on these sub-planes is guided, overshadowed by the Inner Presence, the Transpersonal Self, and is called spiritual activity. Spiritual discernment is a sense which is developed on the third mental plane, the formless plane.[39]

The energy of the increasing number of disciples in all fields of human endeavor puts a tremendous pressure upon the subtle vehicles of those around them who are occupied with the shadows of life. Their bodies are not refined enough to be able to absorb the disciple's energies and use them for higher ideals. These energies either crack them,

---

[37]*The Science of Meditation*, p. 223.
[38]*The Psyche and Psychism*, p. 980.
[39]*Ibid.*, p. 165.

lead them to a life of imbalance between light and darkness, or stimulate their centers to such a degree that they start registering astral impressions. The contact of such disciples with the general public not only stimulates the public, but also leads the public into polarization toward their Souls. Once the Soul is contacted you can have either true psychism, or distorted psychism if your motives and vehicles are not purified and developed. Disciples affect their surroundings through their thought life, through their radiation, through their lectures, songs, books and through contacts of any kind.[40]

When the astral counterpart of the physical senses develops and unfolds on the astral plane, then we say we have psychic powers. Astral senses in most humans are in an embryonic condition. They develop and unfold through suffering, through purification of the emotional nature, through all-giving love, through the experiences of our failure and success, through silence and renunciation, and through developing Soul contact....[41]

...When the lower mental nature is duly developed and the man has started to unfold the higher mental planes or Soul realms and is dedicated to a spiritual life, then the higher psychism starts to express itself....[42]

As the unfolding human soul grows closer to the purity of the Solar Angel, proportionately cleansing himself of his own agelong maya, glamors and illusions, and gaining

---

[40]*Ibid.*, p. 85.

[41]*Ibid.*, p. 55.

[42]*The Science of Meditation*, p. 219.

control over his vehicles, the higher psychic powers begin to shine forth....[43]

Higher psychism starts when the Soul is awakening on higher planes, and Its *mechanisms* are in good order, clean and pure.[44]

...Psychic energy comes via our Soul and gives nourishment to our physical, emotional and mental vehicles. It brings wisdom, love and power to us and charges our aura with fire.[45]

...Divine psychism is the process of the Soul and Monad expressing Themselves in purest simplicity and accuracy in the lower planes. Animal psychism is the leftover remnant of powers from the animal kingdom....[46]

Positive psychism is higher psychism which serves the progress of humanity. It works with the Soul or consciousness aspect of the form, and is sensitive to the impressions coming from the Plan and Purpose of Life. It emphasizes love, light and discipline and is positive for the achievements of humanity.[47]

Psychic energy is a combination of two kinds of energy. One is the energy of Great Bear, transmitted through the Monad; the other is the energy of the Pleiades which fuses with the energy of the Great Bear and is transmitted to us through the Solar Angel.

---

[43]*Ibid.*, p. 220.
[44]*The Psyche and Psychism*, p. 88.
[45]*Ibid.*, p. 1039.
[46]*Ibid.*, pp. 95-96.
[47]*Ibid.*, p. 95.

As Monadic influence increases and Soul fusion goes forward, psychic energy increases in man and creates greater sensitivity in the human aura to receive impressions from higher planetary and solar centers.

The psychic energy in the Cosmos awakens psychic energy in man, which comes into existence when the pure Self — the Great Bear in man — is in harmony with the substance, or with the nature of Pleiades in man. This is why psychic energy connects the individual man with the Cosmos, and makes him an outpost of cosmic consciousness.

For a person the psychic energy is the energy transmitted to his personality from his Inner Guide or Angel. That Guide gives courage, strength, vision, revelation and actual energy to the personality, if it is in the right condition. At the time of joy, aspiration, prayer, striving and meditation, we bring the personality into the right condition in which the Inner Guide can release psychic energy. Psychic energy heals the vehicles, enlightens the mind and expands the consciousness. It shields and protects the personality from many dark attacks and increases the vitality of man. It also creates integration and alignment within man's many vehicles.

To stand in the light of the Inner Guide means to act, to speak, to feel and to think in harmony with the Plan and Purpose of that Inner Guide. Your life expressions must not disturb the symphony of your Inner Guide, if you are expecting Its energy to charge you.

The first source of psychic energy is the Inner Guide. **The Inner Guide radiates three principles:**

a. *Love.* Whenever we act against the principle of love, we create a blockage on the path of psychic energy and create a turbulence which results in many complications within our personality. To act against love means to use dirty criticism, to spread lies about people, or hate, or hurt people in various ways, even in thoughts. Whenever a person is in these conditions, the connecting line between the Inner Guide and human soul is blocked, and it often takes a long time to reestablish the communication between the personality and the Guide.

b. *Intelligence.* Psychic energy needs the substance of intelligence to perform its task properly. Those who think, speak and act in an unintelligent way hinder the flow of psychic energy into their system. To live intelligently means to live a life in harmony with the vision of the Inner Guide.

c. *Will.* Psychic energy cannot manifest fully and pass through planes if the substance of will is lacking in the planes through which the energy will pass. The substance of the will is the best conductive agent for psychic energy. That is why one must develop willpower in order to be a conductor of fire.

These three principles must increase in the life of a human being harmoniously, if he is going to be a disperser of psychic energy.[48]

Striving toward the Hierarchy. Striving produces psychic energy. It orients the whole mechanism toward the Soul. It draws the energy of the Hierarchy. The energy of the Hierarchy is joy, bliss and peace....[49]

...According to the esoteric teaching, the energy [of the seventh ray] coming from outside our solar system is a great contributing factor to the increase of psychism. The energy

---

[48]*Ibid.*, pp. 205-206.
[49]*Ibid.*, p. 246.

of this ray helps the human being to integrate his personality with the Soul, which means integration between the
etheric, astral and mental centers and the causal body. This
unfoldment puts great pressure on these centers and the
physical glands, and it may manifest itself in higher or distorted psychism.[50]

Great artists in all fields of art are true psychics, in the
sense that they can contact the world of greater beauty on
higher planes, and translate that beauty through their intuitional, mental, astral and physical senses and give us the
immortal culture of the ages, in the form of color, sound,
movement, harmony, rhythm, form, meaning and significance. Thus they pave the way for our higher evolution.

A higher psychic is not a slave of the urges and drives of
his glamors, illusions and vanities. He uses his energies to
cause changes in the consciousness of men, and enlighten
their motivation. The higher psychic always deals with the
Soul nature, while the lower psychic is interested with matter and personality fields. Higher psychics are inclusive;
lower psychics are separative.[51]

[Psychism] ... is the manifestation of the powers of the
Inner Guide. Its powers may manifest through a person
when there is an exceptional need for guidance or protection.

The person himself does not possess these powers, but
the Inner Guide within manifests them in certain critical
conditions. The Inner Guide in Oriental wisdom is called the
Solar Angel. A person can show Its power by having Soul
infusion or by witnessing Its power in certain occasions.[52]

---

[50]*Ibid.*, p. 86.
[51]*Ibid.*, p. 72.
[52]*Ibid.*, pp. 76-77.

There are many voices that a psychic may hear, but none of them are valid unless he hears the Voice of Silence, or the Voice in extreme silence. When the vibrations of your physical, astral and mental realms are harmonized and raised to such a degree, they automatically shut off the sense of hearing on the physical and astral planes, and open the hearing on the mental plane.

No one can reach such a stage of silence unless he purifies his personality nature and raises it to extreme integrity, except in rare cases when a great Teacher builds a wall of electricity between your mental ear and personality vehicles and enables you to hear His voice, or the voice of your Inner Guardian.

In each initiation, you enter into a deep silence, and a voice addresses you. It is your Inner Guard that speaks to you first, then your Master; then you hear the voice of Christ, and in a more elevated initiation, you hear the voice of the Eternal Youth.

Meditations, retreats, isolation in certain periods of time from the personality world, complete reticence and mental serenity, renouncement and detachment help you to prepare for the Voice of Silence. Those who are familiar with the Voice tell us that It speaks only about your responsibility in the Divine Plan, and about your sacrificial acts in regard to the Divine Purpose. After each communication, it seals your mouth to total secrecy.

The Inner Voice never reveals the secrets of other people. It instructs you in leadership and in cases of global emergencies and advises you to take those actions which will facilitate the emergence of the Plan.[53]

---

[53]*Ibid.*, pp. 708-709.

To discriminate ... the true voice, one must use pure reason. He must know that the true inner voice of the Real Self never forces, never demands, never flatters never says anything to increase a person's vanities nor the glamor of his being important. Also, It never suggests negativity, separation and fear. It stands for group welfare, unity, sacrifice, duty, labor and group responsibility; it points toward the formless. It gives joy, energy and the will-to-good.[54]

Higher psychism is produced:

   a. When there is purity in the personality vehicles.

   b. When the etheric and higher centers are ready to receive, assimilate and direct energies under the conscious guidance of the enlightened Soul.

   c. When people have paid their past karma through suffering or sacrificial service.

   d. When people have Soul infusion, and are on the way of penetration into the Spiritual Triad.

   e. When people have right motives and have dedicated their life to the service of one humanity.

   f. When people have constructed part of the antahkarana and are busy building higher and higher counterparts of that bridge in many dimensions.

---

[54]*The Science of Meditation*, p. 209.

Higher psychism must be used to:

a. Redeem prisoners of the physical and astral planes.

b. Prove the continuity of human life on higher planes.

c. Be streams of light, love and power for others.

d. Contact the divine prototypes and bring them to the objective plane to guide humanity along the right lines.

e. Build bridges between planetary centers and centers in the solar system.

f. Spread healing energy.

g. Be distributing agents of the purpose of Shamballa on Earth.[55]

...Striving builds a channel for psychic energy. On the other hand, an act to hinder the dedication and striving of other people is an offense to the Inner Guide.[56]

Cultivate detachment. Sometimes sit and think what will happen if everything you love is taken away from you. What will you do on special occasions in which you will be forced to detach? Prepare yourself for detachment. As you detach, you become more Soul and less matter, more joy and *less suffering.*

---

[55]*The Psyche and Psychism,* p. 89.
[56]*Ibid.,* p. 208.

True psychic powers develop if one lives a focused life throughout the year.... Psychism, in reality, is a life *lived as a Soul.*[57]

In lower psychism, you are interested in personalities and their problems. In higher psychism, you are interested in their Soul evolution, Soul destiny. In lower psychism, you work for yourself, and you collect things for yourself. In higher psychism, you work for others, sacrifice and serve.[58]

Higher clairaudience is an advanced form of mental telepathy. This has three stages: In the first stage, it is from mind to mind. Minds communicate with each other and transfer the message to the brain for adaptation. In the second stage, it is the human soul that either sends the telepathic message or receives it. In the third stage, the Solar Angel sends the message to the human soul.

There is another stage where your Master telepathically communicates with you from the Soul level, after receiving permission from your Solar Angel to do so. All these telepathic communications develop very slowly until they reach a stage of perfection through "Spiritual Telepathy."

...Psychometry is the ability to be impressed. The Teacher Djwhal Khul says that:[59]

> ...*Sensitivity or the psychic sense of touch is etheric in nature, is general in expression and must eventually give place to that spiritual impressibility which enables a man, like the Christ,*

---

[57]*Ibid.*, p. 816.
[58]*Ibid.*, p. 88.
[59]*Ibid.*, p. 59.

> *simply to 'know' what is in his fellow man and to*
> *be aware of his condition and of the condition of*
> *life in all forms....*[60]

Planetary or higher psychometry can be achieved when there exists a very high degree of Soul impression. This means the unfolding, developing human soul is fused with the Solar Angel. One unified field of glory is created by this fusion in which the human soul accomplishes the vision of his agelong striving and labor.[61]

Spiritual telepathy is the mental correspondence of physical intuitive perception. This is real telepathy, which is communication between Soul and Soul. When a man transcends personality hindrances and obstacles and functions as a *Soul*, he is able to communicate with the Souls of other human beings.

Time and space disappear for him as far as spiritual telepathy is concerned, and he can tune at any time with a Soul for an exchange of wisdom or service.[62]

---

[60]Bailey, A.A., *Esoteric Psychology*, Vol. II, p. 585.
[61]*The Psyche and Psychism*, p. 160.
[62]*Ibid.*, p. 166.

24

Adverse Effects of Soul Contact

*T*HE INNER GUIDE MAY LEAVE

> *In some cases ... the Solar Angel withdraws and sheds no light upon the problems of man. His purpose in so doing is to give man the opportunity to help himself.*[1]

According to the Ageless Wisdom,

— a person can be born without a Solar Angel.

— the Solar Angel, after being with a person for some years, may separate Itself from the person.

In the first case, the intellect does not develop and the subject remains mentally retarded. The pineal gland of such a person generally remains undeveloped and we are told that for this reason they remain as babies, but the Ageless Wisdom teaches us that their glands do not work properly because their Souls remain inactive.

Some people can look into a person's eyes and recognize whether the Soul is absent or partially withdrawn. If It has left the body, the eyes of the subject are like those of a person who is suddenly awakened and not yet fully conscious, appearing empty and dead. If the Soul is partially withdrawn, the eyes express fear, uncertainty and nervousness.

---

[1] *Cosmos in Man*, p. 49.

I made a special study of a young man who was about nineteen or twenty years old and who had the mind of a child of about two or three years of age. His instincts and passions were awake; he was like an animal. After many psychological tests, I was sure that he did not have an "Angel" — he was unable to imagine or to reason; and could only repeat whatever he heard without understanding the meaning of the words.

It sometimes happens that the Angel is present but the mechanism is so out-of-order that the Angel cannot express Itself through the body; It remains in a suspended state for a while and eventually departs. Or the Solar Angel may leave a person because of his vices. This situation is explained in *The Secret Doctrine* (Vol. III, p. 527), which says:

> *There is however, still hope for a person who has lost his Higher Soul through his vices, while he is yet in the body. He may be still redeemed and made to turn on his material nature. For either an intense feeling of repentance or one single earnest appeal to the Ego that has fled, or best of all, an active effort to amend one's ways, may bring the Higher Ego back again.*

In this case the thread of connection has not been completely severed.

Sometimes the mind can be blinded by materialistic ambitions and selfish thoughtforms, which create a fog or wall between the Soul and man, separating the man from the Real Thinker. The man can only reflect the thoughtforms in space created by other minds. Such people are easily affected by demagogues and may easily be led especially in destructive directions.

A Tibetan Sage says, "...When mind becomes unduly developed and ceases to unite the higher and the lower, it forms a sphere of its own. This is the greatest disaster that can overtake the human unit."[2]

We must not forget that though the Soul is the Inner Light, It can be used for selfish and material purposes. When used incorrectly, a fog or wall is gradually created which prevents communication between the mental body, the mind and the Soul, and in due time man finds himself the victim of contradictory ideas and actions. Such people may attempt suicide or become mentally unbalanced because life has lost its purpose and its plan, and they can see no hope for the future.

"Entities" that take possession of the minds of living people are not Solar Angels or Souls, but "spirits" as they are sometimes called. These entities are usually the "souls" of low-grade men who have passed away, and being entirely enveloped by low-grade thoughts and emotions, they feel a strong craving for earth life. They may approach people who are magnetically in tune with them, occupy their bodies and force them to partake in intense sexual activities, to use drugs and alcohol, and even to commit crimes. The possessed ones may literally hear voices suggesting behavior that is against their better judgment. Unfortunately, they often obey the voices. (I am not referring to the "voices" that one may hear from his subconscious mind or from his reactive mind, but to voices coming from "entities.") There are many such people in mental institutions whom modern physicians are unable to help; they can only record the cases. These patients provide the channel of entry for the entities

---

[2]Bailey, A. A., *A Treatise on Cosmic Fire*, p. 261.

by their own emotional conflicts, resentments, past relations, and obstructed sexual and aggressive energies. By their strong and purifying vibrations, people of great spiritual achievement can help possessed victims and cast such entities out of their energy fields.[3]

The human soul is between the Higher Self and the personality, if he has liberated himself from the personality. Most human beings or souls are lost in the elementals of the body, emotions and mental nature. They do not exist yet, as they do not have independence. They blindly obey what their body, emotions and thoughts want. In this stage there is no conflict with the Higher Self because the Higher Self does not exist for them.

After a person gains a certain degree of liberation from the personality, he receives direct hints, suggestions and impressions from the Higher Self. It is at this stage that conflict starts. The personality pulls him down; the Higher Self pulls him up. Often he becomes like a pendulum between these two poles. Sometimes he tries to resist the pull of the personality; sometimes he resists the pull of the Higher Self on behalf of the personality. It is in such moments that he betrays his Higher Self and falls again into slavery.

Such a battle continues for a long time until the person stands firm in the light of the Higher Self and tries to sublimate the personality, to make it serve the light of the Higher Self.

There are many ways that you betray your Higher Self. The following twelve ways are very common:

---

[3]*The Hidden Glory of the Inner Man*, pp. 29-31.

1. You betray your Higher Self when you work against the decisions you made in the light of the Higher Self. All decisions made in the light of the Higher Self are pro-survival decisions. They are decisions to strive; to work for light, for unity, for beauty; to be harmless, courageous, daring, detached, etc. Once you make a decision in the light of the Higher Self, you must obey your decision. If not, you disobey your Higher Self.

Decisions made in the presence of the Higher Self are very important. The Higher Self looks at your actions to see in what degree you can keep your decision or promise. Your relation with the Higher Self fades away if you do not keep your promises and carry out your decisions.

The same thing happens in your worldly relationships. If you do not keep your promises and decisions, very soon you lose your friendships.

Every decision you make for service and sacrifice, or to unite, uplift and help is a decision made in the light of the Higher Self....

2. You may betray your Higher Self by wasting your physical, emotional and mental energy. These bodies and their energy are given to you to be used to achieve perfection under the supervision of your Higher Self. In wasting and misusing this energy you make the Plan of the Higher Self for you fail.

You also must not waste time. Time is so precious. Delay in your evolution is the greatest mistake. Wasted time makes the efforts of your Higher Self fail or be delayed. Like a supervisor, the Higher Self feels frustrated if an employee cannot complete his job within the given period of time.

3. You betray your Higher Self when you deliberately hurt others, creating obstacles and hindrances on their path. When you hurt someone, you hurt his Higher Self. We must know that all Transpersonal Selves act as one. They are group-conscious. For Them, every human soul belongs to Them. When you hurt others, you hurt your and others' Higher Selves.

We are told that our Angels — the Higher Selves — see the face of the Father every day, and They communicate with each other instantaneously.

You may hurt someone without him being aware of it, but you cannot hide your action from his Higher Self. All that your Higher Self knows is shared with the Higher Selves of others related to you.

4. You betray your Higher Self if you do not follow the discipline given to you by your Teacher. Your spiritual Teacher is the representative of your Higher Self, until you have direct communication with your Higher Self.

Please note that you must obey the discipline given by your Teacher — not his self-will, desires or wishes. Actually, a real Teacher is the interpreter between you and your Higher Self....

5. If you disobey the Teaching, you betray your Higher Self. All true Teaching is given by the Hierarchy, and all Transpersonal Selves are members and executive officers of the Hierarchy. Disobedience to the Teaching is treason.

The Teaching given by Krishna, Buddha, Christ and Their disciples contains the highest wisdom a person can assimilate. Then there is the Teaching given through H.P. Blavatsky, Alice Bailey and Helena Roerich, which reflects the wisdom of great Teachers. The Ten Commandments, the Sermon on the Mount, and the Noble Eightfold Path are precious examples of the Teaching.

Your Higher Self wishes that you study the Teaching and actualize the Wisdom given through it.

All the Teaching is intended to bring you into contact with the Bride within you. Once you have direct, face-to-face contact with your Higher Self, the ways of study change. You find books in Space, classes in higher realms and Teachers in glorious spheres; and written Teaching can no longer offer what your soul needs.

6. You betray the Higher Self by acting against the five major principles — Beauty, Goodness, Justice, Joy and Freedom. Every ugly act, every act of ill will, every act of unrighteousness, every act to destroy the joys of others, and every act to impair the freedom of others is an act of treason against the Higher Self.

No one can defeat a person who is living in the light of the five principles of Beauty, Goodness, Justice, Joy and Freedom. Real success in life is the result of a life lived within these five principles. All pain and suffering dissolve once a person lives within these principles.

Any person, group or nation who works against these principles begins to follow the path of decay, degeneration and destruction. Once a person or a nation is separated from its Higher Self through treason and disobedience, that person or nation thinks, feels and acts against its own survival because the Higher Self withdraws and leaves it with its own karmic destiny.

7. Everyone who increases the glamors and illusions in the world and serves matter betrays his Higher Self.

Lies and falsifications in all spheres of life increase the glamor of the world. Misinterpretation of facts for one's own advantage increases illusions. Worship of matter and material values chains the human heart to the Earth.

One can contact his Higher Self only through clearing his glamors and trying to decrease the glamors of the world. One can contact his Higher Self through eliminating his illusions and decreasing the illusions of the world. One can contact his Higher Self through the elimination of greed and attachment to material values, as glamors, illusions and attachments to matter create an impassable abyss between a person and his Higher Self.

8. You can betray your Higher Self in developing vanities. You cannot contact the Higher Self if you are not yourself. The Higher Self wants to see you as you are, so that It tries to work with you. The Higher Self wants you to know yourself as you are. It is impossible to change yourself unless you know what you are exactly. Vanity covers and changes your face; vanity is a heavy mask.

9. Those who create cleavages work against the Higher Self. Do not create cleavages between good friends, in families or between nations. Try to unite them.

10. Those who play the role of hypocrite betray their Higher Self.

11. Those who waste their sexual energy betray their Higher Self. Do not use your sexual energy to exploit people, to create cleavages, or to gain positions. When sexual energy is wasted, the Higher Self cannot reach your physical, emotional, and mental nature and impress you.

Sexual energy is a very sensitive element in your aura, which is used as an agent of higher impression. Your Higher

Self withdraws from you when It feels that you are destroying the element It needs to contact you. And when the Higher Self withdraws, astral or evil entities possess you and lead you into physical, moral and spiritual destruction.

12. If you use hallucinogenic drugs, alcohol, or hypnotism, you betray your Higher Self. Your Higher Self expects from you not to pollute the Temple in which God dwells.

Your Higher Self does not want you to act and live by a will imposed upon you. It wants you to be free, not only from drugs and alcohol, but also from imposition of others' will, no matter by what name such imposition is called.

How can we come closer to our Transpersonal Self? The answer is very clear:

a. Through regular, daily meditation.

b. Through regular, daily study of the Teaching.

c. Through sacrificial service, done without criticism, complaint or self-interest.

These are three steps which gradually bring you closer to your Inner Lord and make you ready to have the honor of standing in Its presence.

Betrayal of the Higher Self is a very serious matter. It starts slowly and gains momentum, until one finds himself near Niagara Falls. Betrayal is accumulative. Every time an act of betrayal is committed, it makes it more difficult for a person to contact the Higher Self or to draw guidance from It.

People who are interested only in their greed, hatred, revenge, and separatism never consider how they are slowly making their Soul withdraw and eventually depart from them. Some occult books speak about losing our Souls, but they do not clearly explain what is the Soul that we lose.

Actually, when a person dedicates himself to evil for a long time, his Higher Self or his Transpersonal Self leaves him. In ancient literature, the Transpersonal Self is called the Soul. It is this Soul or the Higher Self that one loses, not himself — the human soul.

A person dedicated to evil may lose his Higher Self and slowly identify himself with the elementals of the physical, emotional and mental bodies. Because of the absence of the Higher Self, after the death of the physical body the human soul falls into a state of unconsciousness and fuses with the elementals of the personality. He cannot incarnate any more because, due to his evil life, his permanent atoms have disintegrated and he can no longer form any vehicles with which to incarnate. Instead, he remains an unconscious entity for a long time, until another chance is given to him to build a human body and subtle vehicles, starting from the mineral kingdom.

If he loses his second chance, his destiny is annihilation. Millions of years of labor are wasted and the human soul loses his identity and becomes a part of chaos. This is why the Teaching warns us not to betray the Higher Self, but to step by step follow the directions of Its silent voice and eventually contact it face-to-face. As one of the disciples of Christ put it:

> We see him in a glass darkly ... but one
> day we will see him face to face....[4]

---

[4] *Challenge for Discipleship*, pp. 159-163.

A soul is a sinless entity. It cannot be sick or ill. The causes of illness are not found in the human soul, but in the bodies. The reflection of the Spark of life which exists in the
lower bodies may sin and break the Good Law, the Law of
Love. This reflection may pay the karma and gradually
advance on the path. When this reflection has reached the
stage of Soul infusion, has been tested in the fire, and has
emerged as pure gold, it has become a Master of Wisdom
and a fountain of light, love and power. The evil person, the
harmful one — he who complicates the lives of others, causing them suffering and trouble, and preventing the progress
of his fellowman — is a person who is not yet a Soul or who
is not in contact with his Solar Angel.[5]

We have many unfortunate people in hospitals who have
unbalanced natures, but who also have a drive to live and
express themselves. There is a greater danger. If the mechanism, especially the mind (not the brain) is badly damaged,
the Solar Angel leaves the person for a long period of time.
The result may be mongoloid, retarded children and
deformed births.[6]

If any thoughtform crystallizes in a man's mental space,
it blocks the transmission of energy from the Soul realms....[7]

The Solar Angel leaves the man temporarily when the
person falls into "fright, grief, despair, a violent attack of
sickness or excessive sensuality."...[8]

---

[5]*The Hidden Glory of the Inner Man,* pp. 57-58.
[6]*The Science of Becoming Oneself,* p. 107.
[7]*Cosmos in Man,* p. 260.
[8]*Ibid.,* p. 215.

...Most average people who claim that they are in contact with the Masters, are in illusion. A true Master cannot be contacted until a man establishes conscious contact with his Solar Angel. When he has met his Solar Angel face to face, he is led into the presence of the Masters. Before that time, any real or illusionary contact can have disturbing effects on his vehicles and on his way of life....[9]

The dark brothers carefully watch those disciples who are progressing along the right lines and advancing toward the light of the Soul and toward the Spiritual Triad. Such a disciple is the center of their attention, and they are anxious to harm him in any way possible to hinder the service for which he is dedicated....[10]

In *Esoteric Healing*, the Tibetan Master says:

> *All disease is the result of inhibited soul life, and this is true of all forms in all kingdoms. The art of the healer consists in releasing the soul, so that its life can flow through the aggregate of organisms which constitute any particular form.*[11]

At present a group of psychologists and psychiatrists, with the help of esoteric students, are working on a system to produce soul release and radiation. Along this line, psycho synthesis has made a fine beginning. Through testing and experiences, it has become apparent that psychosomatic illness is the result of an inner, distorted vibration which exists in the subtle bodies and gradually emerges in the form of a malfunction. However, if the causes of illness have

[9]*Ibid.*, pp. 266-267.
[10]*The Science of Meditation*, p. 231.
[11]Bailey, A.A., *Esoteric Healing*, p. 5.

not exhausted themselves through the physical body at the time of death, then on the death of the other bodies these existing causes register themselves in the seed-atoms found in the atmosphere of the soul. When the soul again tries to develop the threefold man, these traces or vibrations create disturbances which cause diseases in the subtle bodies. In due time these diseases express themselves on the physical plane.[12]

Hypnotism destroys the self-determination of the subject and prevents the release of soul-energy, creating walls between planes of mind and emotions and the higher states of man....[13]

The difference between Soul impression and hypnotic possession is very simple. In Soul impression, man strives toward beauty, goodness, truth, purity, inclusiveness, living-ness and freedom. In hypnotic possession, the man heads toward illogical action, crime, lies, depression, separative-ness, death and slavery of many kinds.

In hypnotic possession, there is a forceful drive or urge accompanied with fear and with a martyr's complex. In Soul impression, there is no imposition. It is logical and joyful.[14]

Many hypnotists will eventually find out the damage they are doing to their subjects when they closely observe their subjects' mental, emotional and physical behavior and the state of their consciousness. They must observe primari-ly the behavior of children who demonstrate effects of hyp-notic suggestion from their former lives. Many children demonstrate blind urges, drives and mechanical actions

---

[12]*The Hidden Glory of the Inner Man*, pp. 55-56.

[13]*Ibid.*, p. 54.

[14]*The Psyche and Psychism*, p. 308.

without any apparent reason. They act, they feel, they think and speak in a mechanical way, and do not feel the slightest responsibility for their deeds. Such children must be cleared of these suggestions; this is a task which is very difficult to accomplish.

If they are not cleared they will carry the curse of the hypnotic command with them for a long time, until their consciousness expands through education and esoteric discipline to such a degree that they enter into Soul consciousness. From the Soul plane, they will destroy all past hindrances and blind commands within their nature.[15]

THE DANGER OF MISUSE OF MENTAL FACULTIES

...[Meditation] develops the faculties of discrimination, analysis and synthesis....

As these faculties slowly appear, man could be tempted to use them for his own personal and materialistic ends. This is a great trap on the Path of discipleship. People starting with great aspiration for spiritual visions and beauties may be trapped within worldly, selfish and materialistic activities and pleasures, and eventually lose the Path and become wanderers in the valley of illusions and glamors. They engage in works that feed their ambitions and nourish their pride and vanity, making them the slaves of their lower, selfish natures. Here a great danger appears. The man, instead of directing his mental energies upward toward the Soul, makes them servants of his lower nature, to satisfy the interests of his social environment and his personality interests. This activity eventually builds a wall between him and his Solar Angel, between lower and higher mind....[16]

[15]*Ibid.*, p. 281.
[16]*The Science of Meditation*, p. 228.

The Dark Forces work largely on the etheric plane. They influence the physical body, and create there a number of diseases which are connected with the glands, nervous system and blood stream. A disciple is warned to be alert for his health, and to guard it by focusing his heart on the Hierarchy and Christ, and by living under the light and fire of his Solar Angel, the Angel of the Presence.[17]

Some of the well known Teachers tell us that, "It is hard to keep a right balance between the soul and the personality when the spiritual stimulant is relentlessly high. The rushing into the personal life of soul force is like sunshine in a garden. Weeds as well as flowers emerge."[18]

Once a relationship is established between the personality and the Spiritual Triad, the will energy starts to flow into the personality. We are told that this is very dangerous in the early stages if it is not balanced by the love energy of the Soul....[19]

Virtues are qualities of the Soul, but when they are used for our personal interests, they turn into vices. The energy entering our system is colored by the center where our consciousness is focused.[20]

If at any time an aspirant feels tired, depressed; if he cannot sleep well; if he is nervous or feels fatigue, inertia, drowsiness and does not want to read, to search, to work; if he is in a heavy mood of laziness, he must immediately stop his meditation, slow down his spiritual aspirations, and try to find the causes of his general condition.

[17]*Ibid.*, p. 271.

[18]Blavatsky, H.P., *The Secret Doctrine*, Vol. II, p. 179. (Excerpt from *The Science of Meditation*, p. 40.)

[19]*The Science of Becoming Oneself*, p. 132.

[20]*The Psyche and Psychism*, p. 644.

We are told that one of the causes is mystic devotion: when the aspirant tries to "rise to strive toward the goal," "to reach to the Soul," or "to the beloved vision of the Soul, to the Lord," and so on. When this kind of aspirational meditation is done for a long time with intensity, it causes the lifting or rising of the subtle vehicles, including the etheric, out and above the head. This produces a too loose anchorage of the etheric brain in the physical brain. This condition extends all over the physical body and eventually the aspirant suffers fatigue and inertia and sometimes brain starvation. The etheric underlies the nervous system and the venous system, and in this case does not transfer energy to these two systems. The aspirant feels fatigue, and often falls asleep or drops off in a half sleep or has a mental absence.

The cure for this situation is to change the way the mystic meditates. Thus he must center his attention within the center of the skull where the etheric brain penetrates. Here is the place for anchoring the Soul Thread, or thread of intelligence, where he must sound the OMs, invoking the higher energies to take a firm seat within the *etheric brain* and *keep* them there. This is the seat where the aspirant must turn his attention any time his aspirational nature wants to rise. It is here that he works in the light of the Soul, and thus all work done in the mental body is kept in direct alignment with the brain awareness by keeping the etheric body properly anchored in the physical brain.[21]

The use of drugs in this life will open some centers in the etheric body, overstimulate them and produce an overflow of energy into the corresponding physical organs. In the next life this overflow will continue and will have devastat-

---

[21]*The Science of Meditation*, pp. 225-226.

ing physical and psychic effects. In the present reincarnation the drug user will destroy his brain cells and increase the thickness of the veil between himself and his Soul.[22]

There is another important point to consider when analyzing the driver's role. Sometimes it happens that the carriage and horses — the bodies — are taken over by thieves, who jump on the carriage and drive it wherever they wish. A close examination reveals that these thieves are very often strong thoughtforms of other people, posthypnotic suggestions, engrams, or even disembodied entities, who desire to come in contact with the physical plane for various reasons. At times, these thieves even dare to pretend that they are the Lord, Who is sometimes absent, thus leaving the carriage and horses unattended. The thieves occupy the bodies and use them until their desires are fulfilled; then they leave the horses and carriage in a worn out condition. This can happen because the Lord has not yet gained full control over the bodies....

Many people feel that they are the permanent "I," but this is not true. When people live on the carriage level, they are not identifying with their Inner Lord, and with the Spark behind it. One day a wheel declares itself the real Self; then another day the box proclaims itself to be in charge. One day the axle claims to be the Lord, and on other days even a screw proclaims itself the Lord. The reason for such assumptions is simple. Every part of the carriage reacts as an automaton to external influences. Each influence controls one part of the organism, a nerve center, and acts as its master forcing that part to obey. This influence lasts a short time, or a long time, depending on the nature of the source and

---

[22]*The Fiery Carriage and Drugs*, p. 46.

the circumstances, but every time the influence changes, the controller changes. The same is true of our horses and even of our driver. For example, the horses want to wander around, or the driver goes and seeks his own pleasure when goal-fitting actions are required of them. Each time they do anything that is not in tune with the will of the Inner Lord, they submit themselves to outer influences.

A feeling of hatred, jealousy or self-pity can serve as a dangerous ruler for a long time; a prejudice, a doctrine, an opinion or habit can dominate the mind and act as the ruler. Thus, we see that man cannot be the master of his own destiny until his Lord is fully awake and maintaining full control over his three vehicles or bodies.

Sometimes people say, "I want this," or, "I want that." These people are steeped in a cloud of illusion. It is not the Inner Lord who wants or does not want, but rather an external influence working upon one of man's vehicles that produces negative or positive desires, or various attitudes and expressions....[23]

Hatha yoga ... tightens the link between the physical and etheric, intensifying the substance of the astral body to the point of crystallization. Thus obstacles are created which block the path of Soul contact, and which hinder the process of externalization of the unit of consciousness from etheric-astral into higher mental and buddhic planes.[24]

...Our physical body is floating within the etheric, emotional and mental bodies which are under the rhythm of the Inner Presence. When things go wrong in any of these bodies

---

[23]*Ibid.*, pp. 26-28.
[24]*Cosmos in Man*, p. 127.

through lies, hatreds, jealousies, in wasting precious energies, or in wrong mental activities and negative attitudes, we create disturbances within these bodies. These disturbances, sooner or later, come down and affect the condition of our physical body....[25]

If you can control your physical vehicle through your etheric body or higher mind, your emotions through your Intuitional Plane, your mind by the Soul or Atmic energy, your vehicle is fused with a source of energy and energy is manifested in all your activities, you are fused with a power-house of your being and you are charged with high potential electricity.

Most of us lack energy regardless of how well we sleep or rest. When this is so, it is because the energy lost from or used by the physical vehicle is not replaced by energy from the etheric and higher mental reservoirs. The secret of the abundance of energy is successful alignment and integration of the lower and higher bodies and the infusion of all vehicles with the Soul, and later, infusion with the Spiritual Triad.[26]

The health of our body, the beauty of our heart, and the clarity of our mind depend on the generation and conservation of energy. Through every physical action, through every emotion or feeling, through every thought, we spend or generate energy. When we are cut off from the Inner Light, inner purpose, we become debtful, for we are spending or wasting energy. We generate energy if we are always conscious of our Inner Light which is a Spark of the One Light....[27]

[25]*Ibid.*, p. 161.

[26]*Ibid.*, p. 256.

[27]*Ibid.*, p. 267.

I remember one day when my father, talking about genocide, said, "We knew about their plans. Their whole being
was engulfed by irritation. One could almost feel the poison
they had in their livers. The rattlesnake could no longer bear
the pressure of the accumulated poison; a victim had to be
found."

When I was studying the psychology of genocide I saw
clearly what my father indicated. There was a planned, systematic injection of irritation into the veins of leadership
which produced abundant imperil. This imperil not only
urged them to genocide, but also obscured the light of their
consciousness and the light of their Souls. It is observed that
when they reached the end of their destructive deeds the
leadership and the nation collapsed.[28]

Insanity is the condition of a defective mental machine.
The laws of the Soul are not obeyed, or carried on, and psychic energy is not distributed evenly through the centers.

Sanity is the condition of a well-functioning machine
which operates according to the plan set for the machine.
Thus, the mental body operates through psychic energy, in
accordance with the planned purpose of the Soul, without
any external or internal interference.[29]

...A solemn man immediately feels the shock of the Inner
Guide when he fails to keep all his expressions in harmony
with the law of economy of energy.[30]

We may think that there are people who, for the sake of
their business or for the sake of their various interests, lie,

[28]*The Psyche and Psychism*, p. 261.
[29]*Ibid.*, p. 134.
[30]*Ibid.*, p. 1007.

exploit and steal. Yet their health seems good, and they seem to enjoy life. It is true that average man can survive with his wrongdoing for a while, but eventually he develops serious complications in his mental, emotional and physical health. But this is not so important. The most important thing is that such people cannot advance into the sphere of their Soul, cannot penetrate into the presence of the Great Ones, cannot enter into Ashrams, cannot channel beauty, cannot live a creative life, cannot serve the Hierarchy.

A disciple would rather die than be deprived of such contacts.

A disciple, if he does wrong, immediately feels the reaction of his Soul, of his Teacher, of his Ashram, and enters into a state of inner conflict, with its many consequences.[31]

...Unless the motive is purified, all energies released for action will do wrong work. It is the wrong motive that attracts the attention of the Black Lodge and astral entities. Wrong motive starts a process of disintegration and decomposition of the higher vehicles and their centers, and cuts off Divine Guidance or Soul impression, and makes man prey to the destructive entities of the air.[32]

Contact with higher frequencies can be detrimental for you if first of all you did not have contact with your Inner Guide — your Soul — and prove that contact through a life of Beauty, Goodness and Truth. Unless you have such a contact first, higher contacts (achieved by wrong means) will take you out of equilibrium. You must build first an integrated personality and achieve the state of Soul infusion, and then you become ready for higher contacts.

---

[31]*Ibid.*, p. 797.
[32]*Ibid.*, p. 96.

Higher Teaching creates hypocrisy, insanity and imbalance when it is given to those people who do not have a pure aura, and who do not yet have contact with their Transpersonal Self.[33]

We become effects when we reject the suggestions of our Inner Soul, the Inner Christ, Who is our conscience.[34]

...Like a great beam of light the energy of the *Great Invocation* must be directed into ... dark places....

In doing such a sacred work, we must be very careful not to project our own glamors or illusions toward objects, and not to build any specific thoughtforms about individuals, groups, nations or events. Instead we must stand in the light of the Soul, and release the energy in a general, objective way, toward physical, emotional and mental locations, leaving the energy free to carry out the work of burning, cleaning and clearing away obstacles on the path of progress. By being a clear channel for these energies, events will occur in tune with the Divine Plan, and in accordance with the karma of the point of focus.[35]

Glamors can be dispelled by "analysis, discrimination and clear thinking," that is by holding our mind steady in the light of the Soul, and then focusing that light through the mind into our glamors, located in the astral plane. This means that glamors are dissipated by a Soul-illumined mind. The energy used here by the Soul is the atomic substance or the highest substance of the mental plane. It is a fiery energy which, when focused properly, dries out the dark patches of clouds, the glamors, and annihilates them.

---

[33]*Ibid.*, p. 882.

[34]*Ibid.*, p. 275.

[35]*Triangles of Fire*, revised edition, p. 143.

Our illusions can be dispelled by the Soul when It focuses the energy of intuition on them. Illusions are thought-forms, and they are fiery in nature. The energy of intuition is used to dispel them

Maya is devitalized or redirected by the power of *inspiration*, which is a *form of will energy* accumulated in the Soul. This energy is let loose down the etheric centers, like a burning and healing ray. Through this energy, the Soul puts the centers in harmony with the rhythm of the great pulsating light of the Spark....[36]

When you recognize your glamor, analyze it in the light of the Soul, not in your emotional and lower mental "reasoning." Then focus your Soul-illumined light upon your glamor and try to make it evaporate or disintegrate....[37]

Whenever you are identified with the maya, glamors and illusions of your vehicles you become an *effect*. Whatever you create eternally exists until you put into action another cause to obliterate it. Such an action can be inspired by a Wisdom Teaching, by a Teacher, or by your Inner Lord.[38]

Illusions ... are more mental than astral; yet they can be reinforced by glamors and ill-thought of his enemies.

What can be done in such situations? The disciple must:

1. Find and recognize the existence of the glamor.

---

[36]*The Science of Meditation*, p. 289.

[37]*Christ, The Avatar of Sacrificial Love*, p. 106.

[38]*The Psyche and Psychism*, p. 269

2. Attack it with the arrows of spiritual courage, faith and confidence in the source of life and fire within him.

3. Create opposing images of health, success, victory and joy.

4. Invoke the help of his Master, or the Christ.

5. Spread words of optimism, success and images of future prosperity.

6. Note and then shut out any negative expressions from his associates and himself.

7. See the developing vanities in his associates and with clear sincerity smash them.

8. Know that his destiny is in the hands of his Solar Angel and of his Master, and nothing can interfere with Their decision.

9. Have a special time to stand daily in the light of Christ.

...One of the best methods that his friends can use is holding the disciple in the light of their Soul and in the light of Christ, and thinking in terms of victory, success and health in relation to him....[39]

The Dweller on the Threshold is formed of all our selfish habits, glamors, illusions and maya, of all our desires for material satisfactions, of all our tendencies that are based on separation and the resultant karma, thus forming a great barrier between the Inner Dweller and the unfolding human

---

[39] *The Science of Meditation*, p. 282.

soul. But the *fragment* cannot be imprisoned forever in that condition. *The Magnet* or the Inner Dweller cyclically evokes a response from the *fragment*, and the human soul radiates a deeper aspiration toward more freedom....[40]

In the *New Testament* this episode was given in the example of the rich man, who came to Christ and asked how he could enter into the next stage of awareness. "Go and sell whatever you *have* and give to the poor...." But he was unable to do it, because of his wealth. In esoteric literature to sell means to get rid of the objects that are hindrances on the Path; things that you *have* must be given up to make you to BE.

So all his illusions, glamors and maya stood there as a great hindrance and did not let him pass through the door of initiation, toward the light of the Soul in which he should stay "poor in spirit" — "poor" of illusions, glamors, maya and their totality, the Dweller on the Threshold.

In a sense, the Dweller on the Threshold is the unfolding human soul so dressed in the heavy "wealth" of his maya, glamors and illusions that he is not yet able to make his own decision to reject or thrust them away, so as to enter into the light of the Solar Angel and fuse with It....[41]

The Dweller on the Threshold is removed by the focused will-to-achieve of the human soul and by the reply of the Solar Angel, this time using the will energy of the Spiritual Triad upon the Dweller on the Threshold, thus removing the shell in which the unfolding human soul is present, and bringing it under the light of the Spiritual Triad. The man is now a third degree initiate in full transfiguration.[42]

---

[40]*Ibid.*, p. 43.

[41]*Ibid.*, p. 287.

[42]*Ibid.*, p. 290.

The astral plane is the plane of glamor; it is from this plane that the dark forces operate, possess and control people. It is on this plane that glamors are contacted and even absorbed into our system. It is from this plane that dark forces descend on Earth to prevent progress as far as they can.

That is why in the process of alignment we must bypass this plane, and through our visualization build a golden line of communication between the Soul and the brain....[43]

Distorted psychism, in many cases, can be traced to the misuse of sex energy. The devitalization of the etheric body, nervous system, the brain and other parts of the body prevent the Inner Dweller from contacting Its vehicles and passing psychic energy to them. As the control of the inner energy center over the physical and etheric bodies weakens, entities in the etheric plane try to occupy it for their own use. They possess the sacral center, the solar plexus and also the throat center, and come in contact with the physical plane life to satisfy their urges which remain unsatisfied on the etheric planes.[44]

Distorted psychism is caused:

a. When the energy system is imbalanced.

b. When the wires transmitting the energy currents are broken and we have short circuits.

c. When we allow obsession.

[43]*Triangles of Fire,* revised edition, pp. 7-8.
[44]*The Psyche and Psychism,* p. 104.

d. When the grip of the Soul is loosened on our personality vehicles.

e. When the communication line with the Inner Guide is broken.

f. When there is no aspiration toward toward Hierarchy.[45]

---

[45]*Ibid.*, p. 111.

25

The
Third Initiation

*T*rue enlightenment starts with the Third Initiation, when the subject has become purified in his motives and free from his heavy karma and can consciously contact his Inner Guardian and do Its will....[1]

...[T]he process of enlightenment has three steps:

In the first step, the mental permanent atom irradiates the mental plane as a whole and fuses it with its light. This process affects the emotional plane, cleanses it from agelong glamors, and makes it a pure channel of intuitional love. It is in this degree of enlightenment that the initiate comes in contact with the Plan of his Soul. He becomes conscious of all possibilities in his life; he sees his karmic hindrances, the right way, and the right place to serve.

In the second step of enlightenment, the light of the intuition pours down to the whole mental plane and reveals the Plan for humanity and the Plan for all kingdoms of Nature. The initiate finds his position within the greater Plan and adjusts all his activities according to this revelation.

The Plan is built by the intuitional substance, and as this substantial energy or fire increases within the mental

---

[1] *The Hidden Glory of the Inner Man*, p. 118.

plane, the deeper layers of the Plan unfold gradually in his consciousness....

In the third step of enlightenment, the energy of the Atmic Plane pours down to the mental plane and charges it with the energy of the will. The mental activities express powerful will, and the person now has the energy he needs to carry into fulfillment the revelations that were given to him in the course of his enlightenment. Atmic energy is often called the "progressing light," which carries the initiate into fields of great service and responsibilities. This energy is accumulated in the Soul. It burns agelong maya and releases the person into intense spiritual service.

This whole process of enlightenment takes many years or incarnations.

The Third Initiation, the Initiation of Enlightenment mentioned in the lives of Buddha and Jesus, is the final seal of the achievement of the three phases of the path of enlightenment.[2]

...Buddhists call ... [the Third Initiation or the Transfiguration], *Enlightenment,* in which man gradually unfolds his mental powers, tries to penetrate into the laws of nature, and is given a vision of his true essence. It is during this initiation that the physical, emotional and mental nature is flooded with a great light and energy, coming from the Chalice and from the essence of man. This enables man to stand in the presence of his Angel and have direct communication with It and to bring, through service, the Intelligence, the Love and the Will Energy to the world of men.[3]

---

[2]*Ibid.,* pp. 108-109.

[3]*Christ, The Avatar of Sacrificial Love,* p. 54.

At the Third Initiation the personality is related to the Inner God, and thus it is flooded with the greater light. The Third Initiation is the initiation in which the Dweller on the Threshold is completely destroyed.... The Dweller on the Threshold is the sum total of physical, emotional and mental obstacles on the path, thus blocking the path toward the goal of the disciple. At this stage the Initiate-to-be is standing in front of the Angel but the Dweller on the Threshold, Satan, is there also, standing at his right. Satan is very active but the Solar Angel rebukes him, which means obliterates his power, and the Initiate stands only in the presence of the Angel. It is in this initiation that the personality is completely purified and passes into the glory of the Spiritual Triad, the Angel gaining full communication with the unfolding human soul, the Initiate....[4]

...**The Third Initiation is the result of a triple activity:**

1. The lower mind transmutes the physical body.

2. The Soul transforms the emotional nature and enables it to accept the rays of pure reason or Intuition, and,

3. The Spiritual Triad transfigures the whole personality with its physical, emotional and mental nature. It is in this stage that the will-to-good or the Will of God is gradually unveiled to the Initiate.[5]

---

[4]*Ibid.*, p. 45.
[5]*Ibid.*, p. 75.

26

The Fourth Initiation

*A*t the Fourth Initiation the three innermost petals [of the Chalice] start to open and the man's life becomes a sacrificial service for humanity. He steps into the Fourth Initiation and the pure light of the Inner Divinity, the Monad, pours into his personality and into his environment in great splendor. This pure light eventually consumes the Chalice, the age-old Lotus, and sets free the Solar Angel, the Great Presence....[1]

...It is only in the human kingdom that, through the help of the incoming Lord, the diffused light of the Spark starts to be awakened and to form a consciousness of identity, "I-ness," "self-ness," or a center in itself, an *individuality*.

This blooming or awakening will take ages. The unfolding human soul will pass through initiations (expansions of consciousness) into the stage in which he will be able to see his own inner depth and the vision of his own becoming. He will sense his kingship and consciously will walk toward his throne to rule his kingdom as a conscious Lord, liberating the little lives with which he comes in contact.

This is the stage where the Solar Angel leaves and the Real Man becomes a living Soul. In occult books this stage of achievement is defined as the Fourth Initiation, when the

---

[1]*The Science of Meditation*, p. 192.

Causal Body, or the body of the Presence, is destroyed and the Indweller passes on to higher paths of evolution.[2]

As we know, the Solar Angel helps the Monad until the Fourth Initiation. At that time the Chalice is destroyed and the Guiding Soul, the Solar Angel, is released. Now the Monad must travel the Path on Its own. Always, however, on the Path of Evolution there is to be found One Who stands between the existing condition of the Monad and the Future.[3]

When man reaches the Fourth Initiation, in the process of building the Antahkarana, the monadic energy starts to flow down the Antahkarana and burns the Chalice, releasing its central Fire or Jewel. The man is now resurrected and the Father is seen. From that moment on, the personality is in direct relationship with the Monad.[4]

...The Fourth Degree Initiation is that stage of consciousness in which your Inner Guide leaves you, your causal body is destroyed and for the first time you stand alone, on your own feet.

That is why when Jesus was crucified He said, "My Lord, My Lord, why hast Thou forsaken me?" The Inner Guide was leaving the man, and the man for the first time on his long journey of evolution stood on his own feet, not aided by the Inner Guide.[5]

The departure of the Solar Angel marks a great step forward in man's journey on the Path of Return. When the

---

[2]*Ibid.*, p. 52.

[3]*Cosmos in Man*, p. 56.

[4]*The Science of Becoming Oneself*, p. 137.

[5]*The Psyche and Psychism*, p. 171.

evolving human soul enters into that vast expansion of consciousness called the Fourth Initiation, the Solar Angel leaves the man. The evolving human soul has already built the web of the Triad and is able to function in the awareness of the Spiritual Triad. Man begins to know his own kingship, and the powerful energy of his own Essence releases itself more potently, radiating outward through the Spiritual Triad. When the Solar Angel leaves the human being at the Fourth Initiation, the Temple of Solomon, the Lotus or Chalice, is completely burned away. We are told that at this Initiation, the innermost petals of the twelve-petaled Lotus slowly open and the fire of the spirit sealed within the Monad is released. The fire burns all petals, and flows down uninhibited to the threefold lower unit, galvanizing it into a mechanism capable of performing as an instrument of the Spiritual Triad without the Solar Angel acting as an intermediary between the Triad and the lower mechanism. This is the fiery baptism to which Christ refers in the Bible.

Actually there are three kinds of baptism for the human being: the baptism of water, the baptism of the Holy Spirit, which is at the Third Initiation when the evolving human soul is fused with the Solar Angel, and the third baptism, the baptism of fire at the Fourth Initiation, when the Solar Angel leaves the man to stand alone in full awareness of the Spiritual Triad.[6]

The most interesting occurrence at the Fourth Initiation is the departure of the Guardian Angel and the destruction of the Inner Temple or the Chalice. The One Who guided the steps of the Initiate since individualization now departs giving him a chance to delve deeper into the mystery of his own Self. Once the Causal Body or the Inner Temple is

---

[6]*Cosmos in Man*, pp. 78-79.

destroyed, man does not need to incarnate again in the world of matter....[7]

As man passes from one level to a higher one, the need for symbolic interpretation decreases, and even the Soul, Who is a greater Interpreter in man between the Spark and the personality, eventually vanishes, and man walks in the "clear light of day."[8]

...In the Fourth Initiation the Lotus in the higher mind reaches Its maximum beauty and the innermost petals begin to open with an intense fiery radiation. The Initiate becomes a burning bush of sacrifice and bliss. This Lotus, in the Ageless Wisdom, is called the Causal Body, the Temple of Solomon, or the Temple made without hands. It is a center in the mental body for three kinds of energy: will, love and light. The petals extend into each vehicle carrying these three divine energies.

The Lotus is called a Temple because in it is anchored the Solar Angel, the Inner Presence. It is also called the causal body because within that body are found the seeds of the other vehicles. When man passes away, he leaves his physical, etheric, emotional and mental bodies. On his return to Earth in his next incarnation, it is these seeds which will bring into manifestation the bodies according to their own content. At the Fourth Initiation this Causal Body is destroyed and the Initiate is freed from the physical and lower mental vehicles....[9]

As the blood decreased in Jesus' body, flowing from the wounds in His body, He slowly came out of His body and

---

[7] *Christ, the Avatar of Sacrificial Love,* p. 56.

[8] *The Hidden Glory of the Inner Man,* p. 91.

[9] *Christ, The Avatar of Sacrificial Love,* p. 76.

saw the miracle of the ages: a Chalice with twelve petals above His head and a crown of thorns. He saw a white-blue central fire in it, which was bubbling and slowly penetrating from petal to petal toward the edges, and when the blue and white glow of fire passed the boundaries of the petals, in an amazing conflagration, the whole Chalice melted into the blue sphere in which He saw a Presence holding to His heart a triumphant warrior. The Presence touched Jesus' forehead and said farewell.... In a flash of time, Jesus identified Himself with the warrior and felt a great pain, a pain in "spirit," because of the departure of that Presence. And He said, "Why are you forsaking me?" This was the last renouncement. Then Jesus saw the destruction of the Inner Temple, and the departure from Him of the Agelong Guide. A second later He felt Divine Bliss filling His whole being because He met Himself, within Himself, as a triumphant warrior.

As He was undergoing this rare experience within the sphere of His higher mind, His body was bleeding, the sun was setting and a few of His beloved ones, including the Holy Mother, were watching Him. It was at this moment that in tremendous joy He announced His victory to the world.

"It is accomplished!"

The agelong labor pointing toward the release of His Inner Presence and entrance into His own Inner Being was finished and now greater paths were opening for Him. This is but a glimpse of the glorious initiation through which He passed to become a Fourth Degree Initiate.[10]

---

[10]*Ibid.*, p. 78.

We live as personalities or as reflections "as in a mirror" by the life and consciousness which we draw from our Souls. We aspire toward the Soul, toward Soul-consciousness and the Soul aspires toward the Spirit. This process continues from incarnation to incarnation, until man comes in contact with his spiritual principle and gains victory over the matter aspect of his nature. Having achieved this, the Soul stands aside and proceeds onto Its more advanced duties.

The Solar Angel feels a deep joy when the time for Its release approaches. This is also the time of release for man who now enters into the "kingdom of Souls...."[11]

The destiny of every man is to become a living Soul, eventually making it possible for his Divine Guide, the mysterious Sacrificial One within, to be released from Its age-long labor with us, to perform Its cosmic duties.

[The Solar Angel] ... has led us:

> *From darkness to Light,*
> *From the unreal to the Real,*
> *From death to Immortality,*
> *From chaos to Beauty.*[12]

There is a belief that after a man becomes a Soul, a living, awakened Soul, and releases the Solar Angel, his progress comes to an end and he enjoys eternal peace and bliss as a Soul. This is not the case. The fact is that, after he becomes a Soul, greater horizons open before him. His next step is to start functioning as a Triad, a Spiritual Triad, expressing

---

[11] *The Hidden Glory of the Inner Man,* pp. 44-45.

[12] *Cosmos in Man,* p. 267.

pure reason, love and power; then the man starts to become himself, a *Monad*.[13]

Beyond the mental plane, average man *does not have* any higher mechanism. The intuitional, atmic, monadic and divine vehicles are in embryo in the kernel of the "Monad", but they are not opened yet and have no active existence. The intuitional body, the atmic and monadic and divine vehicles of the Solar Angel which form part of man's nature, do not belong to him, but *they are the vehicles of the Solar Angel*. Until the end of the Fourth Initiation man gradually builds his intuitional, atmic and monadic vehicles out of his own essence, with the corresponding substance of the Planetary Logos. His building is the semblance of the model of the vehicles of the Solar Angel. After these bodies are in some degree built and utilized by the man himself, the Solar Angel leaves him, with Its higher bodies, for higher realms.[14]

In olden days people anointed their kings at elaborate ceremonies and festivals. Usually on that day, the king dressed in great splendor, donned symbolic signs and wore a *crown*. This is analogous to the real man who achieves mastery of life. He wears a very beautiful garb of rare colors, dons brilliant ornaments, and emanates a radiating halo around his head. The garb, the ornaments, and the halo are symbols of the fourth body, the Causal Body, the Body of Glory or the Chalice. On a higher level, this Chalice melts away and man enters into the awareness of the *Triad*, which is built by the three fiery spheres of the higher mental, Intuitional and Atmic seed atoms, through which the Spark can

---

[13]*Ibid.*, p. 54.

[14]*The Science of Meditation*, pp. 52-53.

function. When a man achieves such great realization, he can live without a physical carriage. He can also send away the ordinary horses and the old driver, because the body of Fire now serves as the true vehicle of communication.

This realization is symbolized in the Old Testament when Elijah rode to heaven in a golden carriage, pulled by fiery horses and driven by angels (II Kings 2:11). This analogy shows how the three bodies of man can be transmuted into their higher correspondences in the body of Fire, and how unlimited horizons open before the liberated Lord, toward the true peak of existence.[15]

...Human beings have five rays:

1. Physical ray
2. Emotional ray
3. Mental ray
4. Personality ray
5. Soul ray.

The real ray of a person is his Personality ray. The Soul ray can have a tremendous effect on the Personality ray. On many occasions It will fuse with the Personality ray until this ray flourishes completely and man enters into the Fourth Initiation. At the Fourth Initiation man becomes a Soul, or the diffused monadic light recollects itself and forms a center by itself on the intuitional level. It begins to radiate as the owner or ruler of the form called man. He is now a Soul and because of this achievement, the Solar Angel has departed and the Causal Body has been destroyed. We assume that the ray of this Soul will be the same as the

---

[15]*The Fiery Carriage and Drugs*, pp. 28-29.

major ray of the Personality in the last incarnation before the Fourth Initiation was taken. This assumption would bear out the fact that the Soul rays of advanced Initiates are essentially the same as their monadic rays. If, however, a man is not a free soul, if his Solar Angel is still present, the ray of his soul may differ from his monadic ray....[16]

---

[16]*Cosmos in Man*, pp. 77-78.

27

Externalization

efore thou canst approach the foremost gate thou has to learn to part thy body from thy mind, to dissipate the shadow, and to live in the eternal. For this, thou has to live and breathe in all, as all that thou perceivest breathes in thee, to feel thyself abiding in all things, all things in SELF.[1]

—H.P.B.—

There are four exits by which man can withdraw from his body. In the Ageless Wisdom, we are told that there are three doors in the subtle body through which man can exteriorize himself; there is a door near the solar plexus, another near the heart, and a third at the top of the head. These doors may be used according to the achievement of man.

The first form of exteriorization is death, at which time man draws himself out of his body, away from its magnetic field.

Second, man may withdraw himself at the time of a great crisis, danger or fear, in which case the withdrawal may be either partial or complete. If the withdrawal is partial, it creates glandular and nervous effects and can destroy some parts of the brain and affect the consciousness adversely. Its slight effects may be seen in people whose state of mind is diffused, uncertain, or without much purpose.

---

[1]Blavatsky, H.P., *The Voice of the Silence*, p. 54.

Third, by the use of drugs man sometimes leaves his body. Here anesthetics play an important role.

Fourth, through the advanced technique of meditation and contemplation man can withdraw himself from the body gradually and in a very natural way. Self-hypnosis is a branch of this technique, but creates many problems and does not afford any spiritual usefulness.

In hypnosis the unit of awareness steps out from the sphere of the body through the solar plexus and enters into the lower strata of the astral world.

In conscious withdrawal the awareness unit steps out through the heart center or through the head center. In both cases the awareness unit, the unfolding human soul remembers his experiences in the subtle worlds. As he withdraws from his body, a tiny thread of light extends from the heart center to the awareness unit. This is called the life thread. When it is cut, the body passes away. It is possible that with this thread two other threads extend between the head and the awareness unit, through which all experiences of the unfolding human soul pass to the etheric and dense brain. This is how man remembers his dreams or experiences in the higher astral, mental or even Intuitional planes.

These threads are called the consciousness thread and the Antahkarana. One extends from the Soul to the brain. The other extends from the mental unit to the mental permanent atom, to the Intuitional and Atmic Planes.[2]

The Lotus with its petals controls not only the metabolism of the body through the etheric centers and glands, but it also controls the emotional and mental

---

[2]*The Hidden Glory of the Inner Man*, p. 25.

metabolism. The Lotus with its petals is the agent of transmutation and sublimation; lower forces are refined through the heat (aspiration) it creates. Through this heat, forces are transmuted into emotional, mental and spiritual forces and energies. We must remember that activities and powers of the Lotus petals are relative to their unfoldment and development. There are people who have only a few petals functioning and others who have more. This is the factor which accounts for the difference between an average man and a man of great creativity, a man of great enlightenment.

The unfolding or developing human soul is the Divine Spark in the process of being educated. He communicates with the Inner Guide according to his degree of development, through the knowledge petals. Later, as he proceeds on the path of Initiation, he will be able to communicate with It through the love petals, and, eventually, through the sacrificial petals. The Inner Guide serves as a bridge between the unfolding human soul and his Future — the human Soul in his Monadic awareness.

The vehicles of the human soul are the physical, emotional and mental bodies plus the etheric double. All of these vehicles, together, form the personality of the unfolding human soul. When they are truly integrated and controlled by the human soul, they become a Personality, the reflection of the Monad. The personality is held together by the etheric vehicle and is connected to the Soul and the Spark by two energy lines which in the Ageless Wisdom are called the *life thread* and the *consciousness thread*. The consciousness thread branches off from the life thread which originates in the Monad, in the Core of the man.

The life thread extends to the heart center of the mental, astral and etheric vehicles, to the two lung centers under the breasts, to the spleen, and terminates within the heart. The consciousness thread passes through the Solar Angel, or Soul, to the head centers of the mental, astral and etheric bodies, terminating within the pineal gland in the brain.[3]

When the Sutratma, or life thread, withdraws, the man passes away and the consciousness thread registers all that occurs during the process of the life thread withdrawal. When the consciousness thread withdraws, the man still lives, but enters into a coma. We are told that there are two kinds of comas:

1. There is a coma in which an opportunity is given to the physical life by the Soul to repair its mechanism and restore health. The unconscious state causes the man to be unaware of the pain and complications which the body is undergoing. For example, if you are in a sudden accident and suffer serious injury, you may go into a coma. Such an unconscious state would be caused by the withdrawal of the consciousness thread for a short period during which you would feel no pain.

2. There is a coma caused by the withdrawal of the consciousness thread through a decision made by the Soul to dissolve the physical body. In this instance it would mean that a great battle is taking place between the physical elemental, or physical life, and the Soul. The physical life still wants to hold on to the life thread and avoid disintegration, but the Soul's plan is in direct opposition. This conflict, of course, ends in victory for the Soul's decision, but it may take hours or even a few weeks.[4]

---

[3]*Cosmos in Man*, p. 178.
[4]*Ibid.*, p. 179.

As we know, the Sutratma is anchored in the heart and the Antahkarana in the head. At death the Antahkarana or the consciousness thread withdraws itself from the head center; the thread of life withdraws itself from the heart center; and the physical body starts to disintegrate. If the consciousness thread is still there, man feels the "death chill." The sensitivity of the physical body dies away as the consciousness thread withdraws itself from the head center. The head center is the synthesis of all centers and as the life thread departs from it, all centers in the etheric body correspondingly are affected and are rendered insensitive to their corresponding organs.

When the life thread is withdrawn from the heart to the Soul via the head center, all centers are left without this integrating life; the body starts to disintegrate, and the man passes into his etheric body for a while.[5]

If it is withdrawal of the Soul from the physical plane, the light of the spleen will grow dim and go out, the light of the two lung centers will fade away and finally the flame of life will pass out of the heart.

Sometimes the battle with the Soul is carried on by a disciple (the unfolding human soul) when he thinks that he has much yet to do for the Plan. He does not want to die because of numerous needs of his friends and his followers. His rejection causes some delay, in the form of a coma. When an Initiate passes on, however, there is no fight, no rejection. There is only blissful acceptance of the will of His Soul.

After the life and consciousness threads are withdrawn, the physical body is apparently dead, but real death occurs

---

[5]*The Science of Becoming Oneself*, p. 137.

when the life and consciousness threads withdraw themselves from the etheric body, causing complete disintegration of that body. This is accomplished by an act of the Solar Angel and at that time the physical man is dead. H. P. Blavatsky says:

> At the solemn moment of death every man, even when death is sudden, sees the whole of his past life marshalled before him, in its minutest details. For one short instant the *personal* becomes one with the *individual* and all-knowing Ego [Solar Angel]. But this instant is enough to show him the whole chain of causes which have been at work during his life. He sees and now understands himself as he is, unadorned by flattery or self-deception. He reads his life, remaining as a spectator looking down into the arena he is quitting; he feels and knows the justice of all the suffering that has overtaken him.[6]

The etheric body is formed of energy threads radiating from the Sutratma, from the life thread. Actually, it is a coil of four grades of luminosity in the shape of the physical body. This thread of energy comes out of the center of the Lotus, and as a spider spins its web, the Solar Angel spins it into the etheric body upon which the Lunar Pitris build the physical body. The physical body is formed around this etheric coil. It is the real shadow of the etheric body.

---

[6]Blavatsky, H.P., *The Key to Theosophy*, and abridgement, pp. 102-103. (Excerpt from *Cosmos in Man*, pp. 179-180.)

At the time of death this coil is drawn into the Lotus, and all magnetically attracted cells and atoms, or physical substance, is dissolved into the general reservoir of force and matter. When the etheric coil is withdrawn, it passes into the Lotus and there it serves as a link between the physical permanent atom and the Lotus, keeping the permanent atom alive. Thus the life impulse for the physical body is centralized in the Causal Body, the Lotus, and rooted in the first mental plane, the atomic plane.

When continuity of consciousness is achieved, the process of dying will be a conscious act and the man will be aware, step by step, of the experience of leaving the physical consciousness and entering into the astral consciousness. Such people often know when they will die because the Solar Angel informs them through special contact, and prepares them for the transition....[7]

Ancient tradition tells us that immediately after death, the *Messengers of Death*, the Angels of Death, meet the man and take him to the *Seat of Evaluation*, the *Seat of Judgment*. Some traditions hold that the judge is not really a separate entity, but the light of the Solar Angel under which, for a very short time, the human soul clearly sees the causes he released and the effects which they created upon the physical, emotional and mental planes....[8]

...The developing human soul is connected to the Lotus and his awareness is proportionate to the unfoldment of the Lotus.

---

[7]*Ibid.*, p. 180.
[8]*Ibid.*, p. 181.

The Inner Guide hovers over the Lotus and watches the human soul. It controls his cycles of incarnation and the type of body he must have for each incarnation.[9]

In Deva-Chan the human soul may be on higher or lower mental levels, but he is still in the mental body. If higher, he has closer conscious communication with the Solar Angel through the Lotus; if he is on the lower levels of the mental plane, he will be unconscious of the existence of his Guardian Light, Who, nevertheless, will watch over him faithfully.[10]

During all these periods of out-of-body experience, the Solar Angel observes the activities and responses of the human soul....[11]

It is possible that a person after passing away, can, while in the astral plane, communicate with the physical world through his own Soul or through an advanced disciple....[12]

The Deva-Chanic period mainly impresses upon us the mystery of joy, harmony and simplicity. You can see these three pearls shining in the eyes of a baby, in the tears of a baby, in the smiles of a baby, but slowly, slowly, the dust of life comes and covers these three pearls, and they sink into the heavy layers of our fears, hatred and greed — but they have not been lost! Again and again our Inner Guide will remind us of the three pearls, and if we listen to the Inner Voice, we will start searching for them at all costs....[13]

---

[9]*Ibid.*, p. 181.

[10]*Ibid.*, p. 188.

[11]*Ibid.*, p. 190.

[12]*Ibid.*, p. 214.

[13]*Ibid.*, p. 191.

28

Rebirth

*T*HE CYCLES OF MANIFESTATION

> *Reincarnation is an aspect of the pulsating life of Deity.*
>
> —The Tibetan—

Following the period in Deva-Chan, the mental body is destroyed by an act of will and the man stands for a short time before his Solar Angel. He sees the future as clearly as he was previously aware of the past and present. This takes place immediately before the call of incarnation.

In esoteric Teaching the steps of descent are explained as follows:

1. Man takes the first step toward incarnation.

2. His Soul sounds the note of descent which slowly draws the human soul from the mental plane and brings him to the sphere of the etheric plane, where the etheric centers start to form.

3. His three lower permanent atoms radiate, creating a magnetic field upon which the three vehicles are gradually built, according to the records of the permanent atoms.

4. He chooses his parents, if he is a conscious entity, but if not, he is drawn to whoever can provide entrance to the physical plane....

1.   The first step, which is preparation, is actually a process of detachment from the mental world, from its inhabitants and interests, and a process of making oneself ready for the conditions that are awaiting him on the physical plane.

This experience is like entering deeper and deeper into limitation and isolated loneliness, which is far more distressing than the passing out of the body. This is true because after a man leaves his body, he meets those who were known to him on the physical level. He is also able to see those who are living in the body, and to feel their thoughts and emotions, but when he reincarnates, he loses both worlds; he is no longer in touch with those who are on the subjective side of life, nor those who were related to him in the objective world, unless he has built continuity of consciousness, the bridge which connects the three lower worlds. The Tibetan Teacher says:

> ... *each life is not only a recapitulation of life experience, but an assuming of obligations, a recovery of old relations, an opportunity for the paying of old indebtedness, a chance to make restitution and progress, and awakening of deep-seated qualities, the recognition of old friends and enemies, the solution of revolting injustices and the explanation of that which conditions the man and makes him what he is....*[1]

2.   The second step, the sounding of the note of return by the Soul, is actually the call of return. This note helps the man to detach himself from Deva-Chan, reminding him of

---

[1]Bailey, A.A., *A Treatise on the Seven Rays*, Vol. 1, p. 300.

his responsibilities and his karma waiting for him in the physical world. It also puts into action the permanent atoms, which in due time will build the three lower vehicles.

3. In the third step, the physical permanent atom first builds the blueprint of the etheric body, radiating those tiny lines of energy upon which the physical body will form.

Each permanent atom is like a photographic negative. When the energy of the Sutratma strikes them, their contents are projected out as the corresponding vehicles of the man.

4. In the fourth step, the choosing of parents is sometimes done blindly, if the incarnating soul is not evolved enough to discriminate. Concerning this the Tibetan Teacher says:

> ... *they have also brought too rapidly into incarnation myriads of human beings who were not yet ready for the experience of this incarnation, and who needed longer interludes between births wherein to assimilate experience. Those souls who are unevolved come into incarnation with rapidity; but older souls need longer periods wherein to garner the fruits of experience. They are however open to the magnetic attractive power of those who are alive on the physical plane, and it is these souls who can be brought prematurely into incarnation. The process is under law, but the unevolved progress under group law as do animals; whilst the more evolved are susceptible to the pull of human units, and the evolved come into incarna-*

tion under the Law of Service, and through the
deliberate choice of their conscious souls.[2]

...Regarding the Law of Reincarnation, we should remember these facts:

— Man has a Solar Angel.

— Three of man's permanent atoms are the seeds of his lower bodies.

— Man is the evolving, unfolding human soul, the Spark in the process of liberation.

...A great Teacher suggests that rebirth and reincarnation are misleading terms. He proposes the terms cyclic impression, intelligent purposeful repetition, or conscious inbreathing and out-breathing. The latter expression is especially beautiful. As the Soul breathes out, the form comes into existence. As the Soul breathes in, the vehicles slowly disappear. It is the records in the permanent atoms that are creating a new vehicle. It is not the true man, himself, who is incarnating.[3]

[Referring to the real entity within the vehicles, or to the human soul, *The Bhagavad Gita* says]:

The Indweller of the body is never born, nor does It die. It is not true that, having no existence, It comes into being; nor having been in existence, It again ceases to be. It is the unborn, the eternal, the changeless, the Self. It cannot be killed, even if the body is slain.[4]

---

[2]*Ibid.*, p. 272. (Excerpt from *Cosmos in Man*, pp. 195-197.
[3]*Ibid.*, p. 198.
[4]*Bhagavad Gita*, Ch.2, Vs. 20.

*I*ndex

Bull
> Eye of•288
> of aspiration•288
> sacrifice of•287-288

Call
> answer to•70
> def.•70
> sources of•70

Calling, high•133
Canada•289
Cancer•289-290
> relationship of•289-290

Candles
> Soul drama of three•14-15
> symbol of•17

Car accident, story of•55
Carriage (human body)
> development of•180
> man resembles•179

Cathedral, Notre Dame•221
Catherine of Siena, Saint•110
Cause(s)•252,253-254
> world of•136

Cave
> drama of•75-77
> Soul drama of•14-15
> symbol of•17

Celestial Hosts, explanation of•84
Celibacy, reason for•30
Center(s)
> head•17
>> stimulation of•169
> heart•203,310
>> opening of•172
> higher, activation of•173
> seven, location of•158

Ceremonies, effect of•107
Chain(s)
> def.•51
> moon•37
>> cataclysm of•41
> planets of•35

Chalice•80,144,243,246,282,283,296,405
> building of•157-158
> burning of•132,160,167,400,401
>> words of Jesus•160
> consumption of•399
> content of•122

creation of•132
def.•151
destruction of•317,400,401
formation of•157-161,162
Holy, filling of•143
light and energy from•396
light consumes•170
location of•161
melting of•405
of Jesus•403
opening of•74,247
substance of•162
symbol of, quote A.Yoga litera-
> ture•162-163
treasure located in•161
use treasures of•293
vessel of, qualities mentioned•162
vitality from•205
wisdom of•271

Change, Law of•228
Character, formation of•296-297
Charter, United Nations'•332
Chhaya, def.•84
Children
> Mongoloid, cause of•377
> retarded, cause of•377

Chill, death•413
China•289
Christ•22,23,28,110,118,219,232,275,282,
> 318,346,372,381,401
aspire to•208
consciousness, stage of•21
contact•292
Disciple(s) of, def.•224,349
> (quote)•376
great sacrifice of•45
greater Light•250
inner•4,108,144
> suggestions of•388
invoke help of•390
Jesus, claiming to be•59
Lord•70,143
parable of search for jewel•63
quotes of•21,53,204,227,292,391,
stand in light of•390
symbolic event•248
symbolized•312
Teacher for Hierarchy•346

Core
  Inner•208
  Innermost, help from •343-344
  one with •263
  true•274
Cosmos
  Heart of•70,163
  path to•187
  psychic energy of•359
Courage•206-207
Court, symbolism of outer•314
Creation, purpose of•318
Creativity•323
  def.•232
  ability of•261-262
  form of prayer •232
  Fountainhead of•108
  moment of•106
  process of•228
  sign of•261
  Soul characteristic•228
Creed of Aquarian Educational Group•263
Crisis
  Solar Angel contact during•106
  withdrawal at time of•409
Cross
  horizontal arm of•159
  Jesus on•160
  symbol of•159
  vertical arm of•159
Crown, symbolism of•405
Crucifixion, after•160
Culture
  def.•218
  expression of•218
  living or spiritual •219
  personality•218,219
    examples of•219-220
    result of•219
  Soul
    birth to•220
    expression of•220
    result of•220,221
  Transpersonal of Soul •218
  types of•218
Currents, destructive•iv
Cycle(s)•279-295 (Ch. 18)
  lunar•279

seven-year•310
Cyclopes, three•288
Dance
  in cave drama•14
  Soul drama•14-15
  symbol of•15
  man in
    grey•14
    silver•16
    yellow•16
Danger, withdrawal at time of•409
Dante•218
Days, Ancient of•168
Death
  acceptance of•413
  Angels of•415
  at time of•415
  fear of•334
  knowledge of•415
  Messengers of•415
  occurrence at time of•413
  real, occurrence of•413-414
  rejection of•413
  states of consciousness in•260
  withdrawal by•409
  words of Blavatsky, H.P.•414
Debts, payment of karmic•212
Decision, important•107
Decisions, obedience to•371
Dedication and decision, day of•282
Descent, steps of•417-419
Destiny, Soul•365
Detachment
  achievement of•254
  cultivation of•364
  def.•230
  spirit of•282
Deva-Chan
  detach from•418
  during period of•416
  period following•417
Devas•40
  Fire•87
Development, three stages of•305
Devotion
  fiery•334
  line of•346
  mystic, result of•382

Works by Torkom Saraydarian

A Commentary on Psychic Energy
A Daily Discipline of Worship
Bhagavad Gita
Breakthrough to Higher Psychism
Challenge for Discipleship
Christ, The Avatar of Sacrificial Love
Cosmic Shocks
Cosmos in Man
Dialogue with Christ
Five Great Mantrams of the New Age
Hiawatha and the Great Peace
Hierarchy and the Plan
Irritation—The Destructive Fire
I Was
Joy and Healing
Other Worlds
Sex, Family and the Woman in Society
Spiritual Regeneration
Symphony of the Zodiac
Synthesis
Talks on Agni
The Ageless Wisdom
The Fiery Carriage and Drugs
The Flame of Beauty, Culture, Love, Joy
The Flame of the Heart
The Hidden Glory of the Inner Man
The Legend of Shamballa
The Psyche and Psychism
The Purpose of Life
The Questioning Traveler and Karma
The Psychology of Cooperation and Group Consciousness
The Science of Becoming Oneself
The Science of Meditation
The Sense of Responsibility in Society
The Spring of Prosperity
The Unusual Court
The Year 2000 and After
Torchbearers
Triangles of Fire
Woman, Torch of the Future